Manual SPS

HVAC Design for
Swimming Pools and Spas

First Edition, Version 1.00

ANSI/ACCA 10 Manual SPS — 2010

ISBN # 978-1892765-54-3

The First Edition of ANSI/ACCA Manual SPS is the
Air Conditioning Contractors of America
manual for designing moisture control systems for
indoor spaces that have a swimming pool or spa.

(RA 2017)

(Reaffirmed in 2017 without changes)

**To comment on the content of this manual or for information
pertaining to technical content respond to:**

Glenn Hourahan or Hank Rutkowski

**ACCA
2800 Shirlington Road, Suite 300
Arlington, VA 22206
Voice: 703-575-4477**

Copyright and Disclaimer

This publication and all earlier working/review drafts of this publication are protected by copyright. By making this publication available for use, ACCA does not waive any rights in copyright to this publication. No part of this publication or earlier working/review drafts of this publication may be reproduced, stored in a retrieval system or transmitted in any form by any technology without written permission from ACCA. Address requests to reproduce, store, or transmit to: Chris Hoelzel at the ACCA offices in Arlington, Virginia.

Adoption by Reference
Public authorities and others are encouraged to reference this document in laws, ordinances, regulations, administrative orders, or similar instruments. Any deletions, additions, and changes desired by the adopting authority must be noted separately. The term "adoption by reference" means references shall be limited to citing of title, version, date and source of publication.

Disclaimer and Legal Notice
Diligence has been exercised in the production of this publication. The content is based on an industry consensus of recognized good practices drawn from published handbooks, manuals, journals, standards, codes, technical papers, research papers, magazine articles, textbooks used for engineering curriculums, and on information presented during conferences and symposiums. ACCA has made no attempt to question, investigate or validate this information, and ACCA expressly disclaims any duty to do so. The commentary, discussion, and guidance provided by this publication do not constitute a warranty, guarantee, or endorsement of any concept, observation, recommendation, procedure, process, formula, data-set, product, or service. ACCA, and the document reviewers do not warrant or guarantee that the information contained in this publication is free of errors, omissions, misinterpretations, or that it will not be modified or invalidated by additional scrutiny, analysis, or investigation. The entire risk associated with the use of the information provided by this standard is assumed by the user.

ACCA does not take any position with respect to the validity of any patent or copyright rights asserted in connection with any items, process, procedures, or apparatus which are mentioned in or are the subject of this document, and ACCA disclaims liability of the infringement of any patent resulting from the use of or reliance on this document. Users of this document are expressly advised that determination of the validity of any such patent or copyright, and the risk of infringement of such rights, is entirely their own responsibility. Users of this document should consult applicable federal, state, and local laws and regulations. ACCA does not, by the publication of this document, intend to urge action that is not in compliance with applicable laws, and this document may not be construed as doing so. Nothing in this manual should be construed as providing legal advice, and the content is not a substitute for obtaining legal counsel from the reader's own lawyer in the appropriate jurisdiction or state.

Acknowledgments

The author, Hank Rutkowski, P.E., ACCA Technical Consultant, gratefully acknowledges the help, guidance and encouragement provided by the reviewers and advisors during the Manual SPS project.

Manual SPS, First Edition, Reviewers and Advisors

Original Equipment Manufacturer's

- Doug Branger, Western Regional Sales Manager, Venmar CES Inc.; Dayton, MN
- Kenneth W. Cooper, P.E., Director Special Projects, PoolPak International; York, PA
- Keith Coursin, President, DesertAire Corporation; Germantown, WI
- James Hogan, Product Development Engineer, Dectron, Inc.; Roswell, GA
- Kevin Gebke, New Product Development Engineer, DuctSox; Dubuque, IA

Mechanical Contractors

- Ellis G. Guiles Jr., P.E.; Vice President, TAG Mechanical Systems; Syracuse, NY
- Robert C. Murphy, Jr., President Air Management Solutions, LLC; Bremerton, WA
- George L. Rodriguez, ServTEC Air Conditioning Inc.; Santa Fe Springs, CA
- John D. Sedine; President, Engineered Heating and Cooling; Walker, MI

Consultants / Other

- Ronald Bladen, Code Specialist II; Fairfax County, VA
- Mirza Mohammed Shah, Ph.D, P.E., Advanced Engineering Director, Fletcher-Thompson, Inc.; Shelton, CT
- Larry G. Spielvogel, P.E., Lawrence G. Spielvogel, Inc.; King of Prussia, PA

Other Participants

- Staff Liaison—Technical
  Glenn C. Hourahan, P.E., ACCA; Arlington, VA
- Staff Liaison—Production, Publishing, and Editing
  Christopher N. Hoelzel, ACCA; Arlington, VA

Publishing Consultant

- Page layout and electronic publishing provided by Carol Lovelady, Lovelady Consulting; Roswell, GA

Photo and Graphic Credits

- American Society of Heating, Refrigerating and Air-Conditioning Engineers, Inc. (ASHRAE), 1791 Tullie Circle, N.E., Atlanta, GA 30329
- Dectron, Inc., 10898 Crabapple Road, Suite 103, Roswell, GA 30075
- DesertAire Inc., N120 W18485 Freistadt Road, Germantown, WI 53022
- Lifebreath/Airia Brands, Inc., 511 McCormick Blvd., London, Ontario, Canada N5W 4C8
- Munters Corporation, 79 Monroe Street, Amesbury, MA 01903
- Nautica Air Systems/MSP Technology, 77 Bankside Drive, Centerport, NY 11721
- PookPak International, 3491 Industrial Drive, York, PA 17402
- Thermotech Enterprises Inc., 5110 West Clifton Street, Tampa, FL 33634
- Venmar CES Inc., 2525 Wentz Ave., Saskatoon, Saskatchewan, Canada S7L 309
- Xetex Inc., 9405 Holly St. NW, Minneapolis, MN 55433

Dedication

Professional Dedication

This manual is dedicated to a branch of the HVAC industry that deals with interesting and challenging problems on a daily basis.

Personal Dedication

Producing this manual has been an educational experience. The author sends a large alphabetical thank-you to Kenneth W. Cooper; Keith Coursin and James Hogan.

Overview of this Manual

The First Edition of *Manual SPS*®© provides guidance for projects that range from a hot tub in a home to a large natatorium that has an Olympic-size pool with seating for hundreds of spectators. Even though these projects appear to be quite different, they are identical as far as construction requirements and mechanical system performance requirements are concerned. So for this manual, any enclosed space that has a spa, swimming pool, decorative pool or immersion tub is a natatorium.

This manual does not provide guidance for indoor water parks. The reason for this is that there is no standard method for evaluating the moisture loads for water rides and water toys. In this regard, a swimming pool that has one or two water features (water slide or small water fall) is not a water park.

Finally, the mechanical system must be designed to continuously control the dew point temperature of space air, then measures are taken to control space temperature. If this is not accomplished, moisture can cause visible and concealed condensation, wet sagging ceilings, wet framing, wet structural surfaces, wet insulation, visible or concealed mold and mildew, corroded or discolored fixtures and finishes, rust, or masonry that has been fractured by ice. In addition:

- Dehumidification system must provide indoor air quality and space air motion.
- System materials, components and devices must be compatible with moist, chemical laden air.
- Duct runs must have appropriate insulation and moisture membranes.
- Duct runs must be tightly sealed.
- Mechanical system cost and system operating costs are higher than for comfort applications due to the need to control the dew point temperature of space air and to provide indoor air quality.
- Energy use should be minimized to the extent possible. Higher efficiency will increase installed cost.
- Maintenance requirements and costs are generally higher than for comfort conditioning systems.

Section 1 — Design Issues for Humid Spaces
The mechanical system designer must consider moisture issues, condensation issues, chemical issues and zoning issues. The mechanical system designer is advised to verify that the construction details for an existing structure or a proposed structure are suitable for a natatorium enclosure.

Section 2 — Contract Set Points and Outdoor Conditions
The design value for water temperature, and the related values for indoor humidity and indoor air temperature are contract set points. Outdoor and indoor design conditions for a natatorium are significantly different than the conditions that are used for comfort conditioning. There is a winter design condition for outdoor moisture and temperature (the 99.6% dry-bulb condition). There is a summer design condition for outdoor moisture (the 1% dew point condition), and a summer design condition for outdoor temperature (the 1% dry-bulb condition). Figure A1-1 shows that indoor air temperature is warm (78 °F to 86 °F) and that it has a relatively high humidity ratio year-round.

Section 3 — Space Humidity and Surface Condensation
The mechanical system designer is informed about R-value calculations, vapor retarding membranes, and condensation calculations. The mechanical system designer needs to verify that the architect and/or builder has performed appropriate condensation calculations.

Section 4 — Water Treatment and Water Heating

The mechanical system is designed for appropriate and scheduled water treatment, adequate pool-spa maintenance and diligent water system maintenance. Odors and smells indicate inadequate or improper water treatment, and/or maintenance practices. Water shocking affects the design of the mechanical system (the associated purge cycle requires a large amount of outdoor air for a limited time). Water systems for pools and spas are provided by companies and vendors that specialize in this work. These entities are responsible for water pumping, water circulation, water filtering, water heating and water treatment. They also are responsible for information or estimates pertaining to annual water use, annual sewer charges and annual water heating costs. There are procedures for calculating water heating loads.

Section 5 — Indoor Air Quality and Ventilation

Natatorium air contains chemical compounds caused by water sanitation and safety treatments (or the lack of proper treatment). All efforts to control indoor air quality are based on the assumption of proper water treatment. Engineered ventilation (outdoor air) dilutes the concentration of offensive pollutants. Outdoor air is required for the actual water surface area and the wet deck area, and if there is spectator seating, outdoor air is required for spectators. The outdoor air damper can be closed when the space is not occupied (use low leakage dampers). If the spectator load is large and occasional, consider using a dedicated outdoor air system (DOAS) for spectator events. There may be a temporary ventilation Cfm requirement (purge cycle) for water shocking. Condensation or freezing condensation may occur when cold outdoor air is mixed with warm-humid return air, or air discharged from an evaporator coil. Condensation may occur when heat reclaim equipment processes exhaust air. Condensation droplets must not impinge on a heating coil or heating surface. Mixing boxes must be designed to capture condensation, contain condensation and dispose of condensation. Preheat may be required for cold outdoor air.

Section 6 — Evaporation Load

There is a special procedure for calculating the latent load for the water evaporation at wet surfaces. This load depends on water temperature, space air temperature and humidify, water surface area, water activity and wet deck area. A change in the space temperature and/or humidity has a significant effect on the evaporation load.

Section 7 — Heating and Cooling Loads

Mechanical system design shall be based on comprehensive load calculations that are as inclusive and accurate as possible. A twelve month, twenty-four hour procedure for comfort conditioning is used for everything other than the evaporation load. The latent load for water evaporation load varies with water activity. Latent and sensible load calculations are made for the winter design condition and both summer design conditions. The latent load from evaporation is added to the latent ventilation load, the latent load for spectators, and the latent infiltration load (which can be very small or negligible for a structure that has appropriate construction). Latent outdoor air loads can be large. They are negative during cold weather (moisture loss); may be negative during warm weather (dry climate), or positive during warm weather (climates that have a summer moisture load).

Section 8 — Moisture Control Methods

Space humidity may be controlled by a refrigerant evaporating coil, with dry outdoor air, or by a desiccant wheel. These methods vary in concept, complexity, installed cost and operating cost. The primary concern is matching system capabilities with application needs. If two or more methods provide the required performance, installation cost and operating cost may determine the system of choice. Under certain conditions, it may be possible to assemble a dehumidification system from comfort conditioning components. A dedicated outdoor air system may supplement the space dehumidification system when a large spectator area is vacant most of the time.

Section 9 — Heat Recovery
A significant or relatively large amount of outdoor air may be required for the humid space. The space must be at negative pressure, so the exhaust air Cfm is somewhat larger than the outdoor air Cfm for indoor air quality. Exhaust air may provide a heat recovery opportunity. The latent heat of evaporation is a continuous source of reclaimable heat. Heat recovered by the evaporator coil can be used to heat pool water, and/or supply air (priority may depend on the dehumidifier equipment manufacturer). A dehumidifier may have an air-side economizer. There is no industry standard for quantitative comparisons of energy use, operating cost and return on investment.

Section 10 — Supply Air Cfm
The desired air turnover rate for the humid space ranges from 4 to 8 turns per hour. This amount of supply air Cfm may not equal the Cfm required for the space loads. This difference is reconciled by routing some air around the evaporator coil (through a bypass air damper). The final value for supply air Cfm is determined when the equipment is configured to satisfy both airflow requirements.

Section 11 — Equipment Selection
Performance data for evaporator coil dehumidifiers and desiccant dehumidifiers emphasize moisture removal in pounds-of- water-per- hour units. Data for evaporator equipment also provides values for total capacity and sensible capacity in Btuh units, and values for supply air Cfm and maximum outdoor air Cfm. Data for desiccant equipment provides values for supply air Cfm, maximum outdoor air Cfm and exhaust Cfm. Air to air heat recovery equipment has a Cfm rating and an effectiveness rating. Control dampers have performance curves.

Section 12 — Air Distribution and Space Pressure
Exposed glass (windows, glass doors and skylights) should be completely washed with dehumidified supply air (this may not be possible if the facility has a large amount of glass). Skylights are especially troublesome and should be avoided. Primary and secondary supply air must not blow directly on wet surfaces. The relative location of supply outlets and returns should, to the extent possible, induce low velocity air movement across the surface of the pool water. The humid space must be at negative pressure relative to the outdoors and relative to other spaces, except for the chemicals storage space. These pressure conditions must be in effect at all times.

Section 13 — Duct Systems
Low pressure, low velocity duct systems are typical. Practitioners may use the equal friction method for air way sizing. Use efficient fittings and avoid duct entrance and exit conditions that cause a system effect.

Section 14 — Design Example for a Spa and Pool in a Home
Load calculation for a Spa and small pool in a dedicated room in a Tucson, AZ home.

Section 15 — Design Example for a Pool-Spa in a Motel-Hotel
Load calculation for a Spa and mid-size pool in a dedicated room in a Miami, FL motel or hotel.

Section 16 — Design Example for a Competition Pool
Load calculation for an olympic Pool with space for a large number of spectators Milwaukee, WI.

Appendix 1 — Good Practice
Appendix 1 summarizes the requirements for the architectural project and the mechanical project. Check list items that pertain to preventing building condensation and controlling conditions in the humid space are fully explained in the body of the manual. Appendix 1 check lists may contain some items that are not discussed in the body of the manual, these typical relate to installation and maintenance.

Appendix 2 — Equipment Capacity at Altitude

Appendix 2 explains how heating equipment, cooling equipment and air moving equipment is affected by altitude. The discussion focuses on comfort equipment, but it also applies to dehumidification equipment. For locations above 2,500 feet, altitude adjustment guidance must be obtained from the equipment manufacturer.

Appendix 3 — State Point Psychrometrics

Air state points depend on altitude. Appendix 3 provides formulas for altitude sensitive psychrometrics.

Appendix 4 — Symbols and Terminology

Appendix 4 provides definitions for the symbols and terms used by this manual.

Appendix 5 — Summary of Tables and Equations

Appendix 5 provides a summary of the tables and equations used by this manual.

Appendix 6 — Summary of Dehumidification Methods

Summary of the attributes and capabilities of the various types of moisture control systems.

Appendix 7 — Codes, Stanadrds and References

List of related codes and standards, and documents for additional study,

Appendix 8 — Comfort Conditioning Equipment

Comfort heating-cooling equipment may be used for a pool-spa space if all performance issues can be satisfactorily resolved. These issues are discussed in general, but this is not sufficient for producing a design for a particular application in a particular climate.

Appendix 9 — Equipment Performance Data

Exhibits and discussions of performance data supplement Appendix 6, and conditionally supplement comments made in the body of the manual.

Appendix 10 — Forms and Worksheets

Blank copies of Form DH and Form DC.

Prerequisite Knowledge and Experience

Manual SPS assumes the practitioner is very familiar with comfort conditioning systems, equipment and design procedures. The prerequisites for using *Manual SPS* procedures are summarized here:

- A general understanding of the concepts, components, arrangements, procedures, requirements and terminology that pertain to commercial and residential building construction.
- Extensive experience with commercial load calculation methods and procedures.
- Mastery of psychrometric principles and processes, and related altitude adjustments.
- Extensive experience with designing commercial heating and cooling systems for comfort applications.
- Extensive experience with using manufacturers' performance data to select and size heating and cooling equipment.
- Mastery of air distribution principles, and experience with using manufacturers' performance data to select and size commercial supply air hardware and return air hardware, and associated devices.
- Mastery of duct design principles, and experience with designing low velocity duct systems.
- A general understanding of HVAC controls, control strategies and control cycles.
- Experience with designing HVAC systems that adjust performance to maintain space set points for temperature, humidity and engineered ventilation at full load conditions, and at all part load conditions (i.e., mastery of capacity control issues and strategies).

Table of Contents

Part 1 Design Issues and Procedures

Section 1

Design Issues for Humid Spaces

Section 2

Contract Set Points and Outdoor Conditions

Section 3

Space Humidity and Surface Condensation

Section 4

Water Treatment and Water Heating

Section 5

Indoor Air Quality and Ventilation

Section 6

Evaporation Load

Section 7

Heating and Cooling Loads

Appendix 9

Equipment Performance Data

Appendix 10

Forms and Worksheets

Introduction

By John Sedine

"This project has an indoor pool and hot tub, can you handle that?" This question has shot fear into the hearts of many HVAC contractors over the years. Dealing with the issues that affect the design and installation of mechanical systems for indoor spaces with high humidity loads is no easy task. If a practitioner lacks a true understanding of the unique dynamics of pool applications, these types of projects can become HVAC and building nightmares.

Contractor anxiety stems from not being familiar with the equipment used for pool applications. Specialized equipment is normally needed to handle the large latent loads. Determining space loads and the outdoor airflow rate for engineered ventilation requires special procedures. Additionally, mechanical system designers must solve unique air distribution problems, meet code requirements, be informed about water heating and treatment issues; and after all this, they may have to educate architects, building contractors and building owners.

This manual puts building design, mechanical system design, equipment selection and system installation into proper perspective. It provides guidance that applies to indoor hot tub and pool installations in homes; indoor hot tub and pool installations in hotels; and natatoriums with spectators in schools or public buildings. This manual does not cover indoor water parks due to the number and variety of slides, water toys, and waterfalls because there is no consensus standard for calculating individual and aggregate evaporation loads.

It is not Rocket Science... *But, it does mean that the focus shifts from temperature issues to moisture issues. In other words, you are offering a dehumidification system that happens to provide heating and cooling.*

The design tasks for an indoor pool or spa involve most of the procedures you would use to design an HVAC system for a conventional space. However, a very important difference is that the primary goal is to control the dew point temperature of the space air for all operating conditions that apply throughout the year (or for the months that the system is used to control space moisture). A quick summary of the issues are highlighted below:

Humid Air Must Not Cause Condensation

You must determine the design values for the condition (e.g., dry-bulb temperature and relative humidity) of space air and ensure that the structure is suitable for the application (see Section 1 and Section 2).

Dehumidification Method

You need an understanding of the systems and equipment used for controlling dew point temperature and dry-bulb temperature in an enclosed pool-spa space. In this regard, there are varying approaches for handling the latent and sensible requirements. Geographic location, cost constraints, and details regarding space use and activity play an important part in the type of system that you plan to use. A solution that works for one type of climate and/or application may not be right for some other climate and/or application. In order to work with an owner to provide an adequate dehumidification system, you have to know what types of systems and equipment can do the job (see Section 8)

Indoor Air Quality

Outdoor air for engineered ventilation, exhaust air, and the number of space air changes (space air turns) are critical design issues for pool-spa installations. These items determine space pressure, indoor air quality, and influence the ultimate load on mechanical equipment (see Section 5).

Load Calculations

Pool applications are not as forgiving as a comfort conditioning system for a home or commercial building. You must perform an accurate load calculation that includes the latent load for water that evaporates from pool-spa surfaces and the wet deck area, the sensible and latent loads for engineered ventilation, plus all the load items that apply to a commercial comfort conditioning calculation. You must not use a residential procedure, rules of thumb, or safety factors (see Section 6 and Section 7).

Efficiency and Operating Cost

Energy use and operating cost are important issues and there are code restrictions pertaining to reheat. Heat recovered from humid air and exhaust air reduce energy use and operating cost, but increase installation cost. Systems and equipment vary in their ability to recover energy and to use recovered energy (see Section 9).

Verify Performance and Features

You must use manufacturers' performance data to select and size equipment. You need to ensure that equipment performance is adequate for full load conditions and for all part load conditions. In addition, you must ensure that all surfaces and materials that contact space air are compatible with the moisture and chemicals in the space air (see Section 9 and Section 11).

Protect Fenestration and Swimmers

Exposed glass must be washed with supply air or re-circulated air, and there needs to be some air motion over pool water. Airflow is determined by the type, size and location of the supply air outlets and the return grilles (see Section 12).

Minimize Duct System Effects

You have to properly size and locate duct runs. In general, duct construction and materials must be compatible with increased moisture and chemicals found in pool applications. Some of the specialized dehumidification equipment may have duct work requirements unique to that particular brand. Be sure to factor in any of these requirements in your equipment location and design (see Section 13).

System Commissioning

You have to install it right, start it up right, balance the system, and confirm that everything is working correctly. Following all instructions from the equipment providers is key for a successful installation and subsequent operation.

Okay, now Tell Me What I Really Want to Know

The age-old question is what is the best system that I can put in? The answer is still the same. There are various systems that may provide the desired results, but the selection depends on owner requirements, building constraints, pool use/application, geography, loads, budget constraints, etc., etc., etc.

Begin by surveying the concepts, systems and equipment used in the local area. Talk to people that have experience with the application. Discuss performance, maintenance, operating cost and purchase cost. Evaluate the pros and cons of the various approaches before deciding on a system concept.

For a small indoor hot tub in a residential setting, a simple method could use 100% outdoor air in conjunction with a little more exhaust air, with the system being sized to provide enough air changes to control space humidity. This is a cold weather strategy for all climates and may be a year-round strategy for dry climates. Heat and sensible cooling are provided by additional equipment. Operation can be fairly expensive.

A variation of the preceding strategy is to add a heat recovery ventilator (HRV) to an outdoor air system. This provides the necessary air changes to control humidity and reduces energy use.

Probably the most common strategy is the use of packaged OEM dehumidification equipment that is specifically designed for pools and spas. This equipment recovers evaporation heat from pool water. This equipment also controls the dew point temperature of space air; and it can cool the space, heat pool water, and heat supply air. In colder climates, some form of supplemental space heat is required for cold weather operation. If the peak sensible load is relatively large, additional sensible cooling equipment may be required for hot sunny weather.

Another OEM method is the use of desiccant equipment. This equipment has a dehumidification coil and a desiccant wheel that is reactivated by the heat that is recovered by the dehumidification coil. Additional equipment is required for space heating and sensible cooling.

Finally, under certain circumstances, it is possible for a knowledgeable practitioner, who is well-experienced with HVAC system design and indoor swimming pool requirements, to specify a suitable equipment package, or to assemble a system from a combination of HVAC systems/components that meets all the psychrometric performance requirements, full-load requirements, part-load requirements, materials requirements for chemical-laden air, and energy use requirements.

Mr. Sedine is a principle and owner at Engineered Air Systems, Grand Rapids, MI. He has chaired various ACCA technical committees and is an ASHRAE member. He is a member of the ACCA Board of Directors and served as its Chairman during 2010 - 2011.

Design Team

Enclosed pools and spas produce unique and challenging moisture control, temperature control and air quality problems. They also produce architectural problems and building construction problems. Solutions require a significant investment in engineering time. During this process, a design team has to deal with technical issues and budget constraints.

The design team may include the owner, the architect (or equivalent), the structural envelope builder, the mechanical system designer, and a representative of a packaged dehumidification equipment manufacturer. The team also may include the swimming pool builder, and vendors or suppliers of pool and spa equipment.

The Owner

The owner defines goals and objectives relating to form, function, building cost, operating cost and maintenance requirements. These desires are interdependent and some of them may be incompatible. Team members evaluate the owner's vision, identify conflicting issues and present the owner with a set of options. Final design work (architectural and mechanical) begins after the owner accepts and authorizes a total system concept.

The Architect

The architect has to solve moisture migration problems, interior air containment problems and condensation problems (surface and hidden). In addition, construction materials, fenestration items and interior finishes must be compatible with the ambient moisture condition and the chemicals that are released from the water.

- The team determines the design values for water temperature, space air temperature and humidity, pressure levels for the pool-spa space and for adjacent spaces, and the owner authorizes the values.
- The team determines how fenestration will be blanketed with supply air, and the owner authorizes the concept.
- The architect is advised about the chemicals that will be used to treat and condition pool water or spa water.
- The architect specifies construction materials and techniques that prevent visible and concealed condensation on opaque surfaces and fenestration.
- If the relevant space has to be isolated from adjacent spaces, the architect specifies interior membranes, and interior windows and doors that have appropriate air seals and closing devices.

- The architect specifies materials and finishes that are compatible with the moisture and chemical conditions.
- The architect consults with relevant members of the design team and provides adequate space for dehumidification equipment, pool water equipment, ducts and pipes; plus separate, isolated space for chemical storage.

The Mechanical System Designer

The mechanical system designer is responsible for maintaining temperature, humidity and pressure in the pool-spa space, and may be responsible for the conditions in adjacent spaces. Design activities include load calculations, equipment selection and sizing, routing and sizing ducts and pipes, selecting and sizing air distribution hardware, specifying controls, and so forth.

- The team selects values for water temperature, air temperature and relative humidity for the pool or spa, and the owner authorizes the value.
- The team determines the pressure level for the pool-spa space and for adjacent spaces, and the owner authorizes the values.
- The U.S. Olympic committee recommends some air motion at the water surface for airborne chemical dilution. In this regard, there is no definitive guidance (consensus standard) for controlling and measuring air motion at the water surface. And, even if it could be precisely controlled, the velocity value will be a compromise between the desired velocity for chemical dilution and the preferred velocity for evaporation control. Therefore, the design team may decide to investigate the boundaries of this science, or to accept the result produced by a conventional, properly designed air distribution system.
- The mechanical system designer is advised about the chemicals that will be used to treat and condition the pool or spa water.
- The mechanical system designer provides the team with one or more system concepts (considering input from vendors of dehumidification equipment and other specialized equipment).
- The team selects a system concept and the owner authorizes the plan.
- Mechanical system designers advise the architect about space requirements for installing, maintaining and repairing dehumidification equipment and pool water equipment, space for ducts and pipes; plus separate, isolated space for chemical storage.

Ancillary Guidance

Vendors (or manufacturer's representative) of packaged dehumidification equipment and energy reclaim equipment are a primary source of guidance and design information. Pool or spa contractors, and pool or spa equipment suppliers may provide useful information regarding water treatment and pool equipment.

However, the credibility of any source of guidance, and the suitability of related recommendations, depends on the knowledge, experience and agenda of the source. Therefore, the mechanical system designer has to filter third party guidance. This requires an organized and prioritized understanding of all relevant issues and concepts. Vendors that provide dependable, unbiased guidance are valued members of the design team.

Part 1

Design Issues and Procedures

Design Issues for Humid Spaces

Indoor swimming pools and spas produce a hostile environment. Design procedures and construction details are driven by the need to contain and control moisture and odor, and to prevent condensation. The primary issues are direct wetting, condensation, moisture migration, chemical action, space for mechanical systems and zoning. Commentary on these issues is provided below, Appendix 1 provides a summary of the issues.

1-1 Direct Wetting

For swimming pools, direct wetting is normally limited to the pool deck. Use of suitable deck materials is common practice.

Spas may be public or private, they may be built into the floor, or may be a self contained unit that sits on a floor. In any case, they shall be installed in a room that has suitable floor material or floor covering, and there shall be suitable wall material or wall covering in the vicinity of the tub.

1-2 Condensation

Condensation must not form on visible or concealed surfaces. For any outdoor air condition, indoor surface temperatures and concealed surface temperatures must be warmer than the dew point temperature of humid indoor air that may contact the surface.

- This is easy to say, but may be hard to do, especially for a natatorium that has a lot of glass.
- Where condensation is likely, provide means to drain it without damaging other materials.

Preventing Concealed Condensation

A comprehensive air barrier and a comprehensive vapor retarding membrane prevent moisture migration to concealed surfaces. Condensation must not form on the surface of the vapor retarding membrane.

- Vapor membranes shall be installed near the inside surface of a ceiling, wall, or floor over an open space (a properly installed ground slab is a separate issue).
- The vapor membrane may be an interior finish or construction material that has a low perm rating, or a continuous low-perm membrane that is installed behind the interior finish.

   This manual defines low-perm as 0.10 Grains/Hr · SqFt per InHg, or less.

- Vapor membranes simplify concealed condensation calculations because the surface of interest is the inside surface of the membrane.

- Infiltration must be blocked near the outside surfaces of the enclosed space. Use appropriate construction materials and techniques. If necessary, install an infiltration barrier (air barrier) near outside surface. (A vapor membrane at a warm-wet inside surface blocks infiltration, but local condensation will occur if cold infiltrating air contacts this boundary.)

- Vapor membranes and infiltration barriers must be completely sealed (condensation can occur at, or near, leakage points).

- Building materials and insulation shall be selected and arranged so that the effective R-value of any possible conduction path from an outdoor surface to a vapor membrane keeps the temperature of the membrane surface above the dew point temperature of the air that contacts that surface.

- WUFI-Pro and H.A.M software (see page 12) can be used to evaluate building performance as it pertains to visible and concealed condensation.

Preventing Visible Condensation

Visible condensation can occur at the indoor surface of a ceiling, wall, door or floor; or at the indoor surface of a piece of fenestration (window, glass door or skylight). Visible condensation will not occur if the indoor surface temperature is warmer than the dew point temperature of the indoor air.

- Building materials and insulation shall be selected and arranged so that the effective R-value of any possible conduction path from an outdoor surface to an indoor surface keeps the local temperature of the indoor surface above the dew point temperature of the indoor air (prevent thermal bridging).

- A piece of fenestration has an overall R-value for the whole assembly. For products rated by the National Fenestration Rating Council (NFRC), the overall R-value appears on the product label, in manufacturer's data and in the NFRC catalog. (Performance is actually defined by a U-value. The R-value is the reciprocal of the U-value).

- A piece of fenestration has multiple conduction paths, and each path has its own R-value. For example, there is a R-value for the glass, the sash, the frame, a mullion, or a skylight curb. The overall R-value for the assembly is the effective average of the component R-values.

- As far as visible condensation is concerned, the overall R-value for a piece of fenestration may seem adequate, but local condensation will form if a component R-value is too small.

- For fenestration, the smallest component R-value should keep the temperature of the indoor surface above the dew point temperature of the indoor air.

- Skylights tend to be a problem. If installed, make sure the component R-values are compatible with the design value for the dew point temperature of the indoor air.

- Washing exposed fenestration with supply air reduces the potential for condensation during extreme weather (see Section 12).

  Per Section 2, normal weather is defined by the 99.6% outdoor dry-bulb temperature for heating, with dry outdoor air. Extreme weather is defined as dry outdoor air that is colder than the 99.6% value, or cold weather precipitation (snow on a skylight, for example).

Condensation Calculations for Dry Weather

Condensation potential depends on the dry-bulb temperature and humidity ratio (pounds moisture per pound dry air) of the indoor air. It also depends on outdoor temperature and the thermal resistance of the relevant layers of construction material (opaque or transparent).

- The potential for condensation increases as the humidity ratio of the indoor air increases.

- The humidity ratio of the indoor air tends to increase as water temperature increases.

- The humidity ratio of the indoor air tends to increase with water splashing and the amount of wet deck area.

- For a given water temperature, the evaporation rate and the humidity ratio of the indoor air increase as indoor air temperature decreases.

- The potential for condensation increases as the dry-bulb temperature of the outdoor air drops.

- The potential for condensation increases as the R-values of the building materials decrease, and as infiltration increases.

- Condensation calculations show if building performance is acceptable or needs to be improved.

- Condensation calculations are made for the outdoor design temperature for winter air, and the related indoor design condition.

- After the indoor design condition and building attributes are finalized, the dehumidification system is selected and designed to maintain the desired indoor condition

- The ultimate procedure would search for an integrated design that optimizes building cost, equipment cost, energy use and operating cost, but such studies are technically challenging, time consuming and expensive.

1-3 Moisture Migration

Moisture migrates from a space that has a higher humidity ratio to a space that has a lower humidity ratio. Moisture migrates through most building materials and air. Moisture migration can cause condensation on building surfaces, and leaching in concrete walls (streaky white deposits on the outside of a building).

Surfaces Exposed to Outdoor Air

Condensation will occur if the moisture in warm, humid indoor air migrates toward cold, dry outdoor air and impinges on a surface that is at or below the dew point temperature of the migrating air. Therefore moisture migration from the pool-spa space to the outdoors must be prevented.

- Exposed walls, ceilings and floors shall have a sealed vapor retarding membrane.

- Windows and skylights should have a fixed sash. If a window or skylight is operable, it should have a very tight seal.

- Doors should have a very tight seal, a vestibule with tight seals on both doors is preferred.

Surfaces that Interface with Other Spaces

Condensation will occur if the moisture in warm, humid indoor air migrates to an adjacent space, then to a visible or concealed surface that is at or below the dew point temperature of the migrating air. In addition, moisture migration will increase the latent load on the conditioning equipment that served the adjacent space. If this latent load is incompatible with equipment capability, the space condition will be out of control. Therefore, moisture migration between indoor spaces must be prevented.

- Isolate the humid space from adjacent spaces that have conventional heating and cooling, or no heating or cooling.

- Vertical and horizontal partitions (walls, ceilings and floors) shall have a sealed vapor retarding membrane.

- Partition glass should have a fixed sash. If a window is operable, it should have a very tight seal.

- Partition doors should have a very tight seal, a vestibule with tight seals on both doors is preferred.

Mechanical Systems

Condensation may occur if the moisture in warm, humid indoor air is mechanically collected and transported to an adjacent space that has a surface that is below the dew point of the imported air. Condensation may occur if moisture migrates through a duct system or transfer grille. Condensation may occur in a duct that passes through a cold space if the duct not properly insulated and sealed. The mechanical system design must prevent such occurrences.

1-4 Chemical Action

Moisture is problematic for some metals, for most types of insulation, and for many building materials and finishes. The first line of defense is to make sure that surfaces are never wetted by condensation or splashing. If wetting is likely or possible, use appropriate materials.

Chlorine is used to sanitize water. A deficient amount of chlorine produces forms of chlorinated molecules (chloramines). Other chemicals may be used to improve water clarity and pH. Improper water treatment causes an ammonia or chloramine smell (free chlorine has no odor).

Airborne chemicals form acidic or corrosive solutions when they contact wet surfaces. These solutions attack and destroy common types of building materials, duct materials and mechanical equipment materials. Identify the surfaces that will come in contact with the indoor air and use materials, finishes and equipment that will not be affected by airborne chemicals.

Water-side components such as a pump or water heater will be fouled or damaged if water pH is not controlled. Use equipment that has been designed for swimming pool or spa applications, and provide appropriate water treatment equipment.

1-5 Equipment Location

Humid, chemical-laden air attacks materials, finishes electronics, valves, actuators, motors, etc. Equipment that processes hostile air must be designed and built for this duty. In this regard, the equipment may or may not be designed for installation in the pool space.

- Protecting equipment from chemical laden air adds to its cost, which increases as the number of vulnerable components increase.
- Components in the air processing path must be compatible with pool air.
- Equipment is installed outside the pool space if components or materials that are external to the air processing path can be damaged by pool air.

- Equipment may be installed in the pool space or outside the pool space if every item in the equipment package is compatible with pool air.
- There may be performance, service life and warranty issues if the equipment is not installed in a suitable space.
- The equipment manufacturer is the authority for acceptable equipment locations.

1-6 Equipment Space

A swimming pool and/or spa may need a suitable, nearby space for dehumidification equipment. Additional space is required for water system equipment, water treatment equipment and chemical storage.

- Install dehumidification equipment outdoors, or provide an equipment room or space that is structurally and mechanically isolated from pool and/or spa air and moisture.
- Provide adequate space and access for scheduled operations, for routine maintenance, for service and repair work, and for equipment replacement.
- Adequate space includes space for straight duct runs that produce a well-ordered flow at the inlet and discharge openings of equipment cabinets, blowers and fans.
- Water treatment chemicals shall not be stored in a mechanical or electrical equipment room. Provide a separate, vented storage space near the water treatment equipment. (This guidance appears in codes.)
- The chemical storage space shall not open to, be ducted to, or exchange air with a pool space, spa space, mechanical equipment room or electrical equipment room).
- The chemical storage space shall have an alarm and exhaust fan that continuously monitor and maintain negative pressure with respect to adjacent spaces and the outdoors.
- The merit of having dehumidification equipment and pool water equipment in the same space is debatable (there may be chemical spills, and undisciplined or ignorant maintenance people may use the room for chemical storage).

1-7 Limit the Boundaries of the Humid Zone

Moisture finds its way to spaces that are not protected from moisture migration. Therefore, the boundaries of the humid zone should be purposely limited to the space that contains the moisture generating surfaces.

- Provide partitions, appropriate vapor membranes and air locks for adjacent comfort conditioning spaces and unconditioned spaces.

- Mechanically isolate adjacent comfort conditioning spaces and unconditioned spaces from the humid zone. (Provide separate, totally independent HVAC systems for spaces and areas that are not in the humid zone.)

- Moisture must not move from the humid zone to some other space because of duct leakage.

1-8 Multiple Spaces in the Humid Zone

A desire to create a water scene environment, or to make an esthetic statement, may cause the boundary of a humid zone to include spaces that have nothing in common with the space that produces the moisture. For example, comfort conditioning spaces, eating spaces, lobbies and sleeping spaces may share air with a space that has a swimming pool, reflection pool, water fall or fountain.

In this case, the aggregate space is the humid zone, so the local moisture load may be larger than the normal comfort conditioning load, especially during cold weather. For example, moisture migrating to a sleeping room during cold weather may cause a local condensation problem.

- Spaces are not architecturally isolated from each other if they do not have appropriate vapor membranes and air locks.

- Ancillary spaces in the humid zone may have their own comfort conditioning equipment.

- Comfort systems for ancillary spaces are subject to year-round latent load produced by water evaporation.

- Local temperature control may be possible (more so, if the ancillary space is a partitioned space), but moisture migration may make it difficult, or impossible to control local humidity.

- The equipment that serves the wet surface space must not mechanically export air to adjacent comfort conditioned spaces and unconditioned spaces, and must not mechanically import air from adjacent comfort conditioned spaces and unconditioned spaces.

- The equipment that serves a comfort conditioned space must not mechanically export air to the wet surface space, and must not mechanically import air from the wet surface space.

- A duct run and/or engineered opening (transfer grille, for example) must not air-couple a wet surface space with a comfort conditioned space or an unconditioned space.

  Moisture will migrate through duct work to the dryer space when the blower is off. There may be no migration or some migration when the blower operates, but this is difficult to evaluate by simple calculations.

- The duct runs for mechanical systems that serve the wet surface space, must be tightly sealed (regardless of location).

- Duct runs for a mechanical system that serves a comfort-conditioned space must be tightly sealed if routed through a wet surface space. (This prevents airborne moisture exchange between spaces, duct wall condensation is discussed later in this manual).

- A small shower room can be part of a pool or spa area (use suitable materials if a few lockers are installed in the wet surface space).

- Large locker rooms must be isolated from a pool or spa area. (If not isolated, the exhaust system in the locker room usually draws air from the pool space.)

- If a kitchen or food service area is in the humid zone, it must have its own space conditioning system. The pressure in this space must be less negative than the pressure in the pool-spa space (easy to say, not easy to do as various fans and blower start and stop while various dampers open and close).

- Within the humid zone, local space pressures must be adjusted to control moisture flows, airborne chemicals and odors (as previously noted, easy to say, not easy to do). See Sections 12-3 and 12-4 for space pressure requirements.

1-9 Good Practice

Sections 1-1 through 1-6 provide an overview of the issues and design requirements for swimming pools, spas, and spaces that have wet surfaces. Appendix 1 provides additional guidance and more detail.

Section 2

Contract Set Points and Outdoor Conditions

There are default design values for outdoor dry-bulb temperature and humidity ratio. There are negotiated design values (contract set points) for water temperature, space dry-bulb temperature and space relative humidity. There is a design value for indoor air dew point temperature. There is a design value for the coldest surface temperature at any point on the inside of the vapor membrane surface. These values are interdependent and they determine required building insulation R-values.

- Evaporation rates depend on water temperature, indoor temperature, indoor humidity, water surface area, the air velocity at the water surface and activity level.

- The dew point temperature of the indoor air depends on indoor temperature and indoor humidity.

- The potential for condensation on indoor surfaces, concealed surfaces and the inside surface of the vapor retarding membrane, depends on the dew point temperature of indoor air, outdoor air temperature, and the R-value for the path from the outdoor air to the surface of interest.

- The potential for condensation on ducts and pipes depends on the dew point temperature of the air that contacts the exposed surface and the temperature of the exposed surface. The exposed surface may be the exterior duct or pipe surface (no insulation, or insulated with no vapor retarding jacket), or the surface of a vapor retarding jacket that covers duct or pipe insulation.

- Instantaneous internal loads, envelope loads, ventilation loads and equipment loads depend on evaporation rate, the condition of the indoor air and the outdoor air condition.

2-1 Water Temperature

Pools and spas are used for recreation, relaxation, exercise and physical therapy. The range of acceptable water temperature depends on activity or use, as summarized by Table A5-1.

The owner (or owner's representative, or builder) has the authority to specify the design value for water temperature. However, water temperature affects building design details, mechanical system requirements, construction cost, energy use and operating cost. Therefore, the architectural and mechanical design teams, and the

Range of Water Temperature Values	
Application	Temperature °F
Residential Pool	
Hotel or Motel Pool	76 to 86
Public, Institutional or Rec Pool	
Swimming Competition Pool	76 to 82
Diving Pool	80 to 90
Water Fitness Class	82 to 86
Elderly Swimmers	84 to 88
Therapeutic Pool	85 to 95
Spa or Whirlpool	97 to 104

Copy of Table A5-1

owner's representative should investigate and debate all issues and consequences before specifying the design value for water temperature. Then the building and mechanical systems are designed accordingly.

- The evaporation rate from wet surfaces increases with increasing water temperature (see Table A5-4).

- Higher water temperature encourages a higher indoor air temperature because the comfort of damp occupants is improved when the air temperature is warmer than the water temperature.

- Higher air temperatures decrease the evaporation rate from wet surfaces (see Table A5-4).

- The evaporation rate has a significant effect on the latent load for the conditioned space.

- The dehumidification load increases as the evaporation rate increases (if equipment holds the dew point of space air constant).

- The minimum acceptable R-value for any possible envelope conduction path increases as space dew point temperature increases (to prevent condensation).

- Water temperature affects construction costs because it affects the minimum envelope R-value requirement.

- Water temperature affects mechanical system installation costs and operating costs because the system must control space temperature, indoor humidity and the dew point of the indoor air.

5

2-2 Indoor Design Condition for Humid Zone

Condensation, occupant comfort, biological growth, materials damage, energy use, installed cost and operating cost depend on, or are affected by the indoor design condition. The optimum dry-bulb temperature and relative humidity for one issue of concern may be significantly different than the optimum value for some other issue or concern. These considerations apply:

- The humidity ratio depends on dry-bulb temperature and relative humidity. For a given dry-bulb temperature, humidity ratio increases as relative humidity increases; for a given relative humidity, humidity ratio increases as dry-bulb temperature increases.

- The potential for condensation on indoor surfaces and concealed surfaces increases as the humidity ratio of the indoor air increases.

- Condensation may cause mold and mildew, corrosion, and damage to wood or fabric. This favors a low indoor humidity during cool or cold weather.

- Humidity affects the perception of occupant comfort or discomfort, but this depends on whether a person is bare and wet, or clothed and dry. (Wet people may sit and move on the pool deck; dry, clothed people may sit on the pool deck; dry, clothed spectators may sit in stands.) This also depends on activity level, age and health.

- Envelope construction cost is affected by the maximum value for humidity ratio (conduction path R-values and thermal breaks must prevent condensation).

- The energy load and monetary cost for controlling indoor humidity increases as the design value for humidity ratio decreases (more assets are used to maintain a lower relative humidity).

- An acceptable indoor condition must be maintained during cold weather. This requires a basic amount of equipment, installation cost, energy use and operating cost, which depend on the attributes of the heating and humidity control system.

- A desired indoor condition may be maintained during warm or hot weather. This may be optional or mandatory, depending on the purpose of the faculty, owner preference, and the need to control condensation.

- Year-round conditioning requires additional equipment, installation cost, energy use and operating cost.

- Installed cost and operating cost depend on the use of energy recovery equipment.

Indoor Air Conditions for Occupant Comfort

Application	Dry-Bulb Temp °F	Relative Humidity	Dew Point Temp °F
Residential Pool	78 to 86	50% to 60%	57.8 to 70.5
Hotel or Motel Pool			
Public, Institutional or Recreation Pool			
Competition Swimming Pool			
Diving Pool	82 to 86		61.5 to 70.5
Water Fitness Class	84 to 86		63.3 to 70.5
Elderly Swimmers	86		61.2 to 70.5
Therapeutic Pool			
spa or Whirlpool			

1) Preferred air temperature 2 °F to 4 °F warmer than the design value for water temperature.
2) Maximum air temperature = 86° F
3) Maximum relative humidity = 60% RH
4) Relative humidity may drop below 50% RH when the negative moisture load produced by dry outdoor air Cfm exceeds the positive moisture load for the space.
5) Temperature may drop below set point during water shocking.

Copy of Table A5-2

- For year-round conditioning, the heat from pool water evaporation can be reclaimed by a refrigerant coil (evaporator) and used to heat pool water and/or supply air (pool water and cold-dry supply air require heat most of the time).

Table A5-2 provides a range of temperature and relative humidity values for humid zone comfort. Selecting an indoor design condition is often based on experience because a search for the optimum condition may require a complex, time consuming and expensive trade-off study. These considerations apply:

- Wet occupant comfort is improved when air temperature is a little warmer than water temperature.

- Evaporation is reduced if the space air temperature is a little warmer than the water temperature (2° F is a typical differential).

- A warmer air-water deferential may not be practical for therapeutic applications and spas (85°F to 104°F water temperature). In this regard, observers report therapeutic spaces as warm as 90° F.

- A lower indoor humidity makes it easier to prevent condensation, makes dry spectators more comfortable and makes wet or damp occupants less comfortable.

- Comfort is less of an issue if there is no spectator area. Damp occupants are less bothered by high humidity, and clothed people sitting around a pool tend to tolerate a higher humidity.

- The range of acceptable indoor humidity values is relatively small (50% to 60% RH), but 10% RH can make a significant difference in the minimum conduction path R-value requirement and the dehumidification load.

- A 50% RH value eases the minimum R-value requirement (a significant issue for fenestration, less so for insulated walls and ceilings).

- A 60% RH value reduces the dehumidification load (smaller equipment).

- In any case, the heating, cooling and humidity control system must maintain contract set points for all relevant operating conditions.

- To get started, use an air temperature that is 2°F warmer than the water temperature (90°F maximum) and 60% relative humidity.

2-3 Design Value for Dew Point Temperature

The design value for dew point temperature is determined by the design value for indoor dry-bulb temperature and the design value for indoor relative humidity. After dry-bulb and relative humidity are determined, dew point temperature is read from a psychrometric chart or provided by psychrometric software. Table A5-2 (previous page) correlates dew point temperatures with indoor design conditions.

2-4 Outdoor Design Condition

Design conditions for winter and summer are determined by outdoor dry-bulb and wet-bulb temperatures. For heating, the 99.6% dry-bulb temperature is safer than the 99.0% temperature because even a short period of condensation is not acceptable. For cooling, there is a design condition for the latent load and a separate design condition for the sensible load.

- For the winter heating load and for dew point calculations, use the 99.6% drybulb temperature.

- For the latent load design value and coincident sensible load, use the 1% condition for dew point temperature and mean coincident dry-bulb temperature.

- For the design value for sensible load and coincident latent load, use the 1% value for dry-bulb temperature and mean coincident wet-bulb temperature.

- Outdoor design conditions are provided by ASHRAE weather data on CD.

- If a city, or suitable surrogate city, is not listed on the ASHRAE CD, use the persisting 12-hour dew

Humidity Ratio vs. Altitude		
Condition	Grains at Sea Level	Grains at 3,500 Feet
95°F Dry-Bulb; 75°F Wet-Bulb	98.5	Note 2
95°F Dry-Bulb; 60°F Wet-Bulb	21.5	32.1
0°F Dry-Bulb; 80 % RH	4.4	5.0
70°F Dry-Bulb; 50% RH	54.5	62.0
75°F Dry-Bulb; 50% RH	64.6	73.6
55°F Dry-Bulb; 90% RH Note 3	57.8	65.9

1) Illustrative examples for common conditions.
2) The design value for outdoor wet-bulb significantly decreases as altitude increases.
3) Air leaving an evaporator coil.

Figure 2-1

point temperature for the closest location (see the Climate Atlas of the United States, Version 2.0, published by the national Weather Service).

2-5 Outdoor and Indoor Moisture

The amount of moisture in the air is evaluated as pounds of moisture per pound of air, or grains of moisture per pound of air (a pound of water is equal to 7,000 grains of water). This moisture is called humidity ratio, as listed on the right side of psychrometric charts.

- If indoor dry-bulb temperature and relative humidity are known, humidity ratio can be read from a psychrometric chart.

- If outdoor dry-bulb temperature and wet-bulb temperature are known, humidity ratio can be read from a psychrometric chart.

Humidity ratio (grains of moisture per pound of air) depends on altitude. Use a psychrometric chart for the local altitude, use psychrometric software that adjusts for altitude, or use the Appendix 3 equations. Figure 2-1 shows how altitude affects humidity ratio.

2-6 Moisture Difference Values

Moisture moves from a higher humidity ratio to a lower humidity ratio (by infiltration, engineered ventilation and moisture migration). Moisture is removed when it condenses on a cold surface (forcing air through a cold coil). These migrations and extractions are psychrometric processes, and there is a latent load associated with each type of process.

The size of the latent load depends on the moisture difference values for the wet air condition and the dry air condition. Grains values depend on altitude, so moisture difference values depend on altitude, as demonstrated by Figure 2-2.

- ASHRAE or NOAA weather data provides outdoor dry-bulb and wet-bulb values that can be converted to outdoor grains values that depend on altitude (see Appendix 3).

- Indoor dry-bulb and relative humidity can be converted to an indoor grains value that depends on altitude (see Appendix 3).

- The moisture difference value at altitude equals the difference between the outdoor grains value and the indoor grains value.

Moisture Difference vs. Altitude		
Outdoor-Indoor Condition Sets	Grains at Sea Level	Grains at 3,500 Feet
95°F Dry-Bulb; 75°F Wet Bulb	98.5	~
75°F Dry-Bulb; 50% RH	64.6	~
Moisture difference	33.9	~
95°F Dry-Bulb; 60°F Wet Bulb	21.5	32.1
75°F Dry-Bulb; 50% RH	64.6	73.6
Moisture difference	−43.1	−41.5
0°F Dry-Bulb; 80 % RH	4.4	5.0
70°F Dry-Bulb; 50% RH	54.5	62.0
Moisture difference	−50.1	−57.0
Moisture difference = Outdoor grains - Indoor grains		

Figure 2-2

Space Humidity and Surface Condensation

Airborne moisture can cause visible condensation, concealed condensation and freezing condensation. This may cause mold and mildew, cosmetic damage to interior materials and surfaces, or serious damage to structural materials and surfaces. For extreme cases, part of the structure may crumble or collapse.

3-1 Indoor Humidity

The dehumidification system that serves a pool or spa space must not allow space humidity to exceed 60% RH, or a specified value that is between 50% RH and 60% RH (see Section 2-2). This requirement may only apply to the heating season (summer cooling not provided), or to all seasons of the year (year-round conditioning provided).

3-2 Condensation on Building Surfaces

A 50% RH to 60% RH value for space humidity may not seem unusual because this range of values applies to summer air conditioning applications that have a latent load (the design value for space humidity for dry climate cooling may be 45 % RH or less). However, a space that has 50% RH to 60% RH during the heating season is a significant problem because of the potential for visible and concealed condensation.

- Condensation must not occur during any month of the year or hour of day.

- The maximum dew point temperature for space air depends on the contract set points for space air temperature and relative humidity.

- Condensation problems are not caused by space conditioning equipment that provides appropriate air distribution and maintains contract set points (i.e., a specified dew point temperature).

- If the equipment maintains a suitable dew point temperature, condensation problems are caused by the failure to maintain a suitable building surface temperature (i.e., a surface temperature is colder than the design dew point temperature for space air).

- Condensation calculations made by the architect or building designer must show that building construction techniques, components and materials are suitable for the application (see Appendix 1). The mechanical system designer should obtain and file a copy of these calculations.

- The mechanical system designer should have the architect or building designer provide a signed statement that says the thermal performance of the structure will prevent visible and concealed condensation when equipment maintains the design values for space temperature and humidity.

3-3 Condensation Threshold

Condensation occurs when the dry-bulb temperature of a surface is less than the dew point of the air that is in contact with the surface. This applies to interior surfaces, and to concealed surfaces that contact indoor air due to leakage through structural components.

Condensation also can occur when water vapor migrates through building materials. In this case, condensation occurs when the partial pressure of the water vapor is greater than the saturation pressure of the water vapor (see the 2005 ASHRAE Handbook of Fundamentals, page 23.10). This depends on local dry-bulb temperature because saturated vapor pressure varies with dry-bulb temperature.

Calculations that predict dew point condensation are relatively simple. Calculations that predict vapor pressure condensation are more complex. In this regard, condensation calculations are simplified by making the interior surface of the humid space the vapor membrane surface, or by placing a vapor membrane just behind the interior finish and assuming that indoor air contacts the membrane. (Software is used for more sophisticated calculations. See Section 3-6.)

3-4 Minimum Vapor Membrane Temperature

Building surfaces, cold duct surfaces and cold pipe surfaces shall be protected by a suitable vapor retarding membrane. The dry-bulb temperature at the vapor membrane surface should be about 5 °F warmer than the dew point temperature of the indoor air. This differential is a safety factor that reduces the probability of condensation. For example, Table A5-3 (next page) correlates minimum surface temperature with air dew point temperature for common indoor design conditions.

3-5 Minimum R-Value

The temperature at the inside of the vapor membrane surface depends on outdoor air dry-bulb temperature, indoor air dry-bulb temperature and the R-values of the materials in the heat transmission path (including the air film coefficients). Therefore, indoor dry-bulb temperature and relative humidity determine indoor dew point temperature, indoor dew point temperature determines minimum surface temperature, and minimum surface temperature determines overall R-value. Calculations are made for visible and concealed condensation.

Visible Condensation on Interior Surfaces

Condensation on interior surfaces will not occur if the dew point temperature of the indoor air is lower than the temperature of the coldest indoor surface. The following equation shows that surface temperature (T_s) depends on the overall R-value (R_t) of the structural panel (with the indoor and outdoor air film resistance), the indoor temperature (T_i) and the outdoor temperature (T_o).

$T_s = T_i - (T_i - T_o) \times (K / R_t)$

Where K equals the indoor air film coefficient for still air:
K = 0.68 for vertical surface (horizontal heat flow)
K = 0.95 for horizontal panel or skylight (heat flow down)
K = 0.76 for 45 degree panel or skylight (heat flow down)
K = 0.62 for exposed floor (heat flow up)
K = 0.95 for cold pipes and ducts (heat flow down)

If the thermal envelope complies with energy codes, windows, skylights and glass doors will have a lower R-value than walls, ceilings and exposed floors. R-values for windows, skylights, doors and frames exposed to outdoor temperatures may need to be higher than required by a local energy code.

For example, a double pane, clear glass window (K = 0.68) can have a 1.59 R-value (0.63 U-value), so the temperature at the inside surface is 45.8°F when the indoor air temperature is 80°F and the outdoor design temperature is 0°F. Therefore condensation will occur if the dew point of the indoor air exceeds 45.8°F.

Window R-value including air films = 1.59
Ts = 80 - (80 - 0) x (0.68 / 1.59) = 45.8°F

Overall R-values (with air film resistance) are commonly assigned to ceilings, walls and floors, but window manufacturer's normally publish U-Values Btuh/(SqFt •°F). In this case, the R-value is the reciprocal of the U-value.

Table A5-3 shows that the dew point for a swimming pool enclosure is considerably higher than 45.8°F and that the desired surface temperature is five degrees warmer than the dew point temperature. Therefore the performance of clear, double pane glass is inadequate.

Acceptable window performance is determined for the desired design conditions when the surface condensation equation is solved for R_t ((SqFt •°F)/Btuh). This version of the equation is provided here:

$R_t = K \times (T_i - T_o) / (T_i - T_s)$

Minimum Vapor Membrane Temperature		
Application	**Indoor Dew Point Temperature °F**	**Membrane Surface Temperature °F**
Residential Pool		
Hotel or Motel Pool		
Public, Institutional or Recreation Pool	57.8 to 70.5	62.8 to 75.5
Competition Swimming Pool		
Diving Pool	61.5 to 70.5	66.5 to 75.5
Water Fitness Class	63.3 to 70.5	68.3 to 75.5
Elderly Swimmers		
Therapeutic Pool	61.2 to 70.5	66.2 to 75.5
spa or Whirlpool		

1) Minimum dry-bulb temperature at the inside of the vapor membrane surface to prevent condensation.

2) Indoor dew point temperature depends on the indoor design condition, see Sections 2-2 and 2-3.

3) This surface temperature limitation applies to the coldest point on the vapor membrane surface, which is determined by the lowest conduction path R-value (from the outdoor air to the vapor membrane surface).

Copy of TableA5-3

For example, the design value for pool water temperature is 76°F and the design value for indoor dry-bulb is 80°F, so the window R-values for 50%, 55% and 60% relative humidity are 3.56 (U = 0.28), 4.32 (U = 0.23) and 5.39 (U = 0.19), as demonstrated here:

Outdoor dry-bulb = 0 °F
Pool water = 76 °F and Indoor air = 76 + 4 = 80 °F
Indoor air relative humidity = 50%, 55% and 60%
Indoor air dew point = 59.7 °F, 62.4 °F and 64.9 °F
Safety factor = 5 °F
Surface temperature = 64.7 °F, 67.4 °F and 69.9 °F
K = 0.68
R_t = 3.56, 4.32 and 5.39 (includes air films)
U-value = 0.28, 0.23 and 0.19 (includes air films)

This shows that the window assembly must have a low U-value to prevent condensation when it is 0°F outdoors. If the five degree safety factor is eliminated, the minimum surfaces temperatures are 5°F degrees colder, and the window R_t values are 2.68, 3.09 and 3.60, and the related U-values are 0.37, 0.32, and 0.28.

Note that the minimum R-value requirement (R_t) applies to any point on the interior surface of a window, skylight or glass door assembly. This means that the local R-value at any point on a glass-frame assembly must equal or exceed the minimum requirement.

- The National Fenestration Rating Council (NFRC) U-value rating represents that average performance of the entire assembly. The U-value at a particular point on the surface can be larger or smaller.

- The NFRC U-value rating is for a default frame size, the U-value for some other frame size may be somewhat different.

- The 5°F degree cushion for dew point temperature compensates for small differences in performance at various points on the fenestration assembly.

- Appendix 1 provides methods and materials guidance for envelope construction.

- The potential for condensation is reduced if fenestration assemblies are washed by warm air (see Section 12).

- If the pool or spa space is part of a larger enclosed space, the pressure in the pool or spa area must be negative with respect to other spaces (see Section 1-6 and Section 12-3).

The overall R-value equation for interior surface temperature also applies to opaque panels. In this case, the vapor membrane surface could be a low perm paint or a covering on the inside surface of a ceiling, wall or floor. For example, if the indoor design conditions for the glass example (with a 5°F safety factor) apply to a ceiling, wall or floor, the overall R-value requirements for 50%, 55% and 60% relative humidity are 3.56, 4.32 and 5.39.

Condensation on Exterior of Cold Pipe or Duct

A slightly different version of the overall R-value equation is used for the vapor membrane surface (T_s) of cold pipes and cold ducts. In this case, K = 0.95 (heat flow down a point on the perimeter is the worst case), the indoor temperature (T_i) is replaced by the ambient temperature (T_a), and the outdoor temperature (T_o) is replaced by the fluid temperature (T_f), as demonstrated here:

$$R_t = 0.95 \times (T_a - T_f) / (T_a - T_s)$$

For cooling, water temperature ranges from 40°F to 48°F for chilled water pipe, and air temperature is about 55°F (plus or minus a few degrees) for a cold air duct. For heating, water and air temperatures are warmer than room temperature, so surface condensation is not an issue. (See Section 13-9 for more information on this issue).

For a chilled water pipe, a fluid temperature of 40°F would be a worst case test for outside surface condensation. If the indoor design conditions for the glass example apply to a chilled water pipe, the overall R-values for insulated pipe are 2.48, 3.02 and 3.76.

For a cold air duct, an air temperature of 55°F would be an illustrative case for surface condensation. If the indoor design conditions for the glass example apply to a cold air duct at 55°F, the overall R-values for insulated duct are 1.55, 1.88 and 2.35.

Note: Some indoor units have ducted outdoor-air intakes. Thus, the air in the duct may be considerably below 55°F, so more insulation will be required.

Note that the R-value requirement applies to any point on the insulation's surface, and that the insulation's R-value may be significantly reduced when compressed. Therefore the methods and procedures for installing insulation shall assure that the effective R-value at any point on the insulation is adequate.

Concealed Condensation

Concealed condensation occurs whenever the temperature of a surface or membrane within a wall, ceiling, or floor is below the dew point temperature of the indoor air that contacts the surface. The following equation evaluates the temperature distribution across a structural panel. This equation shows that the temperature at a concealed surface (T_c) depends on the R-value for the path from the vapor membrane to the outdoor air (R_r), the total R-value across the panel (R_t), the outdoor temperature (T_o), and the indoor temperature (T_i),

$$T_c = T_o + (R_r / R_t) \times (T_i - T_o)$$

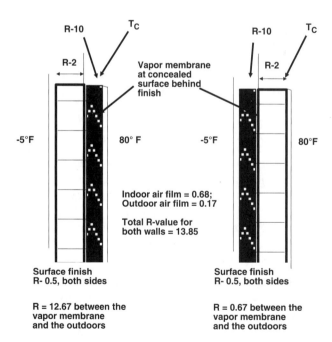

Figure 3-1

Figure 3-1 (previous page) shows two constructions that have the same overall R-value. However, the condensation potential for insulation and retarder at the indoor side of the block is significantly lower than the condensation potential for insulation and retarder at the outdoor side of the block.

- The R-value for the interior finish and the exterior finish is 0.50.
- The R-value for the block is 2.0.
- The R-value of the insulation is 10.0.
- The R-values for the indoor and outdoor air films are 0.68 and 0.17.
- The indoor and outdoor temperatures are 80°F and -5°F.

Insulation and Vapor Membrane near Inside Surface

The following equation estimates the temperature at the vapor membrane surface when the insulation and membrane are near the indoor surface (R-values provided by Figure 3-1). Table A5-3 (two pages back) shows that the desired vapor membrane temperature for a swimming pool or spa enclosure can be about ten degrees lower or three degrees higher than 72.8°F, so this design has adequate performance for some scenarios, and is a little deficient for other scenarios.

Tc = -5 + (12.67 / 13.85) x (80 - (-5)) = 72.8 °F
Desired surface temperatures = 62.2 °F to 75.5 °F

Insulation and Vapor Membrane near Outside Surface

The following equation estimates the temperature at the vapor membrane when the insulation and membrane are near the outdoor surface (Figure 3-1 provides R-values). This design is grossly inadequate. Moist air migrating to the vapor membrane will condense and freeze.

Tc = -5 + (0.67 / 13.85) x (80 - (-5)) = - 0.9 °F
Desired surface temperatures = 62.2 °F to 75.5 °F

Even if a structural panel has a robust R-value, concealed condensation will occur if there is no vapor retarding surface or membrane, or if the surface or membrane is on the wrong side of the structural panel, or if the surface or membrane is improperly installed, cut or damaged.

3-6 Condensation Software

The preceding sections provide simple tools for predicting condensation, and the related examples focused on the winter design condition for a cold climate. However, there are various types of climates and each climate has an outdoor air condition for each month and hour of year. In addition, there are many options for the indoor air condition, many types of fenestration and structural panels,

Building Science Software

The WUFI and H.A.M computer programs evaluate the thermal and hygrothermal performance of building materials and structural panels. Proper use of these programs may require relevant experience and training.

WUFI

The menu-driven PC program WUFI-ORNL/IBP developed by Fraunhofer Institute of Bauphysics and Oak Ridge National Labatory and validated using data derived from outdoor and laboratory tests, allows realistic calculation of the transient hygrothermal behavior of multi-layer building components exposed to natural climate conditions.

WUFI-ORNL/IBP can be used for assessing:

- The drying time of masonry with trapped construction moisture
- The danger of interstitial condensation
- The influence of driving rain on exterior building components
- The effect of repair and retrofit measures
- The hygrothermal performance of roof and wall assemblies under unanticipated use or in different climate zones.

Proper application of WUFI requires experience in the field of hygrothermics and some basic knowledge in the use of numerical calculation methods.

H.A.M

The Heat, Air and Moisture Building Science Toolbox is a computer program that applies building science principles to the design of any cladding and exterior wall system. This program will determine thermal properties and temperature gradients, locate winter and summer dew point temperatures, analyze potential winter and summer wall condensation, determine air leakage rates through openings, determine the effect of height and temperature on stack effect and fan pressurization on the building envelope.

The Building Science Toolbox was developed specifically for architects, engineers, technologists and technicians designing building envelope systems. It contains five building science tools, which are:

- The "R" Value Analysis Tool
- The Condensation Analysis Tool
- The Air Leakage Analysis Tool
- The Building Pressure Analysis Tool
- The Psychrometric Tool

and subtle technical issues that may not be modeled by a simple R-value procedure.

Comprehensive condensation calculations are performed by the WUFI and H.A.M software (see sidebar on previous page). See these sources for related information:

- Search the web for *Künzel & Karagiozis*, and see the Oak Ridge National Laboratories (ORNL's) Buildings Technology Center web site.
- Search the web for *Heat, Air and Moisture Building Science Toolbox*.

3-7 Consequences of Humidity

For health and comfort, 50% RH to 60% RH is best. Even if there is no significant condensation, mold, mildew, bacteria, fungi and viruses tend to grow or thrive when relative humidity exceeds 60% RH (see Figure 3-2). High humidity also causes corrosion and rust.

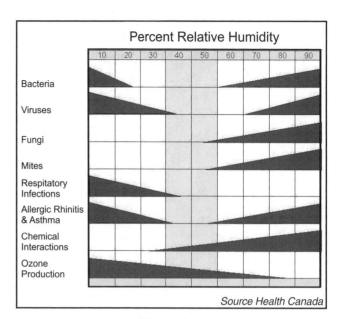

Figure 3-2

Masonry Damage

Damaged Metal Framing

Brick Finish Damage

Damaged Wood Framing

Stain from Condensation

Window Condensation and Damage

Window Condensation

Ice Dam from Moist Exfiltration

Air Leakage Causes Cold Spots

Air Leakage Causes Cold Spots

3-8 Consequences of Condensation

Indoor humidity in the 50% RH to 60% RH range will cause condensation if the thermal performance of the building is deficient. Related problems are listed here:

- Window or skylight glass covered with haze, frames may be stained; or may rot, or corrode.

- Stain or corrosion on interior finishes and metal hardware.

- Mold and mildew on carpets and furniture, on the visible and concealed surfaces of the building, on mechanical system components.

- Stains on exterior finish or masonry.

- Wet ceiling tiles and ceiling insulation.

- Wet wall or ceiling insulation loses most of its effectiveness.
- Electrical wiring problems.
- A ceiling assembly may sag or collapse when soaked with moisture.

- If structural connections and fasteners rust or corrode, framing may fail when exposed to normal wind, snow and rain loads.
- Exterior masonry cracks, splits or breaks off due to freezing condensation.
- Air leakage paths carry moisture to cold surfaces, where it freezes and causes icicles or a ice dam.

Water Treatment and Water Heating

Water treatment chemicals and filters keep pool or spa water clean and safe. Some amount of these chemicals, or products of chemical reactions, are released to the indoor air. Unpleasant odor problems, or serious health and air quality problems are caused by inadequate or unbalanced water chemistry.

4-1 Responsibility

The owner or manager of a swimming pool or spa facility is responsible for water chemistry. In this regard, the mechanical system designer shall state in writing, that acceptable dehumidification system performance is based on the assumption that water chemistry will be properly managed on a day-to-day basis for the life of the facility. Then, contract documents shall show that the owner or manager has acknowledged this responsibility, and understands that failure to perform scheduled tasks could harm occupants, structural components and components of the mechanical system.

The primary issues are free chlorine, combined chlorine, and pH. Figure 4-1 summarizes requirements set by the Association of Pool and Spa Professionals (APSP).

- Odors indicate improper water treatment (chlorine has no odor, humans are sensitive to very small concentrations of combined chlorine, see Section 4-3).

- Bacteria, viruses and biological growth are the consequences of improper water treatment.

- Airborne chemicals and molecules can cause short term, long term or permanent damage to occupants.

- Air borne chemicals can mix with visible or concealed condensation. This corrodes and degrades building surfaces, mechanical system surfaces, increases maintenance cost and reduces equipment life.

4-3 Water Chemistry

Chlorine kills germs, bacteria, viruses, etc., and reacts with biological waste (sweat, urine, feces), natural body oils, skin and hair care products, colognes and perfumes. Chlorine also reacts with ammonia produced by a chemical breakdown of sweat and urine. The by-product is chloramines (monochloramine, dichloramine and nitrogen trichloride), which are measured as combined chlorine.

Combined chlorine and ammonia are hostile agents. Ideally there will be no significant concentrations in the water or air. Chlorine's ability to neutralize ammonia and chloramines depends on water treatment details vs. the type and concentration of contaminants, water pH, the type and amount of dissolved solids, water temperature, the number of people in the pool, pool activity level, etc.

Water Chemistry Requirements						
Issue	**Swimming Pool**			**Spa**		
	Preferred	**Minimum**	**Maximum**[1]	**Preferred**	**Minimum**	**Maximum**[1]
Free chlorine (PPM)	2.0 to 4.0	1.0	4.0 to 5.0	3.0 to 5.0	2.0	4.0 to 10.0
Combined chlorine (PPM)	0.0	0.0	0.2	0.0	0.0	0.5
Dissolved solids (PPM)	na	na	1,500 [2]	na	na	1,500 [2]
Total Alkalinity (PPM)	80 to 100	60	180	80 to 100	60	180
Calcium hardness (PPM)	200 to 400	150	1,000	150 to 250	100	800
pH	7.4 to 7.6	7.2	7.8	7.4 to 7.6	7.2	7.8

1) The US Environmental Protection Agency limit may be 4 parts per million (PPM).
2) 1,500 PPM over startup value
3) See ANSI/APSP -1, -2, -3, -5 and -9; Subject to change without notice, contact the Association of Pool and Spa Professionals.
4) Deficient chlorine causes excessive release of chloramines, foul odors; bacteria, fungus, viruses, etc. not controlled.
5) High pH or high alkalinity causes scale on water heater and pipe surfaces, etc.
6) Low pH or low alkalinity causes corrosion, damages metal parts, damages water heaters

Figure 4-1

This complex relationship is quantified by water testing procedures, then test results determine what chemicals and doses must be added to the water.

- The minimum ratio of free chlorine to chloramines is 10:1. An excessive dose of free chlorine (water shocking) is used when the concentration of combined chlorine is excessive (shocking a pool can make matters worse if not done properly).

- Federal law requires municipal water suppliers to sanitize with monochloramine. Therefore, the combined chlorine in fill water or make-up water may be 20 to 200 times more than the maximum a pool should have. Thus, most pool fills must be shocked immediately after adding water.

- Water purging and water make-up for evaporation may not dilute contaminants (see preceding bullet).

- Water purging increases the amount of heat used for makeup water.

- Water stirring (turnovers) maximizes water treatment effectiveness.

- Filters have a significant effect on water chemistry.

- Ozone treatment reduces the amount of combined chlorine in the water.

- Investigate UV and ionization treatments.

- High pH causes scale that may damage or reduce the efficiency of water heaters, pipes, pumps, etc.

- Low pH water is acidic and corrosive. This can damage water system equipment.

4-4 Chemical Storage

Water treatment chemicals shall be stored in a separate ventilated space (this is a code requirement for many locations). Water treatment chemicals shall not be stored in a mechanical equipment room, electrical equipment room, or any space that opens to a natatorium.

- A transfer duct from the chemical storage room to the pool space or any other space is prohibited.

- The chemical storage room shall have its own continuous exhaust system with a flow or pressure switch that activates a failure light or alarm.

4-5 Materials must Resist Chemical Attack

Mechanical systems have to resist the action of airborne chemicals. Adequate corrosion protection is required for HVAC equipment cabinets, coils, heat exchanges, blowers and shafts, dampers, ducts, supply outlets, return grilles, etc. Provide appropriate metals, finishes and coatings for everything that comes in contact with indoor air.

- Use cupro-nickel materials, brass parts, stainless steel parts.

- Use plastics or cadmium plated steel.

- Use special coatings on heating and refrigerant coils, copper tubing or parts, and steel parts.

- Use plastic ducts and pipe (as permitted by fire codes).

- Use appropriate paints and finishes.

Companies that manufacture mechanical dehumidifiers and desiccant dehumidifiers have experience with materials compatibility problems. Therefore, their literature lists available materials and features, and provides specific installation and maintenance instructions. This guidance is educational because it helps practitioners understand the issues that apply to any type of HVAC equipment or ancillary device.

- Internal components that process chemical laden air must be made of suitable materials, regardless of equipment location.

- The cabinet, various panels, electrical devices, controls, and every other item that is not in the air stream will be exposed to chemical laden air if the equipment is installed in the pool or spa space.

- Materials compatibility problems are manageable when installation instructions specify that equipment be installed outside of a pool or spa space.

- If the equipment is installed outside the pool or spa space, it follows that there must be no air leaks in the internal path though the unit, or in the duct runs to and from the unit (i.e., do not contaminate the ambient air).

4-6 Water Heater Capacity

Figure 4-2 (next page) shows the heating loads for a pool water heating system. For this example, the design temperature for 54,000 Gallons (Gal) of water is 80 °F, and the temperature for fill water or make-up water is 50 °F. The latent evaporation load for pool water is 91,360 Btuh.

Cold Fill Heat

Notice that the water heater must heat cold fill water from 50°F to 80°F. Therefore the cold fill heat (CFH) is the amount of heat required to bring fill water to design temperature, as determined by this equation.

CFH (Btu) = 8.345 x Fill Gallons x TR

Where:
One Gallon of water = 8.345 Lb
Specific heat for water = 1.0 Btu / (Lb·°F)

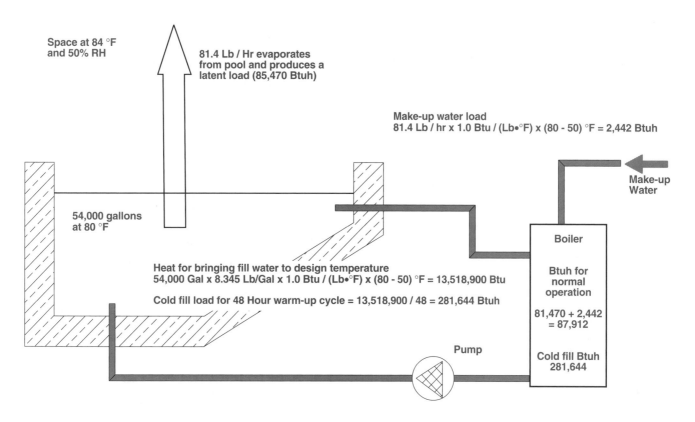

Figure 4-2

Load factor = 8.345 x 1.0 = 8.345 Btu / Gal·°F
TR (°F) = Design water temp - Fill water temp

For this example the total amount of heat that must be added to the fill water is about 13,519,000 Btu.

CFH = 8.345 x 54,000 x (80 - 50) °F = 13,518,900 Btu

Cold Fill Load

Cold fill heat must be added to the water in a reasonable amount of time (discuss this with the owner-manager), which is the warm-up time (WUT) in hours. The warm-up time determines the cold fill load (CFL). For 48 hours, the cold fill load is about 282,000 Btu.

CFL (Btuh) = CFL / WUT

CFL = 13,518,900 / 48 = 281,644 Btuh

Evaporation Load

When pool water is at the desired temperature, it continuously loses heat because of evaporation (this is a latent load to the pool space). If there is no heat recovery equipment, this heat is lost when it is expelled to the outdoors.

Heat must be added to pool water to compensate for evaporation. The latent evaporation load (LEL) depends on the evaporation rate (ER) from Section 6 procedures.

For this example, the evaporation rate (ER) is 81.4 Lb/Hr and the conversion factor is 1,050 Btu/Lb, so the latent evaporation load (LEL) is 85,470 Btuh.

LEL = 1,050 x ER

LEL = 1,050 x 81.4 = 85,470 Btuh

Make-Up Water Load

Notice that about 9.75 gallons per hour (81.4 Lb/Hr) of make-up water is required, and that this flow must be heated from 50°F to 80°F. Therefore, the make-up water load (MWL) is 2,442 Btuh.

MWL = 1.0 x ER x TR

MWL = 1.0 x 81.4 x (80 - 50) °F = 2,442 Btuh

Note: There is a water flow rate for replacing evaporated water and a water replacement rate for pool water chemistry. Use the largest Lb/Hr value to calculate the make-up water load.

Pool Use Load

When the pool is in use, the load on the water heating equipment equals the sum of the evaporation load and the make-up water load. This is the pool use load (PUL).

PUL = LEL + MWL

Where:
LEL and MWL are for the operating condition that pro-
duces the most evaporation. This depends on the number
of people using the pool and their activity level, and on
what fountain, spray, etc., devices are active or inactive.

For this example, the pool use load is about 87,912 Btuh.

PUL = 85,470 + 2,442 = 87,912 Btuh

Water Heater Capacity

Water heater capacity is determined by the cold fill load (CFL) or the pool use load (PUL), whichever is larger. These loads will be different, and can be very different in magnitude. Consider these options if the cold fill load is considerably larger than the pool use load:

- Increase the warm up time (WUT) to reduce the cold fill load.

- The pool use load is a soft number because of various uncertainties. Increase the value by 10% to 15% for equipment selection.

- Use water heating equipment that has staged capacity.

- Use two water heaters, one for cold fill and one for normal operation.

For the example, the cold fill load is much larger than the pool use load. The two loads are more compatible if WUT is increased from 48 hours to 120 hours, and a 1.15 factor is applied to PUL. Now it looks like 100,000 Btuh of output capacity would be about right, providing a five day warmup is acceptable.

CFL for 48 hrs = 281,644 Btuh
CFL for 120 Hrs = 112,658 Btuh
PUL = 87,912 Btuh
PUL x 1.15 = 101,099 Btuh

4-7 Heat Recovery for Water Heating

The latent evaporation load (LEL) is recoverable heat year-round, but an evaporator coil is required to take advantage of the opportunity. For example, if dry outdoor air is used to control indoor humidity, latent heat is just rejected to the outdoors, but refrigeration cycle equipment can capture this heat and use it to heat pool water. Packaged dehumidifier equipment may provide this option (see Section 8-1).

- The unoccupied evaporation load is relatively constant for any outdoor condition because space temperature and humidity set points are fixed values. This is a latent load for an evaporator coil year-round. This load increases when patrons cause splashing and dripping.

- Spectator metabolism increases the latent load. Outdoor air for spectators can increase or decrease the latent load, depending on outdoor air moisture.

- The functional and economical advantage of the latent reclaim option depends on the hour-by-hour size of the latent load through the year.

- The instantaneous latent load on the evaporator coil is converted to reclaimable heat stored in hot refrigerant gas. This heat can be used to heat pool water and/or supply air.

4-8 Condensate for Make-Up Water

Condensation occurs when refrigeration cycle equipment neutralizes the latent evaporation load (LEL). Local codes may or may not allow this to be used for make-up water. If condensate is used for make-up water, it should be filtered and treated before it is returned to the pool.

4-9 Swimming Pool Heat Pump

Swimming pool heat pumps can heat pool water or cool pool water. Units that heat water can be used for indoor or outdoor pools. Units that cool pool water are for outdoor pools (typically for a hot, sunny climate).

- An air-to-water heat pump can extract heat from outdoor air and use it to heat pool water. However, effectiveness and efficiency decrease with decreasing outdoor air temperature, so performance is better in a warm climate.

- A water-to-air heat pump can extract heat from pool water and reject it to outdoor air.

- Water to water heat pumps can perform the same functions.

- For indoor pools, reclaimed heat, fossil fuel heat or electric heat are the common source of water heat for normal operation.

- For indoor pools, fossil fuel heat or electric heat are the common source of cold fill heat and backup heat.

- For normal operation, the benefit of heat pump equipment depends on heating capacity during cold weather, installation cost and annual operating cost, compared to the performance and costs for reclaimed heat, fossil fuel heat or electric heat.

- For cold fill heat, heat pump equipment will be oversized for normal operation.

- The scope of this manual is limited to indoor pools. Information about heat pump packages for outdoor pools is available from a variety of manufacturer's.

Section 5

Indoor Air Quality and Ventilation

Swimming pools require a relatively large amount of outdoor air for engineered ventilation. This produces a significant sensible load on the heating and cooling equipment, and a significant latent cooling load during humid weather.

5-1 Mold and Mildew

Indoor humidity in the 50% to 60% RH range is compatible with human comfort. However, this level of humidity can cause visible and concealed condensation during cold weather, which can lead to mold, mildew and building damage (see Section 3-8).

- The mechanical system tries to maintain 50% to 60% RH in the space all the time (it may be somewhat less than 50% RH during very cold weather).
- The building envelope must be designed to prevent visible or concealed condensation (see Section 3).

5-2 Chemicals Affect Indoor Air Quality

Chemicals are added to swimming pool or spa water for health and sanitation reasons. These chemicals kill germs and combine with organic materials in the water. Some amount of feed chemicals and byproducts of chemical reactions are released to the indoor air. This will cause an air quality problem if the concentration of airborne chemicals exceeds an acceptable limit.

- Chlorine is the primary sanitation and cleaning agent. It kills germs and breaks down contaminants.
- Manufactured contaminants introduced by patrons include cosmetics, perfume, hair spray and body lotion. These may not be completely broken down if concentrations are too high.
- Ammonia and toxins in sweat, urine and feces are chemical contaminants.
- Chlorine may or may not reduce ammonia, toxins and contaminants to basic elements (such as water, carbon dioxide and nitrogen). Success depends on many variables, not least of which is having the right amount of chlorine in the water, and periodic super-chlorination. The use of secondary oxidizers, e.g. U.V., ozone, may help.
- Hostile molecules such as monochloramine, dichloramine, and nitrogen trichloride (trichloramine) form during the sanitation process. Some of these molecules escape to the indoor air. Heavily used pools produce more of these

corrosive chemicals. Super-chlorination on test is necessary to minimize the production

- A sharp smell is actually caused by airborne chloramines that are released to indoor air when water chemistry is not balanced (excessive combined chloramines).
- The airborne chemical problem is exacerbated by water churning and aeration by water slides, water falls, bubblers, fountains, geysers and water mushrooms. The multiplier for the increase in airborne contaminants can range from about 1.5 to more than 5.0.
- Breathing contaminated air may cause noise, throat and pulmonary inflammation and stress the immune system. This depends on the concentration of offending molecules, the length of exposure and the sensitivity of the person breathing the air.

5-3 Spectators Affect Indoor Air Quality

A competition swimming pool will usually have a spectator area. For this application, the number of spectators affects indoor air quality.

- People release moisture, odors and scents, and produce carbon dioxide.
- The seating area may be empty, partially full, or completely full. The engineered ventilation requirement varies accordingly.

5-4 Minimum Outdoor Air Cfm Requirement

The ASHRAE 62.1 - 2007 Standard specifies minimum outdoor air Cfm requirements for commercial and institutional swimming pools. The outdoor air Cfm for the water surface area and wet deck area dilutes chemicals escaping from wet surfaces. The outdoor air Cfm for the spectator area provides outdoor air for observers.

- 0.48 Cfm/SqFt for the water surface area
- 0.48 Cfm/SqFt for wet deck area
- 7.5 Cfm per person for the spectator area

Per Standard 62.1, the outdoor air Cfm for the wet area is added to the outdoor air Cfm requirement for spectators. Base the spectator Cfm value on the largest number of spectators that may attend an event. If the seat count for the spectator area is not known, use 150 people per 1,000 square feet of spectator area to determine maximum occupancy.

- The ASHRAE standard does not provide a rule for determining wet deck area. It is reasonable to assume that the wet deck surface extends two to six feet beyond the edge of the pool.

- The ASHRAE standard does not mention spas. Use 0.48 Cfm/SqFt for water surface and wet deck surface. It is reasonable to assume that the wet deck surface extends three to six feet beyond the edge of the spa. Assume there are no spectators.

- Outdoor air shall mix with the ambient air away from wet surfaces in the room and away from the ambient air near spectators.

- A local code may say that the larger of the ventilation rates (wet surface Cfm or spectator Cfm) is the minimum ventilation rate. In this case, the code authorizes a minimum lawful requirement that is less than the Standard 62.1 requirement (the difference could be relevant during litigation).

- The 0.48 Cfm/SqFt value for wet area assumes that water treatment chemicals and procedures are appropriate and effective.

- A purge cycle is a temporary operating condition that uses 100 percent outdoor air for supply air Cfm (see Section 5-5).

5-5 Purge Cycle

A large dose of chlorine (*water shocking*) may be used to bring unbalanced water chemistry under control. This is done when the space is unoccupied because it produces a high concentration of airborne chemicals that must be purged before the space is occupied. Equipment that has purge cycle capability may flush the space with 100% outdoor air for several minutes to several hours.

Purge Cfm depends on equipment design. In this regard, the maximum outdoor air Cfm for a standard dehumidifier depends on the indoor air quality requirement for normal use. Dehumidifier manufacturers have ways to increases outdoor air Cfm when the desired purge value is greater than the normal use value.

Then, there is the issue of maintaining space temperature and humidity during a purge cycle. Ideally, the condition of the outdoor air entering the space will be compatible with the design set points for space dry-bulb temperature and space humidity.

- Additional heating and cooling capacity may be required for a purge cycle.

- Humid outdoor air may add moisture to space air, dry outdoor air reduces the amount of moisture in space air.

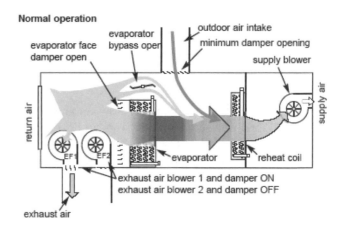

Normal operation

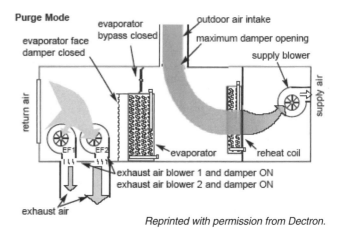

Purge Mode

Reprinted with permission from Dectron.

Figure 5-1

- Significant changes in space air temperature and humidity affect the evaporation rate for wet surfaces. This affects psychrometric energy balances and water chemistry.

- A cold weather purge with 100% outdoor air may reduce the space temperature by several degrees without causing significant condensation because the relative humidity of heated outdoor air is very low and the purge is usually completed in less than 15 minutes.

- Figure 5-1 shows how one dehumidifier manufacturer deals with the purge issue. In this case the OEM has specifications for outdoor air Cfm and entering outdoor air temperature. In addition, when outdoor humidity and temperature are suitable, the purge mode may function as an economizer (uses outdoor air for cooling and dehumidification).

- Discuss equipment arrangements and purge cycle features with the people that sell dehumidification systems and equipment.

5-6 Adjusting Ventilation Cfm

Energy use and operating cost for swimming pool enclosures are important issues, as is equipment cost. A dehumidification system that can adjust outdoor air Cfm to match demand is more expensive to install, but less expensive to operate. Even if the dehumidification system cannot adjust outdoor air Cfm, the use of outdoor air should be minimized.

- If there is no spectator area, outdoor air Cfm is required for the water surface area and the wet deck area. The minimum ventilation requirement is provided by Section 5-4.

- Wet deck area and chemical release depends on pool activity and use of water park devices (sprays, slides, fountains, etc). Design for the worst case. Consider adjusting outdoor air Cfm according to activity level or the concentration of airborne chemicals (if allowed by ASHRAE 62.1).

- If there is a spectator area, the amount of additional outdoor air Cfm for people can be adjusted according to the number of spectators.

- For lowest energy cost, close the outdoor air damper when the space is not in use .

- If outdoor air dampers are closed when the facility is unoccupied, there may be a need to purge contaminants prior to occupancy. This depends on the attributes of the facility. Sometimes, opening the outdoor-air intake prior to occupancy is sufficient (this may required experimentation).

- If there is a spectator area, consider using a dedicated outdoor air system for the spectator area (see Section 5-7).

5-7 Dedicated Outdoor Air System

Pools that have a large spectator area require a relatively large amount of outdoor air Cfm during an event. This requirement may be satisfied by the equipment that dehumidifies space air, but it may be better to use a dedicated outdoor air system (DOAS) for the spectator area.

- The performance of the space dehumidifier can be optimized for normal operations.

- For normal operations, or during an event, the space dehumidifier provides outdoor air for wet water surfaces and wet deck area.

- DOAS equipment provides 100% outdoor air for spectators when there is an event.

- The performance of DOAS equipment can be optimized for spectator ventilation.

- DOAS equipment can be shut down when there is no significant spectator count.

- For spectator comfort, discharge air from DOAS equipment can be a few degrees cooler than space air.

- DOAS equipment will have its own energy conservation features.

- DOAS equipment will have its own air distribution system.

5-8 Exhaust Cfm and Space Pressure

A space that has a pool or spa shall be a separate zone and must be maintained at negative pressure with respect to other conditioned spaces and unconditioned spaces, except for the space used to store water treatment chemicals (see Section 1-6). Space pressure shall be maintained by a supply air fan, an exhaust fan or return air fan, and set of interlocked airflow dampers. The location of the exhaust fan or return air fan, and the capture grille depends on the application.

- An exhaust fan for a pool space may be installed in a roof or wall, in an exhaust duct, or in an air handler cabinet.

- A return air fan for a pool space may be installed in a return duct, or as part of the dehumidification equipment.

- If the pool space does not have a spa, the exhaust air grille or grilles can be installed in the ceiling or a wall. A floor location is undesirable because of the possibility or water getting into a duct run.

- If the space has a spa, the preferred location for an *exhaust air grille* is directly above the spa, and as close as possible to the spa.

- Where capture grilles are located above a spa or hot tub, the attached duct should not connect to an air handler with air heat exchangers. Entrained human skin oil will foul the heat exchangers irrevocably, usually within three to four years.

- Capture grille effectiveness is exponentially reduced as the distance between the tub and the grille increases. For example, a capture grille in a ceiling that is 20 feet above the spa would not be nearly as effective as one that is six feet above the tub.

- The effectiveness of the capture grille increases with face velocity, and so does generated noise. Grille noise is not much of an issue because spas are noisy. Grille face velocity may exceed the 400 Fpm limit that commonly applies to simple comfort condition applications.

- A pool or spa space typically has adjacent locker room spaces. The exhaust Cfm for a dressing room that has lockers is 0.25 Cfm/SqFt. The exhaust

Cfm for a locker room that is not a dressing room is 0.50 Cfm/SqFt.

- Locker rooms and showers should have their own HVAC systems and the space pressure should be less negative than the pool area pressure.

5-9 Air Turnover Rate

One air turnover occurs when all the space air is replaced by supply air in one hour. This is commonly called an air change rate (ACH), but this gets confusing because air change terminology also applies to outdoor air Cfm for ventilation (space air replaced by outdoor air).

The minimum value for space air turnovers is 4 per hour. ASHRAE Standard 62 recommends 4–6 turnovers per hour for non-spectator pools and 6–8 turnovers per hour for spectator pools. Supply air Cfm also depends on space heating and cooling loads (see Section 10).

5-10 Introduction of Outdoor Air

If the humidity in a swimming pool or spa space is controlled by a mechanical dehumidifier, outdoor air may be introduced downstream from the evaporator coil, as demonstrated by Figure 5-2. The rationale for this arrangement is provided here:

- If mixed air enters the evaporator coil, the dry-bulb and wet-bulb temperatures of the entering air depend on the condition of the outdoor air. This has a significant effect on evaporator capacity and coil sensible heat ratio.

- Delivering mixed air to an evaporator coil complicates equipment selection procedure because the coil sensible heat ratio is different than the space sensible heat ratio.

- The space sensible heat ratio, entering air condition and the coil sensible heat ratio are relatively constant for 100% return air.

- One entering air condition and one sensible heat ratio simplifies equipment selection procedures.

- One entering air condition and one sensible heat ratio greatly reduces capacity control problems (the load on the evaporator coil only depends on space use, and is not affected by the condition of the outdoor air).

- Return air is relatively humid (50% to 60% RH), during cold weather.

- If cold outdoor air is mixed with warm, humid return air upstream from the evaporator coil, condensation may occur in the mixing box.

- If relatively dry outdoor air is mixed with return air, the latent load on the evaporator coil is reduced. If the outdoor air is slightly warm , cool or cold, the sensible load on the evaporator coil is reduced.

- The evaporator coil load is reclaimable heat (hot compressor gas may be used for pool water heat and/or supply air). Reducing the load on the evaporator coil reduces the amount of reclaimable heat.

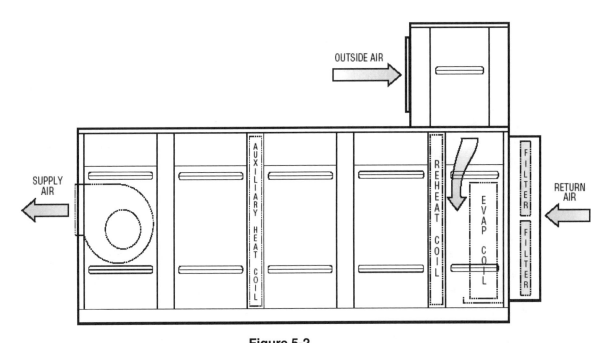

Figure 5-2

Note that the preceding bullet items may or may not apply to systems that use outdoor air for humidity control, and to systems that use conventional comfort cooling equipment for humidity control. Consider this:

- The condensation issue (bullet seven) applies if an outdoor air system mixes outdoor air with return air, and to conventional cooling equipment that processes mixed air.

- The heat reclaim issue (bullet nine) does not apply to a simple outdoor air system or standard cooling equipment because they do not reclaim heat extracted from mixed air.

- The entering condition, sensible heat ratio, equipment selection and capacity control issues (bullets one, two and eight) apply to conventional cooling equipment that processes mixed air.

5-11 Heat Recovery for Ventilation Air

Outdoor air for indoor air quality is required whenever the space is occupied for normal use, and the outdoor air Cfm requirement increases when spectators are present. Space pressure is negative, so exhaust air Cfm is somewhat greater than outdoor air Cfm.

Exhaust air is always warm and humid, so it has significant reclaimable heat during cold weather when heating is required, and less reclaimable heat during warm weather when cooling is required. Some fraction of the heat in exhaust air can be reclaimed by various types of air to air heat exchangers (see Section 9).

5-12 Condensation Caused by Mixed Air

Mold and mildew (as well as materials damage, equipment damage, and frozen moisture) is caused by condensation. Condensation may occur when outdoor air is mixed with warm humid return air, or cool humid air.

Surface Condensation

Condensation occurs if the dew point temperature of air that contacts a surface is warmer than the temperature of the surface. In this regard, pools and spas are radically different than normal comfort heating applications.

- For a pool or spa space at 80 °F dry-bulb and 50% to 60% RH, the dew point temperature for return air ranges from about 60 °F to about 65 °F.

- For a non-pool space, at 70 °F dry-bulb and 20% to 30% RH, the dew point temperature for return air ranges from about 27 °F to about 37 °F.

Saturated Air

Mixing warm humid air with cold air may produce saturated air. In this regard, pool and spa applications are

Relative Humidity for Mixed Air Return Air Mixed with Outdoor Air			
Outdoor Air Fraction	Return Dry-Bulb and Relative Humidity		
	Pool or Spa		Normal
	80°F; 60% RH	80°F; 50% RH	70°F; 30% RH
10%	79% @ -20°F	66% @ -20°F	39% @ -20°F
20%	100% @ -17°F	86% @ -20°F	49% @ -20°F
30%	100% @ 3°F	100% @ -12°F	60% @ -20°F

1) This table shows mixed air relative humidity and the coincident outdoor air temperature (limited to -20°F for this investigation).
2) 30% RH could cause condensation problems for an ordinary structure in a cold climate (used as an upper limit for this comparison).
3) Elevation = Sea level
4) Similar calculations shall be made with altitude sensitive psychrometric software.

Figure 5-3

radically different than normal comfort heating applications, as demonstrated by Figure 5-3.

- For a pool or spa space, mixed air can be saturated for common outdoor air fractions and common winter temperatures.

- Saturation is not an issue for comfort heating applications.

Values for Mixed Air Calculations

Condensation caused by mixed air may or may not be a problem, depending on the type of equipment. If mixed air condensation is an issue, calculations are based on the most severe conditions that may occur.

- Use the combination of space dry-bulb temperature and relative humidity that produces the highest dew point value for indoor air (this depends on the mechanical system's ability to limit space temperature swing and space humidity swing).

- Use the worst-case scenario for outdoor air dry-bulb temperature (this could be 10 °F to more than 30 °F colder than the 99.6% dry-bulb temperature, check local weather data).

5-13 Preheat for Conventional Mixing Box

For conventional equipment, warm humid return air and cold outdoor air are mixed before mixed air passes through heating or cooling equipment. However, Figure 5-3 shows that mixed air can be saturated when the outdoor air is cold or very cold.

Saturated air is unacceptable because moisture is ready to condense. Preheating the flow of outdoor air provides a margin of safety. However, raising outdoor air dry-bulb by 10 °F, 20 °F or 30 °F may not provide as much of a cushion as one may think. As demonstrated by Figure 5-4:

- Mixing 30% outdoor air at 3 °F and 90% RH with 70% return air at 80 °F and 60% RH produces saturated air, so mixed air temperature equals dew point temperature.

- If the flow of outdoor air is heated to 13 °F, the relative humidity of the mixed air drops to 90%, and the difference between the mixed air temperature and the dew point temperature is 3 °F.

- If the flow of outdoor air is heated to 23 °F, the relative humidity of the mixed air drops to 82%, and the difference between the mixed air temperature and the dew point temperature is 5 °F.

- If the flow of outdoor air is heated to 33 °F, the relative humidity of the mixed air drops to 76%, and the difference between the mixed air temperature and the dew point temperature is 8 °F.

5-14 Preheat for Dehumidifier Arrangement

The dehumidifier arrangement (Figure 5-5) introduces outdoor air downstream from an evaporator coil. Dehumidified air is already close to saturation (say, 90% to 95% RH) when it leaves an evaporator coil, so, it is more likely that mixed air will be saturated when cold outdoor air is mixed with evaporator discharge air, as demonstrated by Figure 5-6 (next page).

In addition, some warm humid return air bypasses the evaporator coil, so warm humid return air is mixed with cold outdoor near the top of the evaporator coil (Figure 5-5). Therefore, the mixed air condition near the top of the evaporator coil is equivalent to a conventional mixing arrangement (Figure 5-4).

Figures 5-4 and 5-6 show that condensation may occur, however a dehumidifier manufacturer may say that preheat is not required. This depends on drip pan length and the coldest temperature in the mixed air chamber.

- If there is a long drip pan between the refrigerant coil and the reheat coil, mixed air condensation is captured and drained with refrigerant coil condensation.

- If the mixed air temperature never falls below 32 °F, evaporator coil icing is not a problem.

- Some dehumidifier manufacturers set a 32°F low limit for mixed air temperature.

- Some dehumidifier manufacturers may require preheat when outdoor air temperature is -20°F or colder, regardless of mixed air temperature.

Preheat for Conventional Mixed Air 30% Outdoor Air at 3°F					
Preheat (°F)	OADB (°F)	MARH	MADP (°F)	MAT (°F)	SF (°F)
0	3	100%	54	54	0
10	13	90%	55	58	3
20	23	82%	56	61	5
30	33	76%	57	65	8

1) Sea level; outdoor air at 3 °F and 90% RH; 30% outdoor air; return air at 80 °F and 60% RH.

2) Preheat = Temperature rise for flow of outdoor air
OADB = Dry-bulb temperature of outdoor air that mixes with return air
MARH = Mixed air relative humidity
MADP = Mixed air dew point
MAT = Mixed air temperature
SF = Safety factor = MAT - MADP

3) Similar calculations shall be made with altitude sensitive psychrometric software.

Figure 5-4

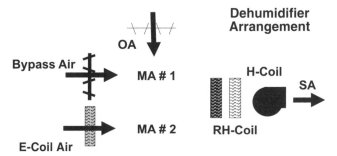

1) MA # 1... Warm humid air bypasses the evaporator coil and mixes with cold outdoor air (Figure 5-4 shows the consequences).

2) MA # 2... Return air that has been cooled and dehumidified by an evaporator coil mixes with cold outdoor air (Figure 5-6 shows the consequences).

Figure 5-5

- An equipment manufacturer may set a limit to the outdoor air fraction, say 30% of supply Cfm, for example.

Study the manufacturer's engineering literature and installation instructions, and discuss outdoor air issues with the engineering department or sales engineer.

- Determine the limit on outdoor air Cfm for normal operation (refrigerant coil dehumidification), and for a purge cycle (if applicable).

- Determine if preheat is required.

- Determine who is responsible for preheat.

- Learn how to size, install and control preheat equipment.

■ Dehumidifier equipment may have an air-side economizer and/or a purge cycle. When these devices operate, supply air Cfm may be 100% outdoor air. Investigate need and/or benefit. If used, conform to guidance and instructions provided by the equipment manufacturer .

5-15 Preheat for Air-to-Air Reclaim Equipment

Air to air heat reclaim equipment (sensible heat only, and total heat) can produce freezing condensation when warm humid air flows through one side of the equipment while cold outdoor air flows through the other side. Use equipment manufacturers' guidance to determine if frost and icing will be a problem. If it is a problem, preheat is one way to prevent frost and icing, but this may not be the only option (see Section 9).

5-16 Hoods and Screens

Moisture causes mold and mildew, and moisture can damage materials and equipment. Rain and snow must not be captured by air intake openings. Provide appropriate caps, goose necks, hoods and screens.

Air intake openings shall not be located in a position that would capture contaminated air, exhaust air, or combustion equipment vent gas. Comply with codes and standards, and comply with equipment manufactures' installation instructions.

Relative Humidity for Mixed Air Evaporator Discharge Air Mixed with Outdoor Air			
Outdoor Air Fraction	**OADB (°F)**	**MARH**	**MAT (°F)**
10%	3		49
20%	19	100	47
30%	23		45

1) Sea level; evaporator coil discharge air at 55 °F and 90% RH; outdoor air at 90% RH.
2) OADB = Dry-bulb temperature of outdoor air that mixes with return air
    MARH = Mixed air relative humidity
    MAT = Mixed air temperature
3) Similar calculations shall be made with altitude sensitive psychrometric software.

Figure 5-6

Section 6

Evaporation Load

Pool and spa applications are unique because of the latent load produced by evaporation. This load depends on water temperature and water churning, space temperature and relative humidity, and the amount of water and wet deck surface area. Air velocity across wet surfaces has a secondary effect, and altitude has no effect.

6-1 Default Evaporation Rate

Table A5-4 lists the default evaporation flux (DEF) in pounds of water per square foot of wet surface. This table is for a normal amount of swimming, splashing and wet deck area. As the table shows, the evaporation flux for one square foot of surface depends on water temperature, space air temperature and space relative humidity. Therefore the default evaporation rate (DER) for the entire wet surface equals the product of the default evaporation flux and the area (A) of the wet surface.

$$DER\ (Lbs\ /\ Hr) = DEF\ (Lbs\ /\ Hr \bullet SqFT) \times A\ (SqFt)$$

For example, 600 SqFt of pool water surface releases 22.44 pounds of water to the indoor air when the water temperature is 80°F and the condition of the pool air is 82°F dry-bulb and 60% RH.

$$DEF\ (Table\ A5\text{-}4) = 0.0374\ Lb/Hr \cdot SqFt$$
$$DER = 0.0374 \times 600 = 22.44\ Lb/Hr$$

6-2 Activity Adjustment

The evaporation flux decreases or increases for different levels of activity. Table A5-5 (next page) provides adjustment factors for various amounts of water churning. Therefore, the evaporation rate (ER) for the wet surface depends on the default evaporation flux value from Table A5-4, the activity factor (AF) from Table A5-5 and the area (A) of the wet surface.

$$ER\ (Lbs\ /\ Hr) = DEF\ (Lbs\ /\ Hr \bullet SqFT) \times AF \times A\ (SqFt)$$

Default Evaporation Flux (DEF)

Water Temperature	Space Air Temperature and Relative Humidity											
	76 °F		78 °F		80 °F		82 °F		84 °F		86 °F	
°F	50%	60%	50%	60%	50%	60%	50%	60%	50%	60%	50%	60%
76	0.0456	0.0364	0.0424	0.0326	0.0392	0.0288	0.0356	0.0246	0.0320	0.0200	0.0280	0.0154
78	0.0482	0.0390	0.0450	0.0352	0.0418	0.0314	0.0382	0.0272	0.0346	0.0226	0.0306	0.0180
80	0.0584	0.0494	0.0554	0.0456	0.0520	0.0416	0.0486	0.0374	0.0448	0.0330	0.0410	0.0282
82	0.0656	0.0564	0.0624	0.0526	0.0592	0.0488	0.0556	0.0444	0.0520	0.0400	0.0480	0.0354
84	0.0730	0.0640	0.0700	0.0602	0.0666	0.0562	0.0630	0.0520	0.0594	0.0476	0.0554	0.0428
86	0.0810	0.0718	0.0778	0.0680	0.0746	0.0640	0.0710	0.0598	0.0674	0.0554	0.0634	0.0508
88	0.0894	0.0802	0.0862	0.0764	0.0830	0.0724	0.0794	0.0682	0.0756	0.0638	0.0718	0.0590
90	0.0984	0.0892	0.0952	0.0854	0.0918	0.0814	0.0884	0.0772	0.0846	0.0728	0.0806	0.0680
102	0.1634	0.1542	0.1604	0.1504	0.1570	0.1464	0.1534	0.1422	0.1496	0.1376	0.1456	0.1328
104	0.1764	0.1672	0.1734	0.1634	0.1700	0.1594	0.1664	0.1552	0.1626	0.1506	0.1586	0.1458

1) DEF = Pounds of water per hour per square foot of wet surface for a normal amount of Swimming, splashing and wet deck area.

2) Table values do not change with altitude.

3) Table values are for about 25 feet per minute air velocity over wet surface (the default for appropriate air distribution, see Section 12).

Air Velocity (Fpm)	5	10	15	20	25	30	40	50
Adjustment Factor	0.92	0.94	0.96	0.98	1.00	1.02	1.06	1.10

Copy of Table A5-4

Activity Factor (AF) for Water Churning	
Application	**AF**
Still water surface	0.50
Residential pool	0.50
Private multi-family, fitness club pool	0.80
Therapy, elderly swimmers pool	0.80
Hotel or motel swimming pool	0.65
Dive or swim competition in progress	0.65
Public swimming pool	1.00
Institutional swimming pool	1.00
Spa or whirl pool	1.00
Water slides Note 2	Speculative
Water fall and collection pool Note 2	No guidance
Fountains	No guidance
Wave pool, water cannon; etc.	No guidance
1) Multiply Table A5-4 values by the applicable adjustment factor. 2) See Sections 6-6 and 6-7.	

Copy of Table A5-5

For example, 600 SqFt of public pool water surface releases 22.44 pounds of water per hour. If the pool is in a hotel, the activity factor is 0.65, so the evaporation rate is 14.6 pounds per hour.

$$ER = 0.0374 \times 0.65 \times 600$$
$$= 14.6 \ Lb/Hr$$

6-3 Evaporation Load

The latent heat of evaporation for water ranges from 1,050 Btu per pound for 76°F water to 1,034 Btu per pound for 104°F water, so a default value of 1,050 Btu per pound is used for the latent load calculation. The latent load for evaporation (LEL) equals the product of the evaporation rate (ER) and the default value for the latent heat of evaporation.

$$LEL \ (Btuh) = 1,050 \times ER$$

For example, the ER value for the previous example is 14.6 Lb/Hr, so the latent load is 15,330 Btuh.

$$LEL = 1,050 \times 14.6 = 15,330 \ Btuh$$

6-4 Caveats and Tendencies

The adjustment for water churning, splashing and dripping depends on what is expected to happen at the pool location. For example, a residential pool that has intensive use may have a 0.7 activity factor.

- The Table A5-5 activity factors account for evaporation from the wet deck area.

- Water evaporates from wet people on the pool deck. The Table A5-5 activity factors account for this affect, and for participant metabolism. (The internal load produced by spectators is a separate calculation.)

- The evaporation rates in Table A5-4 are for a 25 Fpm air velocity at the water surface. This is compatible with the performance of supply air outlets (grilles, registers or diffusers) that are properly selected and installed (see Section 12). An air velocity adjustment (per the Table A5-4 note), is used if the air velocity at the water surface is known.

- Natatoriums with spectator seating have two evaporation rates, one for a competition with many spectators (AF = 1.6) and one for normal enthusiastic use (AF = 2.0) with few or no spectators. Check both cases.

- A pool or spa cover does not decrease the evaporation load because it is assumed to be removed when a pool or spa is in use.

The following tendencies must be considered when selecting pool water temperature and the condition of the space air.

- Evaporation increases as water temperature increases.

- Evaporation decreases as air temperature increases.

- Evaporation decreases as room relative humidity increases.

- Evaporation increases significantly as water agitation increases.

6-5 Water Parks

Water slides, water falls, wave pools, water cannon, water mushrooms, etc. produce large latent loads. At this time (2009), there is no consensus procedure for calculating the evaporation load for such items.

- The concepts in this section apply in general, but there is no standard set of activity factors for water park features, or combinations of water park features.

- The company that provides the attraction(s) may offer evaporation load guidance based on their experience.

- The water park designer, and/or a licenced professional engineer with water park experience should make the evaporation load estimate.

- This market is served by a few companies that have extensive water park experience. Defer to this knowledge (steer potential clients to a qualified organization).

- A natatorium with a simple attraction is not a water park. For example, a swimming pool may have a water slide.

6-6 Open Water Slide

The wet surface area of an open water slide produces a significant latent load. Use half the slide circumference (W) and the slide length (L) to calculate the wet area. The activity factor (AF) for the water slide area is 3.0.

Tube diameter (Ft) = D
Slide width (Ft) = W = (3.14 x D) / 2
Slide length (Ft) = L
Wet area (SqFt) = C x L
Activity factor for the slide area = 3.0
Evaporation rate (Lb/HR) = ER = DEF x 3.0 x C x L
Latent load (Btuh) = LEL = 1,050 x ER

For example, if an open water slide has a 3.0 foot diameter and a 30 foot length, and if the pool water temperature is 80 °F and the condition of the pool air is 82 °F dry-bulb and 60% RH, the latent load produced by the slide is 5,549 Btuh. This load is added to the latent load for the pool.

W = 3.14 x 3 / 2 = 4.71 Ft
L = 20 Ft
Wet area = 4.71 x 20 = 94.2 SqFt
DEF = 0.0378 Lb/Hr•SqFt (see Section 6-1)
AF = 3.0
ER = 0.0378 x 3.0 x 94.2 = 10.7 Lbs/Hr
LEL = 1,050 x 10.7 = 11,235 Btuh

Note: This assumes slide water is pumped from the pool and is about the same temperature as pool water.

Note: The latent load for the water slide is added to the latent load for the pool.

6-7 Closed Water Slide

The discharge opening of a closed-tube water slide can produce a large latent load. In this case, moist air is pushed out of the end of the tube by the slider. This air leaves the tube at about 350 to 500 Fpm and is about 80% saturated (RH equals 80%). This air is about the same temperature as room air, but is more humid than the room air, so the latent load depends on the grains difference value for discharge air and room air.

Grains difference values depend on altitude, so psychrometric calculations are adjusted for altitude. For example, the design condition for the space is 82°F dry-bulb and 60% RH, so the discharge air is 82°F dry-bulb and 80% RH. The corresponding grains difference values for sea level and 3,500 feet are provided by altitude sensitive psychrometric software.

Sea Level
Room Grains (82 °F; 60%) = 98.4
Discharge Grains (82 °F; 80%) = 132.2
Grains difference = 132.2 - 98.4 = 33.8

3,500 Feet
Room Grains (82 °F; 60%) = 112.2
Discharge Grains (82 °F; 80%) = 150.9
Grains difference = 150.9 - 112.2 = 38.7

To calculate latent load, the 350 Fpm discharge velocity is converted to a discharge flow rate (Dcfm). If sliding is continuous, the discharge flow rate depends on tube diameter (D in feet).

Dcfm = Air Velocity (Fpm) x Flow Area (SqFt)
Dcfm = 350 x 3.14 x (D / 2)^2

For example; continuous flow for a three foot tube equals 2,473 Cfm.

Dcfm = 350 x 3.14 x (3/2)^2 = 2,473

If sliding is intermittent, the discharge Cfm is adjusted for the sliding rate (SR) and the sliding time for one trip (ST). For this scenario, the first thing to do is to see if sliding time per minute is less than 60 seconds.

SR = Sliders per minute
ST = Time for one trip in seconds
Sliding is intermittent if SR x ST < 60

If sliding is intermittent, the discharge Cfm adjustment equals the sliding time per minute divided by 60.

Discharge Cfm adjustment = (SR x ST) / 60
Adjusted discharge Cfm = Dcfm x (SR x ST) / 60

For example, for two sliders per minute and a 10 second trip time, the adjusted airflow rate is 824 Cfm.

SR = 2
ST = 10
SR x ST = 20 (less than 60, so sliding is intermittent)
Adjusted discharge Cfm = 2,473 x 20 / 60 = 824

The psychrometric equation for latent heat calculates the latent load for discharge air. This equation is provided below. Note that this equation has an altitude correction factor (ACF) for air density. Table A5-6 (next page) provides approximate ACF values.

Latent Btuh = 0.68 x ACF x Cfm x Grains Difference

For example, the latent loads for continuous and intermittent sliding at sea level and 3,500 feet are computed below. The water slide load is added to the latent load for the pool.

Continuous at sea level (ACF = 1.0)
Latent load = 0.68 x 1.0 x 2,473 x 33.8 = 56,839 Btuh

Continuous at 3,500 Feet (ACF = 0.88)
Latent load = 0.68 x 0.88 x 2,473 x 38.7 = 75,948 Btuh

Intermittent at sea level (ACF = 1.0)
Latent load = 0.68 x 1.0 x 824 x 33.8 = 18,939 Btuh

Intermittent at 3,500 Feet (ACF = 0.88)
Latent load = 0.68 x 0.88 x 824 x 38.7 = 19,082 Btuh

Note: The precession implied by the altitude adjustment greatly exceeds the accuracy of the 350 Cfm, 80% RH assumption. For tube water slides, an altitude adjustment is appropriate, but not absolutely necessary.

6-8 Evaporation Equation

This equation returns the default evaporation flux for one square foot of water surface (activity factor = 1.0).

DER = (2.036 / Y) x (VP$_W$ - VP$_a$) x (95 + 0.425 x V)

Where:
DER = Evaporation rate per SqFt of wet surface
Y = Latent heat of evaporation of water at the surface water temperature (Btu / Lb).
VP$_W$ = Moisture vapor pressure for design water temperature (Psia).
VP$_a$ = Moisture vapor pressure for dew point temperature of room air (Psia).
V = Air velocity over water surface (Fpm); the default value is 25 Fpm

For example, the water temperature is 82° F, the condition of the air is 84°F and 50% RH, and the air velocity at the water surface is 25 Fpm, so the default evaporation rate is 0.0568 Lbs/(Hr • SqFt)

Y = 1,047 Btuh (see Hfg in the 2005 ASHRAE Handbook of Fundamentals, page 6.9)
VP$_W$ = 0.5415 Psia (see Pws in the 2005 ASHRAE Handbook of Fundamentals, page 6.9)
Dew point for 84 °F and 50% RH = 63.34 °F
VP$_a$ for 84 °F and 63.3 °F dew point = 0.28937

Approximate Altitude Correction Factor [1,2]	
Feet	**ACF**
0	1.00
1,000	0.97
2,000	0.93
3,000	0.89
4,000	0.87
5,000	0.84
6,000	0.80
7,000	0.77
8,000	0.75
9,000	0.72
10,000	0.69
11,000	0.66
12,000	0.63

1) Approximate adjustment factors for entering air temperatures associated with comfort heating and cooling processes.
2) Calculations for air-to-air heat exchangers, desiccant wheels heat industrial process equipment, and special heating and cooling applications may require adjustment factors that include the effect of air temperature (see Table A5-7).

Copy of Table A5-6

Use a psychrometric chart or psychrometric software to find values for dew point and VPa.
V = 15 Fpm
DER = (2.036 / 1,047) x (0.5415 - 0.28937) x (95 + 0.425 x 25) = 0.0518 Lbs / (Hr ·SqFt)

Note 1:
The 2.036 constant in the evaporation equation applies when vapor pressure is in Psia units. This constant is 1.0 for InHg units.

Note 2:
The evaporation equation and the associated activity factors (see Table A5-5) are subject to review and revision. Some practitioners have suggested alternative approaches and values to those currently recognized by ASHRAE. See the Bibliography (Appendix 7) for relevant papers.

Section 7

Heating and Cooling Loads

Pool and spa spaces are unique because of evaporation from water and wet deck surfaces. This produces an internal latent load that is added to other building loads and system loads. Section 6 provides a procedure for calculating the latent load for evaporation. Section 5 provides guidance pertaining to engineered ventilation loads. This section deals with procedures for calculating building loads and equipment sizing loads.

7-1 Envelope Loads

A set of building envelope loads may include a roof or ceiling load, wall load, floor load, fenestration load (windows, glass doors and skylights) and an infiltration load. These loads are sensible heating loads or sensible cooling loads, with the exception of the infiltration, which produces a sensible load and a latent load.

Note that moisture migration can produce a winter humidification load or a summer dehumidification load. This is not an issue if the building envelope has an effective vapor retarding membrane (see Section 1). If moisture migration is possible, the latent load is added to the other envelope loads.

7-2 Internal Loads

A large latent load is produced by evaporation from wet surfaces. This is an internal load to the conditioned space. The internal load for a pool or spa space also may include sensible and latent loads produced by people, lights and equipment. Water evaporation has no significant affect on the sensible space load (a boiler, heating element or heat exchanger maintains water temperature).

Dry spectators (male, female and children at rest)
- Default = 245 Sensible Btuh; or practitioner value
- Default = 190 Latent Btuh; or practitioner value

Swimmers in the water or on deck
- The sensible load is ignored (metabolic heat from swimmer goes to water, or causes evaporation from skin when on deck).
- The latent load for metabolic heat, splashing and dripping is embedded in the adjustment for water surface evaporation rate, per Table A5-5.

Lighting and equipment
- See *Manual N*, Fifth Edition, Table 6
- See manufacturer's ratings and performance data.

7-3 System Loads

System loads are produced by blower heat, possibly by engineered ventilation, and possibly by duct runs installed in unconditioned spaces. Blower heat is a sensible load. Duct and ventilation loads may have sensible and latent components.

- For comfort cooling equipment, outdoor air enters upstream from the evaporator coil, so this is a system load. It is important to understand that this is not true for a dehumidifier.
- The typical arrangement for a dehumidifier has outdoor air entering downstream from the evaporator coil and upstream from a reheat coil and a supplemental heating coil (see Figure 5-4).
- For cooling load calculations, outdoor air is a space load that is equivalent to infiltration.
- For sensible heating, outdoor air is a system load if all the heat is provided at the equipment or in the supply air duct (heat not provided upstream from the space is a space load).

7-4 Equipment Sizing Loads

The load for moisture removal, sensible cooling or sensible heating is the sum of the envelope loads, internal loads and system loads. These loads vary with month of year, day of week, hour of day, and depend on occupancy. The equipment sizing load is the largest value experienced during any hour of year.

- For dehumidification, find the maximum latent cooling load for the year and calculate the coincident sensible load.
- For dehumidification, find the minimum latent cooling load for the year.
- For sensible cooling, find the maximum sensible cooling load for the year and calculate the coincident latent load.
- For heating, find the maximum heating load.
- Additional load calculations may be required if the equipment has a purge cycle.
- See Section 2-4 for outdoor design conditions and see Figure 8-8 for an example.

Latent Load

The net latent load equals the sum of all the latent loads (evaporation, occupants, infiltration, ventilation and duct in unconditioned space). This load may be positive (dehumidification required), zero, or negative (humidification required), depending on circumstances.

- Evaporation produces a positive latent load year-round. The size of the evaporation load depends on occupancy (activity factor and wet deck area vs. still water and dry deck).

- Spectators produce a positive latent load during an event (full capacity in dedicated seating). There is no load when dedicated seating is unoccupied (pool space may or may not be in use).

- Since 50% to 60% relative humidity is maintained in the space year-round, outdoor air from infiltration, engineered ventilation and return duct leakage (if applicable) may produce a positive or negative latent load, depending on the moisture content of the outdoor air.

- The latent load for ventilation depends on ventilation Cfm, which depends on evaporation and occupant count (unoccupied, space in use with no spectators, event with all spectator seats filled).

The latent load for infiltration, engineered ventilation and return duct leakage (if applicable) will peak when the monthly dew point temperature peaks. For example, the summer design condition for Akron, Ohio is 85°F dry-bulb and 71°F wet-bulb, which translates to 97 grains of moisture at 1,230 Feet. The persisting 12-hour dew point temperature for August is 75.5°F, which translates to 140 grains of moisture. This means that peak outdoor air moisture can exceed the summer design condition value by a factor of... 140/97 = 1.44.

- ASHRAE weather data on CD provides values for the 1% dew point temperature and the mean coincident dry-bulb temperature.

- Maximum dew point temperatures for locations in the United States for each month of year are provided in the Climate Atlas of the United States. Version 2.0 of this document can be purchased from the National Weather Service. Type NOAA into a web site search engine, then go to the NOAA site and type ... Climate Atlas of the United States... into the NOAA search engine.

Sensible Load for Cooling

The peak envelope load, internal load, ventilation load, duct load (if applicable) and blower heat load for sensible cooling occurs when the outdoor dry-bulb temperature equals the summer design temperature. Normally, there is no discount for cloud cover, air pollution or haze.

- ASHRAE weather data on CD provides values for the 1% dry-bulb temperature and the mean coincident wet-bulb temperature.

- The sensible cooling load for the 1% dry-bulb condition will be larger than the sensible cooling load for the 1% dew point condition (assuming all USA cities follow this pattern).

Sensible Load for Heating

The peak envelope load, ventilation load and duct load (if applicable) for sensible heating occurs when the outdoor dry-bulb temperature equals the 99.6% value for winter design temperature. No credit is taken for solar gain, internal gain or blower heat.

- ASHRAE weather data on CD provide values for the 99.6% dry-bulb temperature.

- Use 90% RH and altitude sensitive, state point psychrometrics to estimate coincident grains of moisture.

Latent Load for Heating

Since 50% to 60% relative humidity is maintained in the space during cold weather (see Section 2), outdoor air from infiltration, engineered ventilation and return duct leakage (if applicable) produce a winter humidification load, which is a negative latent load. However, evaporation from wet surfaces produces a positive latent load (winter dehumidification load). The net latent load equals the sum of the negative latent loads and the positive latent load. The net latent load may be negative (humidification required, but not normally provided), zero or positive (dehumidification required).

7-5 Calculation Tools

Standard load calculation procedures generally apply to swimming pool and spa applications. However, standard procedures do not evaluate the latent load produced by evaporation from wet surfaces. Therefore, Section 6 procedures are used to calculate the latent load for evaporation and this load is added to the latent load from a standard procedure.

- The humid zone shall be structurally and mechanically isolated from the rest of the building.

- ACCA *Manual J* procedures shall not be used for the swimming pool and spa applications.

- Use the latest version of ACCA *Manual N*, 5th Edition for institutional, commercial and residential spaces that enclose a swimming pool or spa, or use a commercial procedure that complies with ASHRAE/ACCA/ANSI Standard 183-2007.

- *Manual N* has an altitude adjustment for infiltration and ventilation loads.

- *Manual N* has procedures for engineered ventilation that features a heat recovery device.

- *Manual N* has a procedure for the latent load produced by moisture migration (not relevant if the structure has an appropriate vapor retarding membrane).

Remember that *Manual N* weather data uses the 1% dry-bulb condition for cooling load calculations. For maximum latent load calculations this value is replaced by the 1% dew point condition, or the persisting 12-hour dew point temperature condition.

In addition, the grains difference values for *Manual N* weather data are for an indoor design condition that is very different than the indoor design condition for a pool or spa application (see Figure A1-1). This means that the grains difference values in Table 1A or Table 1B of *Manual N* cannot be used for pool and spa calculations.

For example, the persisting 12-hour dew point temperature for Akron, Ohio during August is 75.5°F, which translates to 140 grains of outdoor moisture (see the example in Section 7-4). If the indoor design condition is 80°F dry bulb and 60% RH, there are 96 grains of moisture in the indoor air. Therefore the adjusted grains difference value for a pool or spa space is 140 - 96 = 44 grains.

For locations near sea level, you may use a standard psychrometric chart to find grains values for outdoor air and indoor air. For locations at altitude, use altitude sensitive, state point psychrometric software to find grains values for outdoor air and indoor air, or use a spreadsheet implementation of Appendix 3 procedures.

7-6 Sensible and Latent Load Issues

In principle, the design value for indoor humidity (see Section 2-2) must be maintained for every hour of the cooling season (if applicable) and for every hour of the heating season. In practice, indoor humidity may vary between 50% RH to 60% RH for most outdoor conditions, and may be less than 50% when dry outdoor air produces a sufficient negative latent load.

- For pool and spa applications, a year-round system provides dehumidification, sensible heating and sensible cooling. Humidification is not normally provided when dry outdoor air causes a negative latent load.

- The sensible load for heating and the sensible load for cooling vary with month of year and hour of day (because of outdoor temperature, solar gain and internal gain). These loads also depend on the control strategy for the occupied operating mode and the control strategy for the unoccupied operating mode (outdoor air damper position is very important).

- Since the water temperature and the condition of the indoor air are relatively constant, the evaporation rate is relatively constant, so the latent load for evaporation depends on the activity factor and wet deck area.

- Variations in total latent load depend on engineered ventilation, infiltration and return duct leakage (infiltration and duct leakage should be negligible for approved design and construction).

- Latent loads also depend on outdoor moisture, which depends on climate (humid or dry), month of year and hour of day.

- Latent loads also depend on the control strategy for the occupied operating mode and the control strategy for the unoccupied operating mode (outdoor air damper position is very important).

- The net latent load equals the sum of a positive evaporation load and the other latent loads, which may be positive or negative, so the net latent load may be positive, zero, or negative.

- Dehumidification is required when the net latent load is positive.

- Space humidity will balance out at some value that is less than set point (possibly less than 50% RH) when the net latent load is negative. This value can be calculated.

- The water evaporation rate may be significantly affected when 100% outdoor air is used for a purge cycle after water shocking. (This only occurs for a short time, about once a week, usually at night. The dehumidification cycle is not active during the purge cycle, so there may be a short term load excursion when the equipment switches to the dehumidification cycle. (The purge cycle may effect the equipment sizing load.)

7-7 Loads for Intermediate Conditions

The extent of the heating and cooling load investigation depends on the application, on the type of dehumidification system and on the type of equipment. For some cases, the sensible and latent loads for the winter and summer design conditions are sufficient. For other cases, calculations are made for the winter and summer design conditions, and for intermediate conditions.

For example, how will equipment perform when outdoor humidity is low; or when outdoor humidity is high, while outdoor temperature is mild and solar gain is small or negligible? Or, what happens when there is a large variation in spectator count?

Or, a system may use outdoor air to control indoor humidity. In this case, the outdoor air Cfm for humidity control depends on the moisture in the outdoor air. Since the moisture content of outdoor air varies with month of year and hour of day, the outdoor air Cfm requirement must be evaluated for a variety of outdoor conditions.

The point is, load calculations may be made for outdoor conditions other than the winter-summer design conditions. This requires a twelve month, 24-hour procedure.

- ACCA *Manual N*, 5th Edition is a 12-month, 24-hour procedure.

- For swimming pool and spa applications, monthly latent loads depend on the 1% dew point temperature for the month, and monthly sensible loads depend on the 1% dry-bulb temperature for the month

- Monthly design conditions for locations in the United States are provided by the ASHRAE weather data on CD and the *Climate Atlas of the United States*.

7-8 Safety Factors

A load calculation shall aggressively attempt to minimize the load (block, zone or room) to the extent that can be defended by known facts about the performance of the structure, space use, and the performance of system components that produce system loads.

- See Section 2-4 for outdoor design conditions.

- A safety factor shall not be embedded within any part of the procedure or applied to a final value.

- See ACCA *Manual N*, Fifth Edition, Section 2 for a complete discussion of this issue.

7-9 Application

Heating and cooling load calculations are used to select and size space conditioning equipment, or to verify that system or equipment capacity is adequate for a given load condition, or to specify control cycles and control set points. This requires load calculations for the winter and summer design conditions, and may require calculations for a variety of intermediate conditions. This also requires comprehensive equipment performance data, as published by equipment manufacturers.

- Use the winter design condition and the associated loads to size auxiliary heat.

- Use summer conditions and the associated loads to select dehumidifier capacity.

7-10 Load Forms

On the following pages, Form DH and Form DC summarize the output of load calculations for selecting, sizing and controlling dehumidification equipment. These exhibits show the calculations for a natatorium, with

seating for 740 spectators in Milwaukee, WI. Appendix 10 provides blank forms.

Form DH

Form DH (next page) summarizes heating load calculations for three winter day scenarios (maximum water activity with full occupancy; maximum water activity with no spectators; the space is vacant, no water activity, outdoor air damper closed). The purpose of this form is to determine the maximum heating load and the moisture removal loads for the three scenarios.

- The total sensible heating load depends on the space envelope load, the outdoor air Cfm load and the internal load.

- Deduct the internal loads that are required for occupancy (lights, spectators and blower heat); do not take credit for discretionary items; no credit for internal gain when the space is vacant.

  Per ASHRAE Standard 183-2006:
  9.2: Credit for solar heat gains and for internal heat gains shall not be included as part of the calculation of the peak heating load. Exception to 9.2: Where constant or permanent internal heat gains are known to be present in the zone to be heated, the peak heating load may be adjusted to account for these available heat gains.

  Because of thermal storage for radiant heat, the instantaneous internal load is less than the instantaneous internal gain. Load calculation procedures make this adjustment, but the interior thermal mass models do not include a swimming pool.

- Dehumidification equipment does not normally have a problem controlling humidity during the winter, but the minimum moisture load might be useful for capacity control decisions; or to estimate the balance point for space humidity when moisture removal equipment cycles off.

- The net moisture load for cold weather depends on the water evaporation gain, the latent gain for spectators, and the latent loss for outdoor air Cfm.

Form DH also has a space for the values that were used to calculate evaporation loads; and it lists issues that cannot be resolved until equipment is selected. Comments about Form DH and the example problem are provided here:

- Calculations are for the 99.6% dry-bulb condition.

- For a cold climate, outdoor air is very dry at the winter design condition (just a few grains of moisture).

- The moisture removal load depends on the outdoor air Cfm, which depends on space use and the number of spectators.

Heating Load Summary for Dehumidifier Equipment

City >	Milwaukee, WI		Water temperature (°F)			Pool Surface Area (SqFt)			Wet Deck Area (SqFt)		
Altitude	**SqFt**	**CuFt**	**Pool 1**	**Pool 2**	**Spa**	**Pool 1**	**Pool 2**	**Spa**	**Pool 1**	**Pool 2**	**Spa**
692	28,776	575,520	80		102	13,448		80	2,952		108

99.6% Dry-Bulb Loads for Maximum Water Activity and Full Occupancy

99.6% Dry-Bulb		Space		Latent Lb/Hr	Heating Load (Btuh)			62.1 Ventilation		Evaporation	
DB °F	**RH**	**DB °F**	**RH**		**Space**	**OA Cfm**	**Net**	**Count**	**OA Cfm**	**Lb/Hr**	**Btuh**
-5	90%	82	50%	115	+ 112,011	-1,267,259	-1,155,248	740	13,512	666	699,137

Include duct loads, use wet deck area, use maximum activity factors; you may deduct internal loads for lights, spectators and blower heat.

99.6% Dry-Bulb Loads for Maximum Water Activity and No Spectators

99.6% Dry-Bulb		Space		Latent Lb/Hr	Heating Load (Btuh)			62.1 Ventilation		Evaporation	
DB °F	**RH**	**DB °F**	**RH**		**Space**	**OA Cfm**	**Net**	**Count**	**OA Cfm**	**Lb/Hr**	**Btuh**
- 5	90%	82	50%	263	- 69,289	- 746,747	- 816,035	0	7,962	666	699,137

Include duct loads, use wet deck area, use maximum activity factors; you may deduct internal loads for lights and blower heat.

99.6% Dry-Bulb Loads for Vacant Facility

99.6% Dry-Bulb		Space		Latent Lb/Hr	Heating Load (Btuh)			62.1 Ventilation		Evaporation	
DB °F	**RH**	**DB °F**	**RH**		**Space**	**OA Cfm**	**Net**	**Count**	**OA Cfm**	**Lb/Hr**	**Btuh**
- 5	90%	82	50%	285	- 265,714	- 89486	- 355,200	0	954	333	349,569

Include duct loads; outdoor air damper closed with default damper leakage rate; still water; no wet deck area; no deduction for internal loads.

Input for Evaporation Load Calculations

Space Air		Water Temp		DER (Lb/Hr)		Water			Wet Deck		
Dsn RH	**DB (°F)**	**Item**	**°F**	**Dsn RH**	**50% RH**	**SqFt**	**Use AF**	**Still AF**	**SqFt**	**AF**	**Cfm/SqFt**
60%	82	**Pool 1**	80	0.0374	0.0486	13,448	1.0	0.5	2,952	0.0	0.48
		Pool 2									
		Spa	102	0.1422	0.1534	80	1.0	0.5	108	0.0	0.48

1) Design value for space humidity when moisture load is positive = 50% to 60% RH = Dsn RH
2) Default value for space humidity when moisture load is negative = 50% RH
3) Default Evaporation Rate (DER) from Table A5-4; Activity Factor (AF) from Table A5-5

Issues that are Settled During Equipment Selection

1) The default value for outdoor air damper leakage (say, 5% of the maximum Cfm though the damper) is compared to the value for the actual damper, then the load calculations for a vacant space are adjusted if there is a significant difference.
2) The space air turn calculation requires a supply air Cfm value.
3) For dry outdoor air, space humidity may balance at some value that is less than 50% RH, calculate this value.
4) Preheat for outdoor air may be required. If required, determine the heat input value (this reduces the heating load on other equipment).
5) The design values for recovered heat is determined when equipment is selected. This heat may go to water and/or air, which reduces the operating load on other heating equipment, but does not reduce the installed capacity of other heating equipment.
6) If applicable, investigate purge cycle loads and effects, and provide the capability to control space conditions during the purge cycle.
7) Capacity control shall be appropriate for all load ranges (airflows, moisture load, heating load and sensible cooling load).

Form DH

- Outdoor air Cfm for wet surfaces is required when the space is in use. Outdoor air Cfm and internal latent gain increase with spectator count.

- The outdoor air damper can be closed when the space is vacant. There may be damper leakage when the damper is closed (see manufacturer's leakage data).

- Form DH shows that outdoor airflow varies from 945 Cfm (damper closed, with an assumed leakage value) to 13,512 Cfm (with 740 spectators).

- Space humidity drops if the moisture removal load is negative, so 50% RH is used for heating load calculations.

- Form DH shows that for full occupancy during an event, the minimum moisture removal load is about 115 Lb/Hr. It also shows that the moisture removal load is about 263 Lb/Hr when the space is in use with no spectators, and 285 Lb/Hr when the space is vacant.

- Lights, spectators, and blowers add heat to the space when the space is in use. The internal gain defaults to zero when the space is vacant.

- The maximum outdoor air load is 1,267,259 Btuh (outdoor air Cfm for all wet surfaces and 740 spectators), and the maximum space load is 265,714 Btuh. (space vacant, no internal gain).

- The total heating load equals the space load plus the outdoor air load. The total heating load varies from 1,155,248 Btuh (outdoor air Cfm for all wet surfaces and 740 spectators) to 355,200 Btuh (outdoor air Cfm for closed damper leakage when space is vacant).

- Preheat may be required for outdoor air (the heat input value is determined by the equipment manufacturer). Preheat reduces the load on other heating equipment.

- The dehumidifier reclaims heat when it operates, but it may cycle off when the moisture in space air gets too low. When available, reclaimed heat may be used to heat pool water and/or space air.

- Provide auxiliary heat for space air and provide auxiliary heat for pool water. Do not take credit for reclaimed heat when sizing auxiliary heating equipment (discuss with the dehumidifier manufacturer).

- Additional load calculations may be required if the equipment has a purge cycle (100% outdoor air, no internal gains). Additional equipment or equipment capacity may be required for a purge cycle (discuss with the dehumidifier manufacturer).

- Some form of capacity control is required when there are significant variations in outdoor air Cfm, moisture load and heating load (discuss with the dehumidifier manufacturer).

Form DC

Form DC (next page) summarizes cooling load calculations for three summer day scenarios (maximum water activity with full occupancy; maximum water activity with no spectators; the space is vacant, no water activity, outdoor air damper closed). The purpose of this form is to determine the maximum moisture removal load, and the maximum sensible cooling load (the 1% dew point condition and the 1% dry-bulb condition do not occur at the same time).

- Dehumidification equipment that is sized for the moisture removal load may not have enough sensible capacity for the sensible cooling load. In some cases, additional equipment is required for sensible cooling (usually due to a large solar gain from a large glass area).

- The net moisture load for warm weather depends on the water evaporation gain, the latent gain for spectators; and depending on climate, the latent gain or loss for outdoor air Cfm.

- The total sensible cooling load equals the sum of the space envelope load, the outdoor air Cfm load, and the internal load.

See Form DH for the values that were used to calculate evaporation loads, and a list of issues that cannot be resolved until equipment is selected. Comments about Form DC and the example problem are provided here:

- Maximum moisture load calculations are for the 1% dew point condition and the coincident dry-bulb condition. Calculations are made for space in use with maximum spectators, space in use with no spectators, and space vacant.

- Maximum sensible load calculations are for the 1% dry-bulb condition and the coincident wet-bulb condition. Calculations are made for space in use with maximum spectators, space in use with no spectators, and space vacant.

- The moisture removal load depends on the outdoor air Cfm, which depends on space use and the number of spectators.

- Outdoor air Cfm for wet surfaces is required when the space is in use. Outdoor air Cfm and internal latent gain increase with spectator count.

- The outdoor air damper can be closed when the space is vacant. There may be damper leakage when the damper is closed.

- Form DC shows that outdoor airflow varies from 995 Cfm (damper closed, with an assumed leakage value) to 13,512 Cfm (with 740 spectators).

Cooling Load Summary for Dehumidifier Equipment

City >	Milwaukee, WI		Water temperature (°F)			Pool Surface Area (SqFt)			Wet Deck Area (SqFt)		
Altitude	**SqFt**	**CuFt**	**Pool 1**	**Pool 2**	**Spa**	**Pool 1**	**Pool 2**	**Spa**	**Pool 1**	**Pool 2**	**Spa**
692	28,776	575,520	80		102	13,448		80	2,952		108

1% Dew Point Loads for Maximum Water Activity and Full Occupancy

1% Dew Point		Space		Latent Lb/Hr	Evaporator Loads (Btuh)			62.1 Ventilation		Evaporation	
DB °F	**WB °F**	**DB °F**	**RH**		**Total**	**Sensible**	**SHR**	**Count**	**OA Cfm**	**Lb/Hr**	**Btuh**
80	74	82	60%	827	1,420,887	552.945	0.39	740	13,512	514	540,048

Include: Solar load, loads for lights, equipment and spectators; duct loads, blower heat, use wet deck area, use maximum activity factors.

1% Dew Point Loads for Maximum Water Activity and No Spectators

1% Dew Point		Space		Latent Lb/Hr	Cooling Loads (Btuh)			62.1 Ventilation		Evaporation	
DB °F	**WB °F**	**DB °F**	**RH**		**Total**	**Sensible**	**SHR**	**Count**	**OA Cfm**	**Lb/Hr**	**Btuh**
80	74	82	60%	619	1,032,229	381,815	0.37	0	7,962	514	540,048

Include: Solar load, loads for lights and equipment; duct loads, blower heat, use wet deck area, use maximum activity factors.

1% Dry-Bulb Loads for Maximum Water Activity and Full Occupancy

1% Dry-Bulb		Space		Latent Lb/Hr	Cooling Loads (Btuh)			62.1 Ventilation		Evaporation	
DB °F	**WB °F**	**DB °F**	**RH**		**Total**	**Sensible**	**SHR**	**Count**	**OA Cfm**	**Lb/Hr**	**Btuh**
86	72	82	60%	645	1,335,335	658,289	0.49	740	13,512	514	540,048

Include: Solar load, loads for lights, equipment and spectators; duct loads, blower heat, use wet deck area, use maximum activity factors.

1% Dry-Bulb Loads for Maximum Water Activity and No Spectators

1% Dry Bulb		Space		Latent Lb/Hr	Cooling Loads (Btuh)			62.1 Ventilation		Evaporation	
DB °F	**WB °F**	**DB °F**	**RH**		**Total**	**Sensible**	**SHR**	**Count**	**OA Cfm**	**Lb/Hr**	**Btuh**
86	72	82	60%	512	989,786	451,861	0.46	0	7,962	514	540,048

Include: Solar load, loads for lights and equipment; duct loads, blower heat, use wet deck area, use maximum activity factors.

1% Dew Point Loads for Vacant Facility

1% Dew Point		Space		Latent Lb/Hr	Cooling Loads (Btuh)			62.1 Ventilation		Evaporation	
DB °F	**WB °F**	**DB °F**	**RH**		**Total**	**Sensible**	**SHR**	**Count**	**OA Cfm**	**Lb/Hr**	**Btuh**
80	74	82	60%	270	481,484	198,234	0.41	0	954	257	270,024

Outdoor air damper closed, no internal loads, no wet deck area. Include solar load, duct loads, blower heat and default damper leakage load.

1% Dry-Bulb Loads for Vacant Facility

1% Dew Point		Space		Latent Lb/Hr	Cooling Loads (Btuh)			62.1 Ventilation		Evaporation	
DB °F	**WB °F**	**DB °F**	**RH**		**Total**	**Sensible**	**SHR**	**Count**	**OA Cfm**	**Lb/Hr**	**Btuh**
86	72	82	60%	257	493,476	223,706	0.45	0	954	257	270,024

Outdoor air damper closed, no internal loads, no wet deck area. Include solar load, duct loads, blower heat and default damper leakage load.

Form DC

- Milwaukee has humid outdoor air in the summer, so 60% RH is used for cooling load calculations. (For a dry climate, 50% RH may apply when dry outdoor air causes a negative space load.)

- The example shows that the moisture removal load will be about 827 Lb/Hr for full occupancy during an event on a 1% dew point day. It also shows that the moisture removal load is about 257 Lb/Hr when the space is in use with no spectators on a 1% dry-bulb day.

- Sensible internal gain for lights, spectators, appliances and blower heat add heat to the space when the space is in use. Sensible internal gain is blower heat when the space is vacant.

- The total (sensible plus latent) cooling load equals the sum of the envelope load, internal load and the outdoor air load. The total cooling load varies from 1,335,335 Btuh (740 spectators on a 1% dew point day) to 481,484 Btuh (vacant on a 1% dew point day).

- The total sensible cooling load varies from 658,289 Btuh (740 spectators on a 1% dry-bulb day) to 198,234 Btuh (vacant on a 1% dew point day).

- The sensible heat ratio for the cooling loads varies from 0.37 (no spectators on a 1% dew point day) to 0.49 (740 spectators on a 1% dry-bulb day).

- Additional load calculations may be required if the equipment has a purge cycle (100% outdoor air, no internal gains). Additional equipment or equipment capacity may be required for a purge cycle (discuss with the dehumidifier manufacturer).

- Space air turns depend on supply air Cfm. Supply air Cfm equals evaporator coil Cfm plus bypass air Cfm (discuss bypass air options with the dehumidifier manufacturer).

- Reclaimed heat may be used to heat pool water and/or to reheat supply air.

- Some form of capacity control is required when the are significant variations in outdoor air Cfm, moisture load and sensible cooling load (discuss with the dehumidifier manufacturer).

- The dehumidifier reclaims heat when it operates, but it may cycle off when space moisture and temperature conditions are satisfied (depending on the equipment manufacturer's control strategy).

- Consider using a dedicated outdoor air (DOAS) system to supplement the space air dehumidifier when a large amount of outdoor air is required on an occasional basis.

7-11 Auxiliary Heat for Water

The sizing load for auxiliary water heating equipment is not discounted for reclaimed heat (no credit for heat provided by the dehumidifier). The auxiliary pool water heater must take care of the evaporation load plus additional capacity for raising the temperature of make-up water (see Section 4-6).

- Use the largest evaporation load (Btuh) from Forms DH and DC.

- Use the corresponding Lb/Hr value to calculate the makeup water load (i.e., to raise the temperature of entering make up water to pool water temperature).

- If there is water purge cycle, determine the Lb/Hr flow rate for contaminant dilution and compare this value with Lb/Hr value for evaporation.

Section 8

Moisture Control Methods

The mandatory requirements for swimming pool and spa applications are space heating and humidity control (i.e., no condensation). Space cooling is optional, providing there is no possibility of condensation during warm weather. However, space cooling is highly desirable, and common for owner or patron satisfaction; and mechanical cooling provides a useful heat reclaim opportunity (pool water requires heat year-round).

8-1 Packaged Dehumidifier

When thinking about dehumidifiers, there is a tendency to picture the small appliances that are sold at local retail stores. This may have some validity as far as the concept is concerned, but packaged dehumidifiers for engineered systems are substantial and sophisticated products, as demonstrated by Figure 8-1.

Equipment packages come in a large range of sizes and a variety of configurations. Equipment packages have standard features and a variety of optional features.

- Year-round humidity and temperature control
- Moisture removal 4 Lbs/Hr to 925 Lbs/Hr
- Total cooling capacity from 1 Ton to 120 Tons
- 1, 2 or 3 stages of capacity (independent circuits)
- Proportional capacity with specialized equipment
- Evaporator coil with by-pass damper (4 to 8 ATR)
- Evaporator coil has high latent capacity (low SHR)
- Outdoor air for ASHRAE 62.1 ventilation
- Hot-gas reheat coil for supply air
- Hot-gas to water heat exchanger for pool heat
- Outdoor condensing coil (or water equivalent)
- Ducted indoor condensing coil
- Water cooled and glycol heat exchangers
- Independent heat source in unit, or external
- Supply air blower with external exhaust fan
- Internal exhaust fan or return fan
- Air filters (MERV 6 to 8) for return and outdoor air
- Air dampers (return, outdoor and exhaust)
- Exhaust air before and/or after evaporator coil
- Heating coil for tempering outdoor air
- Optional heat recovery for exhaust air
- Temperature and humidity sensors

Reprinted with permission from DesertAire.

Reprinted with permission from Dectron.

Figure 8-1

- Flow switches, safeties and relays
- Sophisticated hot gas valves and controls
- Microprocessor logic controls components
- Materials compatible with chemical environment
- Install indoors, outdoors or on roof

Basic Dehumidifier

Figure 8-2 (next page) shows a basic dehumidifier. This is how it works:

- Warm humid return air enters the evaporator coil every hour of the year (space air is at something like 82°F dry-bulb and 50% to 60% RH all the time).
- There is a sensible and latent load for the evaporator coil most of the time. Even if it is below zero outdoors, air enters the coil at 82°F dry-bulb (or so) and 50% RH (or so), and exits much colder and much dryer when the compressor runs.

- The compressor runs, and the refrigerant coil cools return air when space humidity is above set point. (For OEM swimming pool equipment, compressors may run when the room temperature is above set point, or when pool water is below set point. It all depends on application requirements.)

- Outdoor air introduced downstream from the evaporator coil is equivalent to a space infiltration load. Depending on outdoor air moisture, it can increase or decrease the latent space load.

- Outdoor air Cfm depends on occupancy and spectators. The outdoor air damper can be closed if the space is not in use. If the space is occupied, the outdoor air Cfm shall satisfy the ventilation requirement for wet surface area and spectators.

- If the sum of the negative latent loads for dehumidified air and dry outdoor air exceeds the positive latent load for the space, space humidity drops below set point and a control stops the compressor; then cycles the compressor to hold the space humidity set point. (The compressor runs continuously when space humidity is above a minimum set point, and cycles when the net latent load is satisfied.)

- The total load on the evaporator coil depends on the water evaporation rate (space humidity and temperature have a significant effect), the pool area and wet deck area, the activity factor, the number of spectators, outdoor air Cfm, the condition of the outdoor air, the sensible loads for the building envelope and its internal gains, plus the sensible and latent loads for spectators.

- Capacity control for the compressor and dehumidification coil are required when there is significant variation in the moisture removal load.

  Two (or more) separate refrigeration systems may be installed in one cabinet, or use multiple single-system packages, or multiple two-system packages.

  If the outdoor air load for spectators is relatively large, a dedicated outdoor air system can process outdoor air during events, and a dehumidifier can process space air all the time.

- A hot gas coil adds heat to the supply air if mixed air is too cold for the sensible space load (an air temperature control calls for heat).

- There will be conditions when the heating capacity of the hot gas coil is deficient, so an independent source of heat is installed in the cabinet or external to the cabinet. This is supplemental heat for the space temperature control.

- Evaporator coil Cfm is determined by the design values for moisture loads, sensible cooling loads, and the details of the coil design.

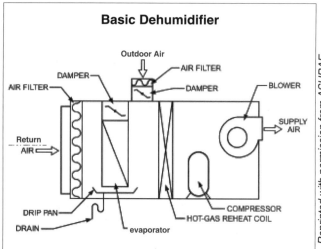

Basic Dehumidifier

Reprinted with permission from ASHRAE.

1) Exhaust provided by separate system. Set-points for space dry-bulb and relative humidity maintained year-round.
2) The primary purpose of the equipment is to remove moisture from return air, so the latent space load is the dominant equipment sizing factor.
3) The evaporator coil extracts sensible and latent heat from return air year-round (entering air condition relatively constant). Extracted heat, plus the heat of compression is rejected heat.
4) When heating is required, rejected heat can be used to heat supply air (by hot gas coil). Additional heat may be required (independent heat source not shown).
5) When cooling is required, rejected heat can be used for hot gas reheat when supply air temperature is too cold for the sensible cooling load.
6) Rejected heat can be used to heat pool water (hot gas to water heat exchanger not shown by diagram).
7) The way rejected heat is used depends on product capability and configuration.
8) Excess rejected heat is routed to an outdoor condenser (not shown by diagram).
9) There is a significant load on the evaporator most of the time. The variation in cooling load depends on variations in the latent space load (caused by splashing and spectators) and the outdoor air load (which can be positive or negative).
10) If the drying effect of the outdoor air can cause space humidity to fall below set point, the compressor cycles by authority of the space humidity control. The output of the hot gas coil is controlled by the space temperature control.
11) The evaporator by-pass damper optimizes the performance of the evaporator coil and hot gas coil. The compressor may be external to the air handler cabinet.
12) Distance between evaporator coil and hot gas coil is designed to prevent water carry-over to hot coil, plus a long drip pan captures moisture produced by mixing cold outdoor air with bypass air and dehumidified air.

Figure 8-2

- The bypass damper above the evaporator coil optimizes the airflow through the evaporator (which may be as low as 200 Fpm for maximum dehumidification) and the hot gas coil (much higher velocity for more heat transfer, appropriate refrigerant pressure and temperature rise).

- The air that flows through the bypass damper (or slot) increases the supply air blower Cfm and the air turnover rate for the conditioned space (four to eight air exchanges per hour are desirable for indoor air motion).

- Pool water needs heat most of the time. A hot-gas to water heat exchanger can provide this heat.

- The need for supplemental water heat depends on how the equipment package uses reclaimed heat.

- The priority for using hot gas heat depends on the equipment manufacturer. Some prefer to use hot gas for air reheat first, then use what is left over for water heat, some do the opposite. Listen to both arguments and decide for yourself.

- An independent source of water heat is required for cold-fill and back-up heat.

- When there is more hot gas heat than required for air heat, water heat, or air and water heat, excess heat is rejected to an outdoor air condenser (or water equivalent).

- The compressor, evaporator coil, and all the components and controls for hot gas circuits are provided by the equipment package manufacturer.

- Evaporator coil capacity, coil Cfm and compressor size depend on the maximum moisture removal load, the maximum total cooling load and the maximum sensible cooling load for the year (see Sections 7-9 and 7-10).

- Evaporator coil sensible heat ratio depends on the design values for the sensible and latent loads. Dehumidifier values tend to be much lower than comfort cooling values (0.50, or so, is common).

- Outdoor air Cfm is equivalent to a space infiltration load because outdoor air enters down stream from the evaporator coil. This makes the coil sensible heat ratio equal to the space sensible heat ratio if there are no return duct loads (ducts shall be tightly sealed and adequately insulated).

- One sensible heat ratio for the space and the coil is desirable because the coil loads and the space loads are satisfied by the same leaving air condition. (This is a compelling reason to minimize duct leakage loads and wall conduction loads.)

Dehumidifier Configurations

Dehumidifier products have various configurations and features, which may be proprietary or peculiar to a given brand. Figure 8-3 and Figures 8-4 through 8-7 (following pages) show products that enhance the performance of a basic dehumidifier (Figure 8-2).

Component attributes and arrangements solve technical problems and/or reduce operating cost. In regard to cost, a decision to do this or that depends on first cost,

Hot Water Coil in Unit and Optimized Exhaust Air

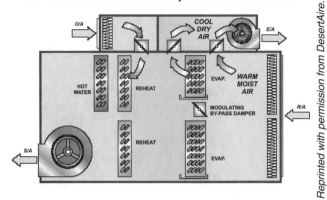

Hot Gas for Air and Water plus Heat Rejection

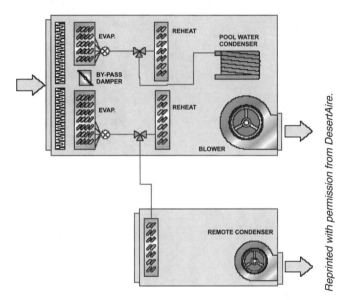

Reprinted with permission from DesertAire.

Figure 8-3

operating cost, maintenance cost and return on investment. Common technical issues are summarized here:

- The dehumidifier equipment and ancillary components must have fundamental capabilities, which are; moisture removal (space humidity control), space temperature control, outdoor air for Standard 62.1 ventilation, adequate space air turns, energy recovery and space pressure control.

- Ancillary components may be heating equipment for air (reheat coil and post heat), heating equipment for water, heat rejection equipment, an exhaust fan or return fan, heat recovery for exhaust air, an air-side economizer, interlocking controls and safeties, etc.

- A refrigerant coil acting on return air reclaims latent heat from water evaporation year-round.

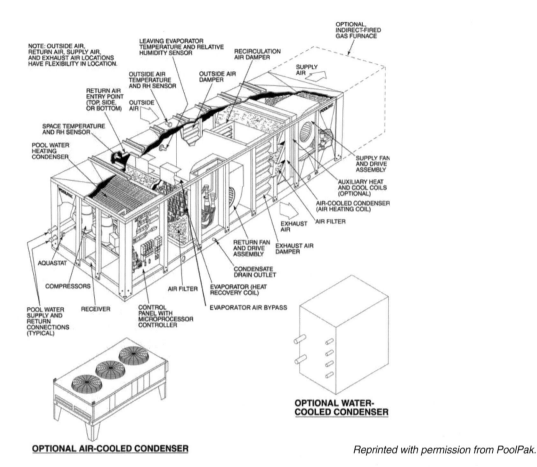

NOTE: OUTSIDE AIR, RETURN AIR, SUPPLY AIR, AND EXHAUST AIR LOCATIONS HAVE FLEXIBILITY IN LOCATION.

LEAVING EVAPORATOR TEMPERATURE AND RELATIVE HUMIDITY SENSOR

RECIRCULATION AIR DAMPER

OPTIONAL, INDIRECT-FIRED GAS FURNACE

SUPPLY AIR

OUTSIDE AIR TEMPERATURE AND RH SENSOR

OUTSIDE AIR DAMPER

RETURN AIR ENTRY POINT (TOP, SIDE, OR BOTTOM)

OUTSIDE AIR

SPACE TEMPERATURE AND RH SENSOR

POOL WATER HEATING CONDENSER

SUPPLY FAN AND DRIVE ASSEMBLY

AUXILIARY HEAT AND COOL COILS (OPTIONAL)

AIR-COOLED CONDENSER (AIR HEATING COIL)

AIR FILTER

EXHAUST AIR

RETURN FAN AND DRIVE ASSEMBLY

EXHAUST AIR DAMPER

AQUASTAT

COMPRESSORS

CONDENSATE DRAIN OUTLET

AIR FILTER

EVAPORATOR (HEAT RECOVERY COIL)

POOL WATER SUPPLY AND RETURN CONNECTIONS (TYPICAL)

RECEIVER

CONTROL PANEL WITH MICROPROCESSOR CONTROLLER

EVAPORATOR AIR BYPASS

OPTIONAL AIR-COOLED CONDENSER

OPTIONAL WATER-COOLED CONDENSER

Reprinted with permission from PoolPak.

Figure 8-4

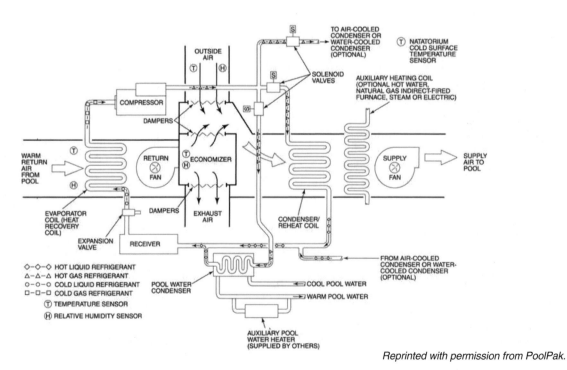

TO AIR-COOLED CONDENSER OR WATER-COOLED CONDENSER (OPTIONAL)

(T) NATATORIUM COLD SURFACE TEMPERATURE SENSOR

OUTSIDE AIR

SOLENOID VALVES

AUXILIARY HEATING COIL (OPTIONAL HOT WATER, NATURAL GAS INDIRECT-FIRED FURNACE, STEAM OR ELECTRIC)

COMPRESSOR

DAMPERS

WARM RETURN AIR FROM POOL

RETURN FAN

ECONOMIZER

SUPPLY FAN

SUPPLY AIR TO POOL

EVAPORATOR COIL (HEAT RECOVERY COIL)

DAMPERS

EXHAUST AIR

CONDENSER/ REHEAT COIL

EXPANSION VALVE

RECEIVER

FROM AIR-COOLED CONDENSER OR WATER-COOLED CONDENSER (OPTIONAL)

◇−◇−◇ HOT LIQUID REFRIGERANT
△−△−△ HOT GAS REFRIGERANT
○−○−○ COLD LIQUID REFRIGERANT
□−□−□ COLD GAS REFRIGERANT
(T) TEMPERATURE SENSOR
(H) RELATIVE HUMIDITY SENSOR

POOL WATER CONDENSER

COOL POOL WATER

WARM POOL WATER

AUXILIARY POOL WATER HEATER (SUPPLIED BY OTHERS)

Reprinted with permission from PoolPak.

Figure 8-5

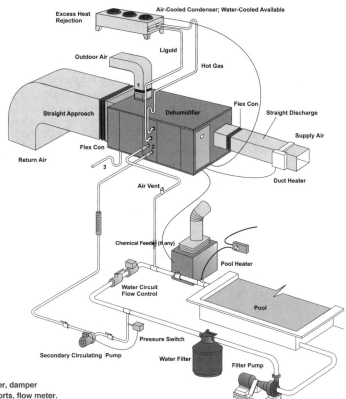

1. Outdoor air flexible connection, filter, damper
2. Pool water isolation valves, gage ports, flow meter.
3. Condensate P-Trap

Reprinted with permission from Dectron.

Figure 8-6

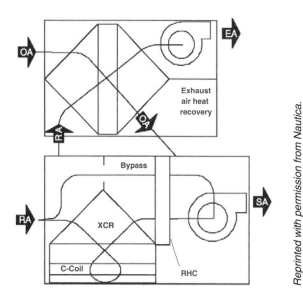

Reprinted with permission from Nautica.

1) Humid return air (RA) flows though the warm side of a plate heat exchanger (XCR) and loses sensible and latent heat.

2) Partially dehumidified air flows through a cooling coil (c-coil) for final dehumidification, then cold dry air flows through the cold side of the heat exchanger and gains sensible heat (partial reheat).

3) Dehumidified air with partial reheat flows through a hot water reheat coil (HWRH), then to the space.

4) Hot compressor gas rejected to a water cooled condenser (WCC).

5) A hot water loop provides heat for pool water (PWH), spa water (SWH), or heat is rejected to the outdoors (HR).

1) Some return air goes through heat exchanger (XCR), cooling coil and reheat coil (RHC).

2) Some return air bypasses the dehumidification device and goes through the reheat coil.

3) Some return air goes through the exhaust air recovery module.

4) Outdoor air gains heat from exhaust air and is mixed with bypass air and dehumidified air.

Figure 8-7

This heat can be returned to pool water year-round, and it can heat or reheat supply air.

- Water can be heated by a hot gas to water heat exchanger. Air can be heated by a hot gas coil. Excess heat is rejected through another condenser.

- Inserting outdoor air downstream from the refrigerant coil maximizes heat reclaim ability, and limits variations in the condition of the entering air, which stabilizes the coil sensible heat ratio.

- Bypass air (around the refrigerant coil) provides flexibility, as far as space air turns are concerned.

- Post heat can be in the cabinet (electric coil, hot water coil, steam coil or gas furnace); or it could be external, and may be provided by others.

- Occasionally (not common), additional cooling is required during warm sunny weather. Post cooling may be in the cabinet (cooling coil fed by separate condensing equipment); or it could be external, and may be provided by others.

- Outdoor air Cfm shall equal or exceed the Standard 62.1 requirement. This is normally significantly less than the supply air Cfm.

- Depending on the situation and product, preheat for outdoor air prevents condensation or freezing temperature in the mixed air section. The preheat device may be external, and might be provided by others.

- If outdoor air is dry enough, an air-side economizer can be used to control space humidity. (This is an economic issue... How does free humidity control with outdoor air, and water heating with fuel equipment, compare with free water heating, and humidity control with electric cooling equipment).

- Outdoor air requires exhaust air. (This is a different issue than the air side economizer. When the space is occupied, outdoor air is introduced to the space year-round, so air is exhausted year-round.)

- There are various ways to reclaim heat from exhaust air. Some dehumidifier products use a heat recovery device, one product varies the exhaust air path (exhaust air expelled upstream of the evaporator coil for cooling and downstream of the evaporator coil for heating).

- Capacity control may be provided by separate refrigeration circuits in one cabinet.

- Consider using DOAS equipment for 100% outdoor air when occasional events draw a large number of spectators.

- The exhaust fan or return fan for controlling space pressure may be in the dehumidifier cabinet, or it could be external, and may be provided by others.

- The equipment may use 100% outdoor air for a purge cycle if there is no air side economizer. (The purge Cfm may exceed the supply air Cfm for normal operation.)

- There may be two exhaust fans in the cabinet (one for normal outdoor air Cfm, two for 100 percent outdoor air purge cycle).

- Methods and arrangements do have an effect on operating cost (compare product performance).

- Gas-phase filters (for odor and chemical control).

- The equipment may return filtered condensate to the pool (if allowed by local code).

Dehumidifier Loads

For simple comfort conditioning, an accurate load calculation is a mandatory requirement for equipment selection. This produces a heating load value for a winter design day, and sensible and latent load values for a summer design day. If equipment performance is compatible with the loads, space temperature and humidity are maintained on a design day (additional measures may be required for part load operation).

Load calculations for dehumidifier equipment are different than comfort cooling calculations because space humidity must be controlled for every hour of the year while the sensible load varies from a maximum heating load to a maximum cooling load. Therefore a load investigation (i.e., a search for worst case scenarios) for dehumidifier equipment sizing requires a set of conditional load calculations.

- There are two outdoor design conditions for summer (1% dew point and 1% dry-bulb), and one winter condition (99.6% dry-bulb).

- For any of the three outdoor design conditions, the facility may be vacant, in use with no spectators, or in use and populated with spectators.

- Evaporation loads, outdoor air loads and internal loads depend on water activity and the number of spectators.

- Internal loads for lights and equipment that are not pool-related usually do not apply when the space is vacant.

- Section 7-10 provides load calculation forms for dehumidifier equipment.

Dehumidifier Selection

The dehumidifier equipment manufacturer will use indoor and outdoor design conditions, load calculation output, required ventilation rates and site altitude to select and size equipment. Space air turns and outdoor air preheat are additional considerations. An example of information that would be useful to an equipment manufacturer is provided by Figure 8-8 (the pool has no spectator seating for this example).

Moisture removal is the primary mission. If sensible capacity is deficient, the dehumidifier manufacturer will either increase the size of the dehumidifier, or help the practitioner select and size supplemental cooling equipment (dehumidifiers have adequate moisture removal capacity and adequate sensible capacity for most applications). The dehumidifier manufacturer also considers or investigates these issues before proposing concepts and tendering quotes.

- The design set point for indoor humidity may range from 50% RH to 60% RH.

- Space humidity may balance out at some value less than 50% RH when a necessary flow of dry outdoor air Cfm causes a negative latent load.

- Consider using DOAS equipment for an application that has a large number of spectators.

- Investigate the outdoor air preheat requirement (if applicable, select and size preheat coil to prevent condensation or freezing in the mixed air section).

- Preheat for outdoor air may be provided by heat recovery equipment.

- Report on space air turnover rate (see Section 5-9).

- Select, size and control supplemental heat.

- Select an exhaust fan or return fan for space pressure control (determine location, size and co-ordinate control of supply fan and second fan).

- Evaluate water heating options (select and size auxiliary equipment, dehumidifier control logic controls auxiliary heat to minimize energy use).

- Select, size and control the outdoor air condenser (or water equivalent).

- Evaluate energy conservation opportunities and trade-offs (supply air reheat, water heating, reclaim exhaust air heat, outdoor air economizer).

- Provide outdoor air ventilation (purge cycle) for water shocking.

- Provide a condensate recovery system.

- The practitioner may be presented with two or more options that have different technical and economic benefits.

8-2 Outdoor Air Method

Outdoor air can be used to control the moisture in a pool-spa space. Figure 8-9 (next page) demonstrates the concept for equipment that mixes outdoor air with return air upstream from components that add or remove sensible heat (a common comfort conditioning configuration).

Dehumidifier Sizing Information						
Loads	**Cooling**				**Heating**	
M - Moisture	1% DP		1% DB		99.6% DB	
H - Heating T - Total cool S- Sens cool	**Occ**	**Uocc**	**Occ**	**Uocc**	**Occ**	**Uocc**
M (Lb/Hr)	104.7	45.2	86.3	39.1	6.2	12.4
H (Mbtuh)	~	~	~	~	203	119
T (Mbtuh)	166	82	160	84	~	~
S (Mbtuh)	56	35	69	43	~	~
SHR (S/T)	0.34	0.42	0.43	0.51	~	~

Location: Milwaukee, WI; Elevation 723 Feet
Indoor condition: 82.0 °F; 50% RH; 81.7 grains
Winter condition: 96.6% = -7 °F; 3.1 grains
Dew point condition: 71.4 °F; 80 °F db; 74 °F wb; 120.4 grains
Dry-bulb condition: 86.0 °F; 72 °F wb; 98.5 grains
Pool 1 water: 78 °F; Activity factor 1.6; Area: 1,800 SqFt
Pool 1 volume: 9,000 CuFt; Cold fill or make-up water: 50 °F
Pool 2 water: None
Spa water: None
Wet deck area: 900 SqFt
Water park equipment: None (no slides, fountains, etc)
Spectators: None (no dedicated spectator seating)
Outdoor Cfm occupied: 1,296; Closed damper leakage: 432 Cfm
Total plan area for space: 2,700 SqFt
Ceiling height: 20 Ft; Space volume: 54,000 CuFt

Figure 8-8

Psychrometrics for the Outdoor Air Method

Figure 8-10 (next page) shows psychrometric process lines for mixed air. Looking at Figures 8-9 and 8-10, the condition of the mixed air (MA) depends on the condition of the return air (RA), the condition of the outdoor air (OA), the effect of preheat or the sensible recovery device (if applicable), the supply air Cfm (SA), and the outdoor air cfm (OA). The mixed air condition is the condition of the air entering the evaporator coil (in cooling mode) or the heating coil (in heating mode).

- Mixed air calculations depend on altitude.

- Figure 8-10 geometry applies to any climate for heating (the mixed air line always slopes from lower left to upper right), but only applies to dry climates for cooling (for humid climates the mixed air line slopes from lower left to upper right).

- The return air condition equals space condition if there is no return duct load (or make adjustment).

- Outdoor air Cfm conditionally depends on latent load (see below), return air grains and outdoor air grains, or equals the ventilation Cfm (largest value).

- Supply air Cfm is determined when the heating-cooling equipment is selected. Return Cfm equals supply Cfm minus exhaust Cfm.

Outdoor Air Cfm for Space Humidity Control

A flow of outdoor air controls space humidity, providing the dew point of the outdoor air is usefully less than the desired dew point of the space air. The conditional flow rate (Cfm_{oa}) depends on the latent space load, altitude, the humidity ratio of the space air, and the humidity ratio of the outdoor air, according to this equation.

$$Cfm_{oa} = Latent\ Btuh\ /\ (0.68 \times ACF \times \Delta GR)$$

Where:
Latent Btuh = Latent space load
ACF = The altitude correction factor
ΔGR = Indoor air grains - Outdoor air grains

For example, if the space air is at 80°F dry-bulb and 50% to 60% RH, and if the outdoor air is at 20 °F dry-bulb and 90% RH, the flow of outdoor air for 1,000 Btuh of latent load varies from to 15.5 to 23.3 Cfm, as demonstrated by Figure 8-11 (next page).

Range of Operation Depends on Climate

For humidity control, the outdoor airflow rate goes to infinity as the grains difference value goes to zero. Therefore, outdoor air can only be used when the humidity ratio of the outdoor air is usefully lower than the humidity ratio of the indoor air. This means that the range of operation of an outdoor air system depends on the climate and season of year.

Figure 8-12 (next page) shows approximate average outdoor air condition lines for a very humid climate (New Orleans, for example), for a moist climate (Indianapolis or Atlanta, for example), and for a dry climate (Phoenix, for example). Figure 8-12 also shows moisture lines for 80°F dry-bulb and 50% RH, and 80°F dry-bulb 60% RH. Note that for a humid climate or moist climate, the moisture content of the outdoor air is usefully lower than the space air when the outdoor temperature is cool or cold. Therefore, the value of the outdoor air method is limited to the heating season for humid climates. However, the outdoor air method can be used year-round for a dry climate.

For example, a space is in a humid climate at sea level, and space air is maintained at 80°F dry-bulb and 60% RH (92.1 grains). The design value for grains difference might range from 5 grains to 20 grains, so the maximum outdoor air Cfm values for 1,000 Btuh of latent load may range from 294 Cfm to 74 Cfm, as demonstrated by Figure 8-13

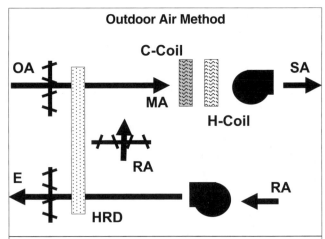

Outdoor Air Method

1) Outdoor air must be usefully drier than space air.
2) Outdoor Air (OA); Exhaust Air (EA); Return Air (RA); Mixed Air (MA); Supply Air (SA); Heating Coil (HC); Cooling Coil (C-Coil). Heat Recovery Device (HRD)
3) Return fan (or exhaust fan) required for space pressure control.
4) Constant supply Cfm, constant return Cfm.
5) OA-EX-RA dampers adjusted by space humidistat, subject to minimum position stops for indoor air quality.
6) Heat input incrementally adjustable to assure cold supply air never enters space (modulate heating capacity, or use controls that approximate modulating control).
7) Sensible cooling for dry climate (outdoor air used for humidity control). The cooling load can range from maximum to zero, so provide an appropriate set of capacity controls.
8) Space thermostat controls output of heating or cooling device.
9) Sensible heat recovery device saves energy; Cfm through HRD varies as humidistat adjusts outdoor air Cfm.
10) Mixing cold outdoor air with warm humid return air shall not cause condensation (see Sections 5-10 and 5-12). A heat recovery device may or may not provide adequate preheat.
11) Air temperature entering the heating coil or cooling coil depends on outdoor temperature, damper positions, preheat and/or HRD performance (make sure water coils will not freeze).

Figure 8-9

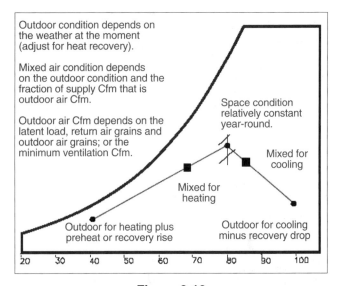

Outdoor condition depends on the weather at the moment (adjust for heat recovery).

Mixed air condition depends on the outdoor condition and the fraction of supply Cfm that is outdoor air Cfm.

Outdoor air Cfm depends on the latent load, return air grains and outdoor air grains; or the minimum ventilation Cfm.

Space condition relatively constant year-round.

Mixed for cooling

Mixed for heating

Outdoor for heating plus preheat or recovery rise

Outdoor for cooling minus recovery drop

Figure 8-10

(next page). And, Figure 8-12 shows that a 5-Grain difference may not control space humidity if the outdoor temperature exceeds 67°F, or 65°F for a 10-Grain system, and so forth.

Worst-Case Dehumidification Load Scenario

Figure 8-13 summarizes a train of thought that applies to other scenarios. For example, the climate could be moist or dry, the design value for space humidity can range from 50% RH to 60% RH, and the design value for space dry-bulb temperature can range from 78°F to 86°F. In addition, outdoor humidity can be higher than indicated by Figure 8-12 because Figure 8-12 shows average weather, not wet, rainy weather (outdoor humidity 90% RH to 99% RH with outdoor dry-bulb above freezing). Therefore, the practitioner has to make some decisions:

- Design for average weather (determined by local weather data for outdoor temperature bins) and let space humidity drift upwards for short periods of very wet weather.

- Design for extreme outdoor humidity (95% RH to 99% RH for outdoor temperature bins) to prevent an upward excursion caused by short periods of very wet weather.

- If the design is based on average weather, design for 50% space humidity so space humidity can drift between 50% RH and 60% RH for short periods of very wet weather.

- If the design is based on extreme weather, design for 60% space humidity to minimize latent load.

- Double up on safety by designing for very wet weather and 50% RH.

Outdoor Air Cfm Vs. Outdoor Temperature

The outdoor air Cfm for humidity control rapidly decreases as the outdoor air temperature gets colder because the minimum airflow rate depends on the humidity ratio of the outdoor air. This is confirmed by Figure 8-12, which shows that the moisture difference for space air and outdoor air dramatically increases as outdoor dry-bulb temperature drops.

For example, a space is in a humid climate at sea level, and space air is maintained at 80°F dry-bulb and 60% RH (92.1 grains). Figure 8-14 (next page) shows that grains difference values increase and outdoor air Cfm values decrease, as outdoor air temperature drops.

Minimum Value for Outdoor Air Cfm for Heating

The minimum outdoor air Cfm for heating could be determined by the space humidity control requirement or the indoor air quality requirement. The outdoor air Cfm value for space humidity control is determined by

Space Conditions Dry-Bulb = 80 °F				
	Sea Level		5,000 Ft	
Space RH	DP (°F)	Grains	DP	Grains
50%	59.7	76.5	59.7	92.2
60%	64.9	92.1	64.9	111.1

Outdoor Conditions Dry-Bulb = 20 °F				
	Sea Level		5,000 Ft	
Outdoor RH	DP (°F)	Grains	DP	Grains
90%	17.9	13.5	17.9	16.2

Grains Difference (ΔGR)		
Space RH	Sea Level	5,000 Ft
50%	63.0	76.0
60%	78.6	94.9

Outdoor Air Cfm per 1,000 Btuh Latent Load		
Space RH	Sea Level (ACF = 1.0)	5,000 Ft (ACF = 0.84)
50%	23.3	19.3
60%	18.7	15.5

1) Contract set point for space humidity from 50% RH to 60% RH
2) Typical outdoor humidity for cold weather = 90% RH
3) Grains values from altitude sensitive psychrometric software
4) *Outdoor Air Cfm = 1,000 Btuh / (1.1 x AC x ΔGR)*

Figure 8-11

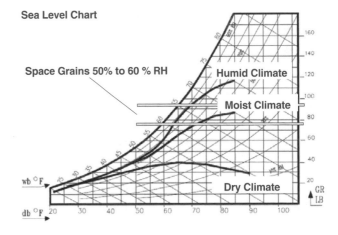

Sea Level Chart

Space Grains 50% to 60 % RH

Humid Climate

Moist Climate

Dry Climate

Figure 8-12

applying the concepts discussed above. The outdoor air Cfm value for indoor air quality is determined by Section 5 guidelines and procedures.

- The maximum outdoor air Cfm for humidity control is calculated for the minimum grains difference value selected by the practitioner (Figure 8-13 shows the procedure).

- If outdoor air Cfm is reduced as outdoor air temperature drops, the minimum outdoor air Cfm for humidity control is calculated for the winter design dry-bulb temperature for the building location (Figure 8-14 shows the procedure).

- The outdoor air Cfm value for indoor air quality will normally be different than the Cfm value for humidity control.

- The minimum value for outdoor air Cfm is the larger requirement (Cfm for humidity control vs. Cfm for air quality).

Minimum Value for Outdoor Air Cfm for Cooling

For a dry climate, outdoor air can be used to control space humidity during the cooling season. This is confirmed by Figure 8-12, which shows the humidity ratio of the outdoor air is much lower than the humidity ratio of the space air during the cooling season.

The procedure for determining the minimum value for outdoor air Cfm for cooling is essentially the same as the heating procedure. The difference is that, calculations are based on the humidity ratio of the outdoor air at warmer outdoor temperatures.

Heating Load and Cooling Load for Outdoor Air

Cold, dry outdoor air must be heated to the space dry-bulb temperature. This produces a sensible heating load for any climate. Warm, dry outdoor air must be cooled to space dry-bulb temperature. This produces a sensible cooling load for a dry climate.

For a given outdoor air Cfm, the size of the outdoor air heating load or sensible cooling load depends on outdoor air temperature. If there is no heat recovery equipment, values for the outdoor air heating load or cooling load are provided by these equations:

H-Btuh = 1.1 x ACF x Cfm$_{oa}$ x (Space db - OA db)
S-Btuh = 1.1 x ACF x Cfm$_{oa}$ x (OA db - Space db)

Where:
H-Btuh = Sensible heating load for outdoor air
S-Btuh = Sensible cooling load for outdoor air
ACF = The altitude correction factor
Cfm$_{oa}$ = Outdoor air Cfm for a given outdoor temperature
Space db = Space dry-bulb temperature
OA db = Outdoor air dry-bulb temperature

Controlling Outdoor Air

Figure 8-15 (next page) shows that a large amount of heating capacity is wasted when a system uses the maximum amount of outdoor air for cold weather conditions (2,402 Cfm for this example). Therefore, the flow of outdoor air should be throttled as outdoor temperature drops. If the

Maximum Outdoor Air Cfm for Humidity Control[1]

Design Value ΔGrains[2]	Outdoor Air Properties[3]			Cfm per 1,000 Btuh[4]
	Grains	Approx RH	Limiting Dry-bulb	
0	92.1	87	69	Infinite
5	87.10	88	67	294
10	82.10	89	65	147
15	77.10	87	64	98
20	72.10	84	63	74

1) Average outdoor humidity for humid climate, space at 80°F dry-bulb and 60% RH, sea level air.
2) ΔGrains value is a design decision made by the practitioner.
3) Read from humid climate line on Figure 8-12.
4) Cfm$_{oa}$ per 1,000 latent Btuh = 1,000 / (0.68 x 1.0 x ΔGR)

Figure 8-13

Outdoor Air Cfm Vs. Outdoor Temperature[1]

Outdoor Dry-Bulb	Indoor Grains	Outdoor Grains[2]	ΔGrains	Cfm per 1,000 Btuh[3]
65		82	10.1	146
55		50	42.1	35
45	92.1	34	58.1	25
35		24	68.1	22
25		17	75.1	20

1) Average outdoor humidity for humid climate, space at 80°F dry-bulb and 60% RH, sea level air.
2) Read from humid climate line on Figure 8-12.
3) Cfm$_{oa}$ per 1,000 latent Btuh = 1,000 / (0.68 x 1.0 x ΔGR)

Figure 8-14

outdoor air Cfm for humidity control falls below the Cfm for indoor air quality, throttling stops and airflow is maintained at a fixed value as outdoor temperature gets colder (300 Cfm for this example).

For a dry climate, significantly less outdoor air Cfm is required for humidity control when the outdoor temperature is above 35°F because outdoor humidity is relatively low (see the dry climate line on Figure 8-12). Also note that sensible heating is required when the outdoor temperature is less than the space dry-bulb temperature (80°F for this example), then sensible cooling is required for warmer outdoor temperatures. Figure 8-16 (next page) shows the heating and cooling loads for a dry climate when the position of the outdoor air damper is controlled by a space humidistat.

- Use a space humidistat to control the outdoor air damper (coordinate the action of the return air damper and exhaust air damper).

- Use minimum position stops to set a low limit for outdoor air Cfm (maintain indoor air quality).

- Condensation must not occur when cold outdoor air is mixed with warm humid return air. Provide adequate preheat (see Section 5-13), or use one piece of equipment for return air and separate equipment for outdoor air and exhaust air.

- Use a heat recovery device to reduce the sensible load for outdoor air.

Heating Load Vs. Outdoor Temperature[1]				
Outdoor Dry-Bulb	Delta Grains[2]	Required OA Cfm[3]	Btuh for Req Cfm[4]	Btuh for Max Cfm[5]
65	10.1	2,402 (max)	39,640	39,640
60	32.1	756	16,630	52,854
55	42.1	576	15,850	66,067
45	58.1	418	16,079	92,494
35	68.1	356	17,637	118,921
25	75.1	323	19,547	145,348
15	81.1	300 (IAQ)	21,450	171,775
5	86.1	300 (IAQ)	24,750	198,202
-5	88.1	300 (IAQ)	28,050	224,629

1) Average outdoor humidity for humid climate, space at 80°F dry-bulb and 60% RH, sea level air. Latent load = 16,500 Btuh Wet surface area = 600 SqFt;. Ventilation Cfm = 0.5 x 600 = 300
2) Based on the humid climate line on Figure 8-12.
3) Cfm_{oa} for latent load = 16,500 / (0.68 x 1.0 x ΔGR)
   Above 15 °F dry-bulb, outdoor air Cfm for humidity control; for 15 °F dry-bulb or lower, outdoor air Cfm for ventilation.
4) $Btuh_{req}$ = 1.1 x 1.0 x Cfm_{req} x (80 - OA_{db})
5) $Btuh_{max}$ = 1.1 x 1.0 x Cfm_{max} x (80 - OA_{db})

Figure 8-15

Optimizing the Outdoor Air Method

The outdoor air method provides year-round humidity control for a dry climate, but only provides cold weather humidity control for a humid climate. During cold weather, a substantial amount of heat is used to temper incoming air. For warm weather, a substantial amount of sensible cooling is used to cool incoming air. To save energy, exhaust air heat can be reclaimed while controls optimize outdoor air use. In this regard, outdoor air Cfm conditionally depends on the airflow rate for humidity control and the airflow rate for indoor air quality.

Heating and Cooling Load for a Dry Climate[1]				
Outdoor Dry-Bulb	Delta Grains[2]	Required OA Cfm[3]	Heating Btuh[4]	Cooling Btuh[5]
105	72.1	337		9,255
95	66.1	367	~	6,057
85	60.1	404		2,221
75	54.1	449	2,467	
65	52.1	466	7,685	
55	55.1	440	12,110	
45	62.1	391	15,043	
35	69.1	351	17,382	~
25	75.1	323	19,547	
15	81.1	300 (IAQ)	21,450	
5	86.1	300 (IAQ)	24,750	

1) Average outdoor humidity for dry climate, space at 80°F dry-bulb and 60% RH, sea level air. Latent load = 16,500 Btuh Wet surface area = 600 SqFt;. Ventilation Cfm = 0.5 x 600 = 300 Outdoor damper controlled by humidistat. No heat recovery.
2) Based on the dry climate line on Figure 8-12.
3) Cfm_{oa} for latent load = 16,500 / (0.68 x 1.0 x ΔGR)
   Above 15 °F dry-bulb, outdoor air Cfm for humidity control; for 15 °F dry-bulb or lower, outdoor air Cfm for ventilation.
4) Heating Btuh = 1.1 x 1.0 x Cfm_{req} x (80 - OA_{db})
5) Cooling Btuh = 1.1 x 1.0 x Cfm_{req} x (OA_{db}- 80)

Figure 8-16

- Air-to-air heat recovery equipment that acts on exhaust air reduces sensible outdoor air loads and saves energy.

- When the space is occupied, the outdoor air Cfm shall not be less than the minimum ASHRAE 62.1 requirement (see Section 5-4).

- Outdoor air Cfm may exceed the ASHRAE 62.1 requirement when outdoor conditions are correct for space humidity control.

- When outdoor conditions are favorable, adjust outdoor air Cfm to control space humidity.

- The heat of evaporation for pool water is not reclaimed when the surfaces of air-to-air recovery equipment are dry. There is some latent recovery when surfaces are wet (for cold climates, effectiveness is reduced by defrost cycles).

- Basic air-to-air recovery does not take advantage of a significant energy saving opportunity because most (or all) of the water evaporation heat is expelled to the outdoors.

- Pool water evaporation heat is replaced with heat provided by water heating equipment.

- Mixing cold outdoor air with warm, humid return air may cause condensation (preheat for outdoor air may be required).

Figure 8-17 shows an example of a reclaim concept without comment on its features and capabilities. When there is interest or need, the practitioner should search for suitable concepts and products and discuss performance and economic issues with product manufacturers.

8-3 Desiccant Method

Figure 8-18 (next page) provides an example of desiccant equipment that dehumidifies return air for a pool space. For this configuration, reactivation heat is provided by hot refrigerant gas (return air that carries pool water chemicals shall not pass though equipment that uses a natural gas burner for reactivation heat).

Figure 8-18 shows an enthalpy wheel feature. This may be installed in units that process 100% outdoor air, but is not applicable to units that process return air (space air flows though both side of the wheel).

Figure 8-18 shows that the desiccant dehumidifier module processes return air and discharges dry air that has a somewhat neutral, or slightly warm temperature. Additional downstream equipment is required for engineered ventilation, space heating and sensible cooling.

- Dehumidified return air is mixed with outdoor air to satisfy the ventilation requirement.

- When there is a sensible heating load, heat is provided by ancillary equipment.

- When there is a sensible cooling load, cooling is provided by ancillary equipment.

The desiccant method is better suited for dehumidifying outdoor air than for dehumidifying return air. For example, a desiccant unit could provide 100% outdoor air dehumidification for pool space that has a large spectator area (the DOAS unit would only operate when spectators are present).

8-4 Comfort Conditioning Equipment

Under certain conditions, it may be possible to assemble a dehumidification system from comfort conditioning components. Appendix 8 provides some general guidance, but this information is not comprehensive, definitive or adequate.

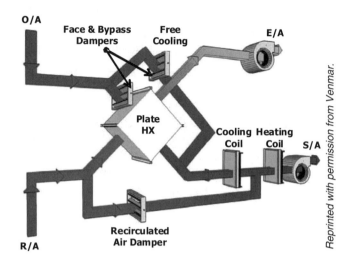

Figure 8-17

8-5 Selecting a Method

Selecting the best method for a given application requires a lot of calculations and a lot of experience. Relevant comments are provided here:

- When selecting a method, the mandatory concern is the system's ability to control space humidity, space temperature and space air quality for any outdoor condition and any occupancy. This means that control strategies, component performance and overall system performance must be investigated and validated for every possible operating condition.

- There may be more than one solution to the space air conditioning problem. After feasible methods are identified, consider system efficiency and system costs.

- Make sure that adequate reclaim heat is available when needed, that it is always distributed in the amount needed, and that there is a way to reject heat that is not needed.

- Compare annual energy inputs, installation cost, operating cost, and maintenance cost for candidate systems.

- If energy use estimates are made, they must be determined for the actual climate, the actual application, and the actual system by an hourly simulation or a sophisticated bin-hour calculation that accounts for all time-dependant, condition-dependant variables.

- Use local utility rates for energy use and demand load charges to estimate energy cost.

- Use performance attributes, and operating cost, installation cost and payback estimates to choose a dehumidification system. (Supplemental heating equipment is normally required. In some cases, supplemental sensible cooling equipment may be required. In some cases, a dedicated outdoor air system may be required, or be a desirable option.)

  - *All materials, controls and wiring that are intentionally or inadvertently exposed to humid, chemical laden air must be compatible with the hostile environment. (Consider equipment location, internal equipment cabinet leakage and external equipment cabinet leakage.)*

  - *Pounds per hour moisture removal is adequate for the full use, 1% dew point condition.*

  - *Sensible cooling capacity is adequate for the full use, 1% dry bulb condition.*

  - *Sensible heating capacity is adequate for the winter 99.6% design condition.*

  - *Moisture removal capacity, sensible cooling capacity and sensible heating capacity are adjusted to track load changes for any use-occupancy condition, and any outdoor condition.*

  - *The dew point temperature of space air is controlled every hour of the year.*

  - *When space is occupied, the ASHRAE 90.2 ventilation rate is maintained for any indoor condition and any outdoor condition.*

  - *An adequate space air turnover rate is maintained for any occupied condition, and any outdoor condition.*

  - *Space pressure is maintained for any operating condition, for all hours of the year.*

  - *Outdoor air must not cause saturated air or condensation when mixed with return air.*

  - *If applicable, the method for air reheat is in compliance with codes and standards.*

  - *Reclaiming and using the heat of evaporation for pool water is a fundamental energy and op-cost issue.*

  - *Reclaiming exhaust air heat is a consideration.*

  - *An outdoor air economizer is a consideration.*

  - *If applicable, the maximum outdoor air Cfm value is compatible with water shocking (i.e., equipment has an adequate purge cycle).*

  - *Chemical laden air shall not pass through a flame.*

  - *The practitioner shall verify that, for any possible operating condition, equipment and controls provide the desired energy balance for equipment that collects heat, for equipment that distributes heat, and for equipment that rejects excess heat.*

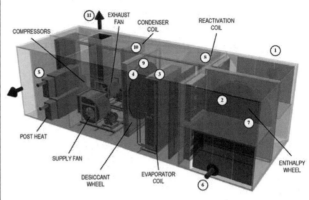

Desiccant Wheel Reactivated by Hot Gas

Reprinted with permission from Munters.

1) Return air enters the unit and passes through a filter.
2) Enthalpy wheel not applicable when processing return air (efficiency option for units that process outdoor air).
3) Return air cooled and dehumidified by direct expansion coil, leaving air is near saturation, condensate goes to drain.
4) Additional moisture removed from air by desiccant wheel, air temperature rises due to reactivation heat.
5a) Dehumidified air is mixed with outdoor air to satisfy ventilation requirement (details not shown in graphic).
5b) Heat added to mixed air by supply air heating equipment, if there is a heating load (post heat).
5c) Heat extracted from mixed air by supply air cooling equipment, if there is a sensible cooling load (details not shown in graphic).

Note: The dehumidification process starts at point 1 and ends at point 4. The ventilation and temperature control process starts at point 4 and ends at point 5. In other words, a desiccant unit dehumidifies return air and feeds dry, warm air to a comfort heating and cooling unit that provides ventilation, heating and sensible cooling.

6) Air from the pool space (exhaust air) enters unit and is filtered.
7) Enthalpy wheel not applicable for return air dehumidification.
8) Air from the pool space is heated by a hot gas coil (reclaiming heat extracted by the point 3 evaporator coil).

Note: Reactivation heat shall not be provided by a gas burner, because chemical laden air from a pool space shall not contact an open flame. This is no problem when a hot refrigerant gas coil provides reactivation heat, but this means that heat for pool water evaporation is provided by ancillary equipment. However, a gas burner can be used when desiccant equipment process chemical free air (100% outdoor air, for example).

9) Exhaust air removes moisture from desiccant wheel and adds heat to desiccant wheel.
10) Exhaust air extracts heat from condenser coil.

Note: The first portion of the heat of compression is use to reactivate the media, the balance of the heat of compression is rejected to exhaust air. Therefore, the ambient air temperature at the heat rejection coil is relatively mild all the time (avoiding the low ambient problem for an outdoor condenser).

11) Exhaust air discharged from unit.

Figure 8-18

  - *Installed cost varies, depending on the system and the equipment, but the preceding bullet items are mandatory requirements, so compare solutions that satisfy all the requirements.*

8-6 DOAS Ventilation for Events

Consider using a dedicated outdoor air system (DOAS) when a facility accommodates a large number of spectators. This way the space dehumidification system takes care of normal space loads and normal ventilation loads all the time, and DOAS equipment takes care of the additional ventilation load when there is an event.

Outdoor Air Load Issues

If outdoor air is drier than space air, DOAS ventilation produces a negative latent load for the space and the space dehumidifier. Therefore, this is a line item load for the with-spectators load calculation for the space dehumidifier.

When outdoor air is more humid than space air, DOAS equipment dehumidifies spectator air, so there is no latent space load (roughly) and no load on the space dehumidifier. Therefore, the line item load for the with-spectators load calculation for the space dehumidifier is zero.

The total amount of outdoor air Cfm equals the Cfm for spectators plus the Cfm for wet surfaces. The outdoor air Cfm for wet surfaces is provided through the space dehumidifier, so this is a line item load for the space-in-use load calculation for the space dehumidifier.

Depending on outdoor conditions, the sensible and latent loads on DOAS equipment can vary from their maximum design day values to zero, or they can be negative. The flow of outdoor air shall be continuous (no on-off control), so an appropriate method of capacity control is required to maintain the desired leaving air condition.

Discharge Air Issues

DOAS equipment processes 100% outdoor air. If the outdoor air is too humid, it cools the air, dehumidifies the air and reheats the air. If outdoor air is dry and warm, it cools the air. If outdoor air is dry and cold, it heats the air. Discharge air moisture and temperature are important issues.

- Discharge air will have about the same moisture content, or be drier than space air. For occupant comfort, it can be a few degrees cooler than space air.

- The sensible and latent loads for spectators can be loads on the DOAS equipment. The specification for the condition of the discharge air can be adjusted accordingly.

- If the temperature of the air leaving the DOAS equipment is higher or lower than the space air temperature, the DOAS equipment will impose a positive or negative sensible load on the space dehumidifier. Therefore, minimizing discharge air temperature swings is an important issue.

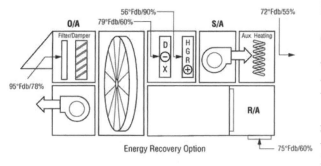

Reprinted with permission from DesertAire.

Figure 8-19

- Various methods are used to reheat air without using additional energy. Some methods produce a significant variation in the condition of the air leaving the DOAS equipment.

- Adjustable reheat minimizes swings in discharge air temperature and dew point temperature. Adjustable reheat is provided by face-and-bypass (good control), or by staging the capacity of hot-gas reheat coil (control depends on steps), or by a hot-gas reheat coil with variable capacity (best control).

- Fixed reheat produces relatively large swings in discharge air temperature and dew point temperature. Fixed reheat may be provided by a heat pipe, an air-to-air heat exchanger, or a hot gas coil that has a fixed capacity.

Efficiency Issues

The efficiency of a DOAS unit is significantly improved by exhausting air through a heat reclaim wheel. This configuration is demonstrated by Figure 8-19.

- An enthalpy wheel is used for climates that produce a dehumidification load. It cools and dehumidifies incoming air to some extent, which reduces the load on the refrigerant coil.

- For dry climates, or cold weather, an enthalpy wheel reduces the negative latent load to the space, and preheats incoming air.

- A sensible wheel can be used for a dry climate.

- Designs vary, depending on the equipment manufacturer.

Other Issues

DOAS equipment can supply outdoor air directly to the space through its own air distribution system, or it can feed neutral outdoor air to another heating-cooling unit. The first option is used for DOAS equipment that operates during spectator events. Other issues of concerns are listed here:

- The distance between the refrigerant evaporator coil and the reheat coil should keep moisture off the reheat coil, and minimize re-evaporation in general. Check to see if the equipment has this feature.

- The DOAS unit does not process chemical laden air, but the air moving side of the equipment is exposed to chemical laden air when the equipment is not in use.

- Do not install equipment in a space filled with chemical laden air unless the equipment has been designed for such a location.

- Heat reclaim wheels have condensation and icing issues.

- Different types of media are used with enthalpy wheels, one type may be preferred over other types.

- Discuss technical issues and installation issues with the equipment manufacturer, and follow instructions.

Heat Recovery

Per square foot of conditioned space, swimming pool and spa applications tend to be energy hogs. If outdoor air is used to control space humidity, the heating and cooling loads for outdoor air can be high to extremely high for many hours of the year. If an evaporator coil controls space humidity, a reheat coil helps control space temperature. Recovery equipment reduces outdoor air loads, and using hot condenser gas for reheat is compatible with codes that prohibit the use of new energy for reheat. In addition, the heat of evaporation for pool water has to be replaced by the pool water heater. A refrigerant coil can recover the latent heat of evaporation and return it to the pool water.

9-1 Air-to-Air Heat Recovery Devices

Space conditioning systems for swimming pool and spa applications tend to process a relatively large amount of outdoor air. This replaces warm, humid exhaust air (about 80°F and 50% RH to 60% RH), which produces a reclaim opportunity for an air-to-air heat exchanger.

- For natatoriums, air-to-air heat recovery should just transfer sensible heat to entering air because adding moisture is counter-productive.

- Air-to-air recovery can reduce primary equipment size, energy load and operating cost, but this increases installation cost and maintenance cost. Payback is an important consideration.

- The minimum value for outdoor air Cfm depends on the flow rate for indoor air quality. This may or may not be large enough to justify air-to-air recovery equipment.

- If outdoor air is used to control space humidity, the maximum flow rate for moisture control can be much larger than the flow rate for indoor air quality. This tends to justify air-to-air recovery equipment.

- For heating, the air-to-air recovery benefit increases as the climate gets colder.

- For cooling, the air-to-air recovery benefit increases as the climate gets warmer.

Equipment

Modular, self-contained heat exchangers minimize the complexity and cost of a recovery system. Examples of plug-in devices are provided by Figures 9-1, 9-2 and 9-3. All three devices are equivalent in concept.

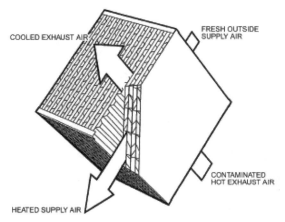

Fig. 4　Fixed-Plate Cross-Flow Heat Exchanger

Figure 9-1

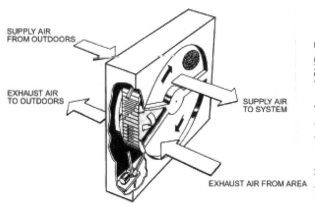

Fig. 6　Rotary Air-to-Air Energy Exchanger

Figure 9-2

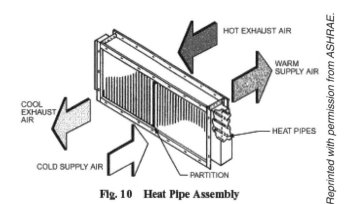

Fig. 10　Heat Pipe Assembly

Figure 9-3

Reprinted with permission from ASHRAE.

- They extract heat from exhaust air, while adding reclaimed heat to entering air, or vice-versa for cooling.

- They use dehumidification system fans to force air through each side of the device. This increases the fan power requirement.

- Device performance is summarized by an effectiveness rating that is sensitive to fan power.

Figure 9-4 shows that two air-to-water coils in one water piping loop can move heat from exhaust air to entering outdoor air (air filters for coils not shown). The advantage is that the coils do not have be close to each other, or oriented in the same plane. The disadvantages are that a complete hydronic system has to be designed and installed, the pump consumes power, and an increment of fan power is required to move air through the coils.

Effectiveness Rating

The following equation shows that the dry effectiveness rating equals the actual amount of heat transfer divided by the total amount of available heat. This rating applies to devices that recover sensible heat, and to devices that recover sensible and latent heat, but this guidance is limited to plate exchangers for sensible heat.

SER = Recovered heat / Available heat

Where:
SER = Sensible Effectiveness Rating (dry operation)
Recovered heat (Btuh) = Heat added to cold outdoor air entering the equipment, or heat removed from warm outdoor air entering the equipment.
Available heat (Btuh) = The difference between discharge air heat and entering air heat.
Available heat calculation is based on the smaller Cfm value and the smaller specific heat value for air.
For design calculations, the difference in the specific heat of air can be ignored.
The SER value is provided by manufacturer's performance e data.
SER rating values range from about 0.45 to about 0.85.

For example, the location is at sea level; 500 Cfm of outdoor air enters the device at 35°F and 600 Cfm of exhaust air enters the device at 80°F. If the SER value is 0.65, outdoor air leaves the device at 74.3 °F.

Smaller Cfm = 500
Maximum temperature difference = 80 - 35 = 45 °F
Available heat (Btuh) = 1.1 x 1.0 x 500 x 45 = 24,750
Recovered heat (Btuh) = 0.65 x 24,750 = 16,088 Btuh
Temperature rise = 16,088 / (1.1 x 1.0 x 500) = 29.3 °F
Leaving air temperature = 45.0 + 29.3 = 74.3 °F

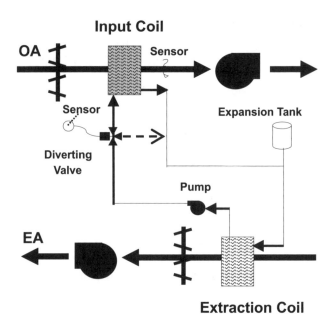

Heat Recovery Loop

Figure 9-4

Condensation and Freeze Protection

Warm, humid exhaust air flows through the air-to-air heat exchanger. Condensation will occur when a surface temperature drops below the dew point temperature of the air passing over it.

For example; if the conditions of the previous example apply, and if the exhaust air has 60% RH, condensation will occur at the exhaust side of the heat exchanger, and the temperature of the exhaust air is close to freezing.

Heat removed from exhaust air = 16,088 Btuh
Exhaust Cfm = 600
Temperature drop = 16,088 / (1.1 x 1.0 x 600) = 24.4 °F
Leaving air temperature = 80 - 24.4 = 55.6 °F
Exhaust air dew point (80 °F, 60% RH) = 64.9 °F
Condensation will occur.

Condensation can increase or decrease heat recovery as summarized by Figure 9-5 (next page).

- Condensation transfers some latent heat to the exhaust side of the equipment, which becomes sensible heat on the outdoor air side of the equipment.

- Some type of freeze protection (defrost cycle, or some method to reduce the amount of heat transfer) may be required for cold weather operation.

- Freeze protection reduces the amount of reclaimed heat during cold weather.

The equipment requires features that deal with condensation.

- The equipment shall have a drain pan and condensate piping to a suitable drain.

- Construction materials and surface finishes shall be appropriate for a wet, chemical laden environment.

Cross Contamination

Ideally, the two air streams should not mix. In practice there may be some leakage, but the amount is relatively small and the consequences are not significant.

- Plate exchanger leakage: None when new, may leak with age (to 5.0 IWC pressure difference)

- Rotary exchanger leakage: None to 5%

- Heat pipe leakage: None to a few percent, depending on installation details.

Air-Side Pressure Drops

System fans force air through the heat exchanger. The exhaust side of the heat exchanger produces a pressure drop for the return fan or exhaust fan. The outdoor air side of the heat exchanger may produce a pressure drop for the supply fan. Component pressure drops increase fan load, which affects the design values for blower wheel speed and blower motor horsepower.

- Component pressure drop information is provided by manufacturer's performance data. (Recovery equipment pressure drop ranges from about 0.10 to about 1.0 IWC, depending on the type of device and the product's effectiveness rating.)

- Determine the pressure drop for the return-side air path (there are two paths if outdoor air is mixed with return air before it enters the blower).

- Determine the pressure drop for the supply side air path.

- Determine the pressure difference across the blower.

9-2 Dehumidifier Reclaim for Exhaust Air

Dehumidifier manufacturers's use various methods to reclaim exhaust air heat. A given method may be unique or proprietary. All methods improve system efficiency and increase equipment cost.

Figure 9-6 shows equipment that has a heat recovery loop, which may be refrigerant heat pipe system or a pumped glycol system. The concept is self explanatory. The manufacturer has conditional specifications for airflow rates and entering air temperature.

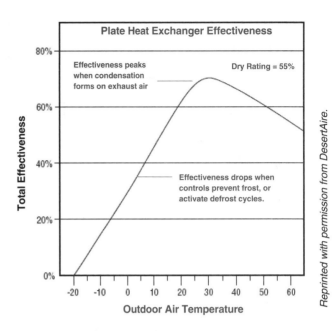

Figure 9-5

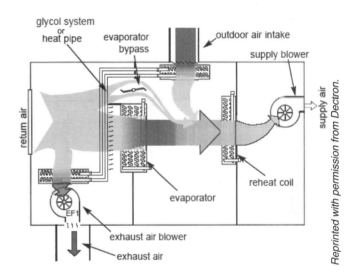

Figure 9-6

Figure 9-7 (next page) shows a concept that is favored by one manufacturer. It optimizes efficiency by exhausting return air before it enters the evaporator coil, or after it leaves the evaporator coil, depending on outdoor air temperature.

- When the space requires heat, return air flows through the evaporator coil, which extracts usable sensible and latent heat from return air, then some air is exhausted upstream from the reheat coil at point A. Concurrently, replacement air (raw outdoor air) enters the system at point A.

- When the space requires cooling, air is exhausted upstream from the evaporator coil at point B,

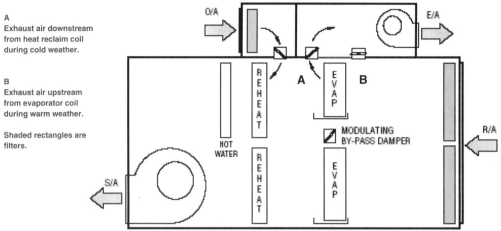

A
Exhaust air downstream from heat reclaim coil during cold weather.

B
Exhaust air upstream from evaporator coil during warm weather.

Shaded rectangles are filters.

Reprinted with permission from DesertAire.

Figure 9-7

which reduces the load on the coil (the demand for recovered heat is less in warm weather). Concurrently, replacement air (raw outdoor air) enters the system at point A.

- The equipment manufacturer that offers this option provides the control logic and controls.

Figure 9-8 shows a plate heat exchanger. These modules come in various configurations. An equipment manufacturer may add a module to a basic dehumidifier, or the heat exchange device may be part of an integrated design.

9-3 Reclaiming Condenser Heat

Section 8 explains how a dehumidifier evaporator coil captures the sensible and latent heat in return air. Section 8 also shows how hot condenser gas is used to heat pool water and supply air.

- The heat content of hot condenser gas includes the heat produced by compressor shaft power.

- Pool water evaporates year-round, so it is a sink for reclaimed heat year-round. (This is an attractive opportunity because of continuous demand, and because the amount of latent heat released by the pool water is roughly equal to the water heating load.) Excess reclaimed heat can be used to heat supply air when air-side heat is needed.

- When the space requires heat, reclaimed heat can be used. Excess reclaimed heat may be routed to pool water when water heat is needed.

- When the space requires sensible cooling and the sensible cooling load is less than the sensible capacity of the equipment, a portion of the reclaimed heat can be transferred to the supply air (as reheat). Excess reclaimed heat may be routed to pool water.

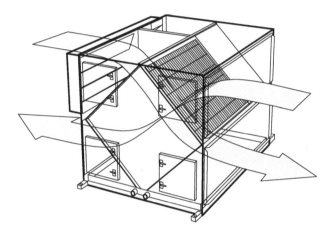

Reprinted with permission from XeteX Inc.

Figure 9-8

- The dehumidifier manufacturer will set the priority for using reclaimed heat. Water heating may be the first priority, with excess heat going to supply air, or vice versa.

In all cases, the primary technical concern is the energy balance for the entire system and the energy balance for each component of the system, for every possible operating condition that will occur during the year.

- Where is heat reclaimed, and how much heat is available at that point in the system?

- Where can reclaimed heat be used, and how much heat is needed at that point in the system?

- What must be done when the required space and pool water heating load is greater than the amount of reclaimable heat.

- What is the load on the ancillary heating device, or the load on the ancillary heat rejection device?

- What is the maximum and minimum load on each device that is in the system?

- How does device performance adjust to part-load conditions that range from a maximum load to a minimum load (which may go to zero)?

In addition, there are control strategy issues and economic questions about installation cost, operating cost, energy saving, avoided operating cost and payback. In most cases, a practitioner will benefit from the knowledge and experience of a company that produces equipment packages for swimming pool and spa applications.

9-4 Dehumidifier with an Economizer Cycle

Figure 9-9 shows a dehumidifier that has an outdoor air economizer. If the outdoor air condition and other conditions are favorable, using outdoor air for dehumidification can be less expensive than operating refrigeration equipment. These conditions determine if the economizer provides a useful benefit.

- The outdoor air has to be usefully drier than space air. (The minimum differential for a given latent load depends on the maximum outdoor air Cfm.)

- A control strategy that requires pool water heating by refrigeration cycle heat is not in effect when the economizer is available for free cooling.

Blower Power for Economizer Units

The maximum exhaust Cfm for a basic dehumidifier depends on the maximum outdoor air Cfm for ventilation, which is normally much less than the supply air Cfm. A dehumidifier that has an air-side economizer might have to exhaust 100% of the supply air Cfm for certain conditions.

- Fan stall may occur when one exhaust fan has to operate over a wide range of Cfm values.

- It may be that one fan cannot be used for normal exhaust and 100% exhaust, even if it has a variable speed drive.

- Some equipment manufacturers use two exhaust fans. One operates when the economizer is not active, and both operate for economizer cooling. This solves the fan stall problem, and it saves fan energy.

Cold Dry Air Exhausted by Economizer Units

During warm weather, the outdoor air condition may not be suitable for economizer operation. For this scenario, the compressor operates and outdoor air Cfm is at the value required for indoor air quality. This means that an equivalent amount of air must be exhausted from the system, and this occurs downstream from the evaporator

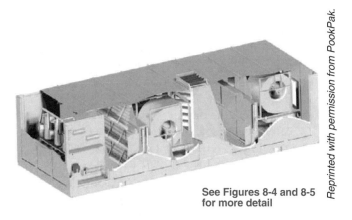

Reprinted with permission from PookPak.

See Figures 8-4 and 8-5 for more detail

Figure 9-9

coil. Therefore, fully conditioned air is discharged to the outdoors when the compressor operates during warm weather. This, to some extent, reduces the effectiveness of the economizer feature.

- Because a natatorium has unusual indoor conditions (see Figure A1-1) there are a lot more heating hours than cooling hours for many parts of the country.

- If heating is the dominant operating mode, discharging cold air during cooling is less of an issue.

- The reduced complexity of a set of economizer dampers is beneficial from a maintenance standpoint.

9-5 Simple Outdoor Air System with Recovery

Companies that produce heat recovery equipment suggest various schemes for controlling moisture and temperature in a pool or spa space. Figure 9-10 (next page) shows a concept, related commentary is provided here:

- An outdoor air system favors a dry climate because there is a useful grains difference value year-round. If the climate has significant summer humidity, it is a cold weather solution for space humidity control (see Figure 8-12).

- Loss of humidity control is technically acceptable if this does not cause condensation on an interior or concealed surface when the space humidity is above set point. This should be checked.

- Loss of humidity control may not be acceptable, as far as occupant comfort is concerned.

- The outdoor air Cfm for dehumidification is determined by the maximum moisture load and the grains difference design value for space air and outdoor air.

- When the outdoor air damper is open, the return air damper is closed, so supply air Cfm must equal outdoor air Cfm.

- Space air turns depend on supply air Cfm, which depends on outdoor air Cfm. If space air turn rate is too low, the design value for outdoor air Cfm can be increased, but there are practical limits to this strategy (equipment size, fan power, and the cycling rate of the outdoor air damper).

- This is an on-off system, as far as outdoor air is concerned. There is no air quality ventilation when the outdoor air damper is closed. (Outdoor air Cfm may be excessive when the damper is open, so this is a compensating affect. However, commercial building codes require continuous outdoor air when the space is occupied.)

- The concept foregoes the year-round opportunity to reclaim the heat of evaporation for pool water.

- Plate heat exchanger efficiency is degraded by defrost cycles.

- Post heat, or some form of space heat is required during cold weather.

9-6 Recovery Economics

Reclaimed energy has no benefit if there is nowhere to use it at the moment. Therefore, there must be a simultaneous need for reclaimed energy, or some way to store it for later use. Natatorium applications with their continuing need for moisture removal and pool water heat, and the prevalent need for supply air reheat and space heat provide important energy recovery opportunities.

Sources of Reclaimable Heat

Pool water evaporation is the primary source of reclaimable heat. The evaporation rate can be relatively constant for casual use of a private pool, or it can depend on the activity factor for a commercial, public or private pool.

Exhaust air is a significant source of reclaimable heat. Exhaust air Cfm may depend on the amount of outdoor air for indoor air quality, or the amount of outdoor air for space humidity control.

- For negative space pressure, exhaust air Cfm is somewhat more than outdoor air Cfm.

- If outdoor air is not used for humidity control, outdoor air Cfm varies from the amount needed for wet surfaces to the amount needed for wet surfaces and a full spectator count. (The outdoor air damper is closed when the space is vacant.)

- If outdoor air is used for humidity control, outdoor air Cfm varies from the minimum value for indoor air quality (space in use with no spectators) to the maximum value for humidity control.

1. VENTILATION MODE

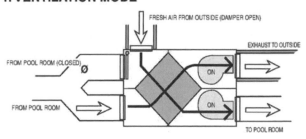

2. RECIRCULATION MODE

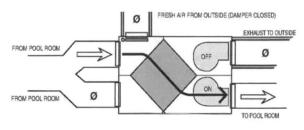

3. DEFROST MODE

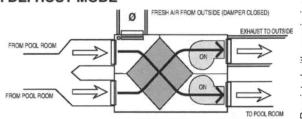

For a dry climate, a common cooling coil (as far as sensible heat ratio is concerned) may provide space cooling (outdoor air controls moisture, the cooling coil controls temperature). Concept viability must be verified by relevant design calculations and equipment selection procedures; it also depends on operating cost.

For hot, humid summer weather, the performance of a common cooling coil may not be compatible with the sensible heat ratio for the sensible and latent loads. This is exacerbated by a plate heat exchanger that decreases sensible load.

Figure 9-10

- Outdoor air is a conditional source for dehumidification capacity and/or sensible cooling capacity. Conditioning with an air side economizer is not free, because of blower energy.

Sinks for Reclaimed Heat

Pool water needs heat year-round. At any given time, the heating load is roughly equal to the amount of reclaimable evaporation heat.

Supply air needs heat most of the time. Heat is required for cold weather, and reheat may be required when there is a net cooling load. Supply air loads are not necessarily coordinated with the availability of reclaimable heat.

Excess heat must be rejected to an external sink. This may be an outdoor air condenser or water equivalent.

Outdoor Air Systems

Outdoor air systems control space humidity during dry weather. Dedicated heat is required for cold weather. Humidity is not controlled during humid weather, there is no summer cooling, and water evaporation heat is not reclaimed. System efficiency is improved by reclaiming heat from exhaust air when conditions are right.

- Dry outdoor air can be used for space humidity control. This saves considerable mechanical system energy, but may require more blower power than a mechanical dehumidification system.

- Dehumidification performance is extremely sensitive to climate. Space humidity may not be controlled for large blocks of time, as demonstrated by Figure 9-11.

- For dehumidification, outdoor air Cfm is decoupled from the space heating load. When there is a net heating load, dedicated equipment must heat supply air or space air.

- Dedicated sensible cooling equipment is required when space humidity is controlled with outdoor air and there is a net sensible cooling load.

- If conditions are favorable, the exhaust air reclaim benefit increases with increasing exhaust air Cfm and the duration of the exhaust cycle.

- Outdoor air Cfm and exhaust air Cfm will vary with the water evaporation load (for best seasonal efficiency), and there is a low limit Cfm for indoor air quality.

- In general, an outdoor air system is the least expensive to purchase and install, but the most expensive to operate.

Mechanical Dehumidifiers

A mechanical dehumidifier controls space humidity year-round, pool water is heated year-round, sensible space cooling is provided during warm weather, supplemental heat is required for cold weather. For normal operation, outdoor air Cfm is determined by the ventilation load. The refrigerant evaporator coil bypass air feature is compatible with desired space air turn values.

Mechanical dehumidifiers are designed to reclaim water evaporation heat. System efficiency may be improved by an air side economizer when conditions are right. System efficiency may be improved by reclaiming heat from exhaust air when conditions are right.

- Return air carries water evaporation heat to a evaporator coil, then it goes to the compressor, then to hot discharge gas. This heat can be returned to the pool water by a hot-gas-to-water heat exchanger. There is an excellent time and

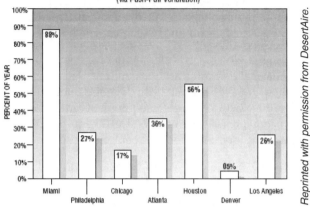

Figure 9-11

capacity match between sink load and source capacity because they are one in the same.

- Hot gas also contains the sensible heat extracted by the evaporator coil, and the heat equivalent of the mechanical shaft power delivered to compressor.

- A hot gas to air coil can reheat supply air. Hot gas reheat replaces the excess sensible heat that is extracted when a dehumidification coil operates on return air. The alternative is to use a dedicated reheat coil that consumes purchased energy.

- As a last resort, excess hot gas heat is rejected to outdoor air, or the water equivalent.

- Outdoor air is needed when the facility is operational and exhaust air Cfm is somewhat more than outdoor air Cfm, so exhaust air provides a significant reclaim opportunity.

- For certain outdoor air conditions, it may be less expensive to dehumidify with outdoor air. In other words, space humidity is controlled with outdoor air, and purchased energy is used for pool water and supply air. The viability of the scheme depends on many parameters. Climate and relative fuel cost are key issues.

- The goal is to optimize the design for the facility and the location.

- In general, a mechanical dehumidifier system is more expensive to purchase and install, but less expensive to operate.

DOAS Equipment

Facilities with a large seating capacity may have empty seats most of the time. This means that outdoor air Cfm and occupancy loads are at nominal values most of the time, and at a much larger values once in a while. If space humidity is controlled by a mechanical dehumidifier, two or more units may be installed, but a substantial amount of this capacity is off line when there are no spectators.

A combination of dedicated outdoor air equipment and mechanical dehumidification equipment may be a better strategy for a facility that has a large spectator count. This way, the space dehumidifier equipment can be optimized for normal conditions and the DOAS equipment can be optimized for the outdoor air requirement during events.

- DOAS equipment can process outdoor air year-round (supply air is compatible with space air).

- DOAS equipment is shut down when there is no spectator load. (The mechanical dehumidifier takes care of the normal outdoor air loads).

- DOAS equipment can adjust outdoor air Cfm for the spectator count.

- Heat can be reclaimed from exhaust air.

Summary

Energy use and operating cost depend on local climate, facility attributes and use, and local utility rates.

- There are a multitude of technical and performance issues for the type of dehumidification system.

- There are various configurations, options and control issues for a given type of dehumidification system.

- Equipment costs depend on what products are purchased and where they are purchased. I

- Installation cost depends on location and on who does the work.

In other words, a comprehensive and fully documented comparison of energy use, installed cost and operating cost for a multi-climate country is not available. Even if it were, it is rendered obsolete when fuel cost, pricing schedules and technology change.

Section 10

Supply Air Cfm

There is a supply air Cfm for the desired air turnover rate for the space, a mathematical supply air Cfm for the heating load at the winter design condition, a mathematical supply air Cfm for the sensible cooling load at the summer design condition, and a mathematical supply air Cfm for the maximum latent load (moisture removal) condition. These airflow rates are relevant to design calculations, but the actual supply Cfm value for designing the air distribution system and duct sizing is obtained when manufacturer's performance data is used to select equipment.

The supply air Cfm for the desired air turnover rate for the space can be significantly different than the supply air Cfm for a load. And for mechanical dehumidifiers, the optimum Cfm for the refrigerant coil is typically different than the optimum Cfm for the hot gas reheat coil. Coil Cfm issues are reconciled with bypass air.

10-1 Supply Air Cfm for Space Air Movement

Authoritative guidance recommends four to six air turnovers per hour for non-spectator pools and six to eight turnovers for pools that have a spectator area. This provides vigorous indoor air motion and effective air mixing. The supply air Cfm for the desired air turnover rate (ATR) and space volume, is determined by this equation:

$$Supply\ Air\ Cfm = ATR \times Volume\ in\ CuFt / 60$$

The following section shows that supply air Cfm depends on heating and cooling loads. So there is a design Cfm for load and a design Cfm for air turnover, and these values may be significantly different.

If the load Cfm value is significantly less than the ATR Cfm, the desired ATR value can be provided by a separate air circulation system, by bypassing excess air around heat transfer devices, or by installing a separate air circulation system. Ideally, the supply air Cfm issue is reconciled within the equipment cabinet. For example, a mechanical dehumidifier may have bypass arrangements that allows four to eight turnovers.

10-2 Supply Air Cfm for Design Loads

To maintain dry-bulb temperature set point, the sensible heating capacity or sensible cooling capacity of the supply air Cfm delivered to a room or space must equal the heating load or sensible cooling load for the room or space. This relationship is summarized by these equations:

$$SHL = 1.1 \times ACF \times Cfm \times (SAT - TSP)$$
$$SCL = 1.1 \times ACF \times Cfm \times (TSP - SAT)$$

Where:
SHL = Sensible heating load
SCL = Sensible cooling load
ACF = Altitude correction factor
Cfm = Supply air Cfm
SAT = Supply air dry-bulb temperature
TSP = Thermostat set point

To maintain relative humidity (RH) set point, the latent humidifying capacity or dehumidifying capacity of the supply air Cfm delivered to a room or space must equal the humidification load or the dehumidification load for the room or space. This relationship is summarized by these equations:

$$LHL = 0.68 \times ACF \times Cfm \times (SAG - IAG)$$
$$LDL = 0.68 \times ACF \times Cfm \times (IAG - SAG)$$

Where:
LHL = Latent humidification load
LDL = Latent dehumidification load
ACF = Altitude correction factor
Cfm = Supply air Cfm
SAG = Supply air grains
IAG = Indoor air grains

The preceding equations show that there are two Cfm values for heating and two values for cooling. This is because there is a Cfm for the sensible load and a Cfm for the latent load. So the question is, how can two loads be satisfied by one Cfm? This depends on two sets of fixed values, and a set of variables that are controlled by the space conditioning system.

- The thermostat set point (TSP) and the humidistat set point (IAG) are fixed values (contract set points).

- The sensible and latent space loads are what they are (unless mechanical-system-designer feedback pertaining to architectural concepts and construction details is used to design an equipment-friendly structure).

- For constant Cfm, the controlled variables are supply air temperature (SAT) and supply air grains (SAG). This requires devices such as heating coils, refrigerant evaporator coils, reheat coils, desiccant wheels, etc.

10-3 Supply Air Cfm for Equipment

Swimming pools and spas are more complicated than common comfort applications because cooling load calculations are made for two outdoor conditions (the 1% dew point condition and the 1% dry-bulb condition), and there is a heating load. Therefore, for constant supply air Cfm, one Cfm value has to be compatible with two sets of sensible and latent cooling loads, a heating load, and the desired air turnover rate for the space.

The primary method for controlling space humidity may be a mechanical dehumidifier, a modulating outdoor air damper, conventional cooling equipment, or a desiccant dehumidifier (see Section 8).

- If a mechanical dehumidifier or desiccant dehumidifier is used, the practitioner works with the equipment manufacturer to produce a set of load values (see Figure 8-8), and allows the equipment manufacturer to select equipment. This determines the design value for supply air blower Cfm.

- If the outdoor air method is used, the practitioner produces a set of load values and designs the system. At some point in the procedure, the practitioner selects a supply air blower, or an equipment package that has a blower. This determines the design value for supply air Cfm.

- If conventional cooling equipment is used, the practitioner produces a set of load values and designs the system. At some point in the procedure, the practitioner selects an equipment package that has a blower, and determines the design value for supply air Cfm.

10-4 Specialized Knowledge is Required for Pool and Spa Applications

Designing an outdoor air system, or a conventional cooling equipment system, is not a trivial task because there are multiple load calculation scenarios, a space air turnover requirement, an outdoor air Cfm for air quality that depends on pool activity and spectator count, an outdoor air preheat issue, water heating issues, energy use issues, and materials compatibility issues. In addition, adequate system performance must be verified for all relevant part-load conditions and part-load sensible heat ratios.

- Dehumidification equipment manufacturers are familiar with these problems. They provide equipment configurations and sizes that have the desired performance and features (see Sections 8-1, 8-3, 8-5 and 8-6).

- Designs based on conventional equipment will have to use similar strategies and concepts to

Dehumidifier Sizing Information

Loads	Cooling				Heating	
M - Moisture H - Heating T - Total cool S- Sens cool	1% DP		1% DB		99.6% DB	
	Occ	Uocc	Occ	Uocc	Occ	Uocc
M (Lb/Hr)	104.7	45.2	86.3	39.1	6.2	12.4
H (Mbtuh)	~	~	~	~	203	119
T (Mbtuh)	166	82	160	84	~	~
S (Mbtuh)	56	35	69	43	~	~
SHR (S/T)	0.34	0.42	0.43	0.51	~	~

Location: Milwaukee, WI; 723 Feet
Indoor condition: 82.0 °F; 50% RH; 81.7 grains
Winter condition: 96.6% = -7 °F; 3.1 grains
Dew point condition: 71.4 °F; 80 °F db; 74 °F wb; 120.4 grains
Dry-bulb condition: 86.0 °F; 72 °F wb; 98.5 grains
Pool 1 water: 78 °F; Activity factor 1.6; Area: 1,800 SqFt
Pool 1 volume: 9,000 CuFt; Cold fill or make-up water: 50 °F
Pool 2 water: None
Spa water: None
Wet deck area: 900 SqFt
Water park equipment: None (no slides, fountains, etc)
Spectators: None (no dedicated spectator seating)
Outdoor Cfm occupied: 1,296; Closed damper leakage: 432 Cfm
Total plan area for space: 2,700 SqFt
Ceiling height: 20 Ft; Space volume: 54,000 CuFt

Copy of Figure 8-8

control humidity and air quality, and to minimize energy use and operating cost.

Dedicated dehumidification equipment is more expensive than comfort conditioning equipment, but the premium pays for experience, performance and efficiency.

- Dehumidifier manufacturers have extensive experience with the right way to do things.

- Dehumidifier manufacturers have a large collection of war stories. This knowledge finds it way into design procedures and installation instructions that prevent similar mistakes.

- Equipment manufacturer's provide turnkey solutions for various design and materials problems.

- Based on experience, they can suggest configurations and options that reduce energy use and lower operating cost.

- It boils down to... pay now or pay later.

Section 11

Equipment Selection

The guidance in this section focuses on dehumidification equipment, air dampers, and heat reclaim devices. There also is guidance for heat reclaim equipment and comfort heating and cooling equipment.

11-1 Dehumidifiers

One dehumidifier package can control space temperature and humidity, heat pool water and heat supply air. Basic concepts are summarized below. See Section 8-1 for more information.

- The compressor and evaporator coil operate year-round to extract sensible and latent heat from approaching air, which will be 100% return air for a space dehumidifier (or, 100% outdoor air for an outdoor air dehumidifier).

- If the space requires sensible cooling, hot gas heat is used for pool water heat and for supply air reheat (or, vice versa).

- When there is a system heating load, a space dehumidifier only recovers latent heat (sensible heat extracted from return air is replaced with an equivalent amount of heat at the hot gas coil, or by another source of heat).

- If the dehumidifier has a water-heating option, the maximum heating load for hot gas depends on the worst-case scenario for the simultaneous demand for water-side heat and air-side heat.

- The hot gas reheat coil does not normally have adequate air-side heating capacity for all load conditions. This depends on the size of the water heating load, the space heating load, the outdoor air load, other system loads, and the size of the latent load on the evaporator coil.

- Supplemental heat is almost always required. This can be in the form of a heater or heat exchanger in the equipment, or separate equipment can be used (provide capacity to maintain design temperature with no help from the hot gas coil).

- Economics determine the best use of hot gas heat. If water heating has first priority, the dehumidifier controls activate water heat first, then use the remaining heat for space air, or vice-versa.

- Supplemental heat for air (or water, if air has first priority) is required when the total heating load exceeds hot gas capacity.

- There is no latent heat recovery if the pool is drained, so supplemental heat or an alternate heat source must satisfy 100 percent of the space heating load when the facility is inoperative (the outdoor air damper will be closed and space temperature can be 70 °F, or lower).

- Supplemental water-side heat is required. There will always be some time where the dehumidifier is either down for repair, maintenance or is just too small for the water load.

- A boiler, or pool water heat pump, heats pool water when the dehumidifier cannot satisfy the water heating load.

- Consider the cold fill load when sizing an independent source of pool water heat.

- Comprehensive back-up pool heat is useful if the cooling equipment has to be shut down for repair.

- If the heating capacity of the hot gas is greater than the sum of the water heating load and the reheat load, some (or all) hot gas heat is rejected at a remote air-cooled or water-cooled condenser.

Efficiency Benefit

Dehumidifiers reclaim latent heat during any season of the year because there is always a lot of moisture in the return air (the year-round set point for indoor humidity is 50% to 60% RH). The motor shaft power delivered to compression provides an additional increment of reclaimable heat.

- Latent heat absorbed by the evaporator coil flows to the compressor, and a proportional fraction of mechanical heat is added at the compressor.

- The total amount of compressor heat is available for heating supply air (space heat or reheat) and/or pool water.

- Equipment manufacturers have software that evaluates energy use and operating cost benefits.

Use Performance Data to Select Equipment

Since the key equipment component is a refrigerant evaporating coil, performance data could look something like the data for a comfort cooling unit (see Figure A9-5). However, the standard performance matrix is not used for dehumidification equipment because moisture removal is a primary concern, because entering air conditions are limited to the set points for space temperature and humidity (outdoor air is introduced down stream from the evaporator coil), and because equipment capacity may depend on two or three condensing coils in two or three environments.

An example of dehumidifier performance data is provided by Figure 11-1. To select equipment:

- The total latent load for water evaporation, other internal gains (typically spectators), and outdoor air is calculated for the 1% dew point condition and the 1% dry bulb condition (Section 2-4 and Section 7), and the maximum values are noted.

- The maximum latent load is converted to a Lbs/Hr moisture removal load and compared to the Lbs/Hr rating for the dehumidifier. (Note that the basic rating is for air at 82°F dry-bulb and 60% RH, but the graph provides a conditional set of values).

- After finding a unit that has adequate moisture removal capacity, the sensible loads for the 1% DP condition and for the 1% DB condition are compared to the sensible capacity of the equipment.

- If the equipment has adequate moisture removal and adequate sensible capacity, outdoor air Cfm capability is compared with the outdoor air cfm requirement, and supply air Cfm is used to calculate a space air turn value.

- For basic applications, a successful candidate satisfies the moisture removal requirement, the sensible capacity requirement, the outdoor air requirement, and the air turn requirement. This may require some excess cooling capacity.

Finalize Equipment Selection

Work with the equipment manufacturer to finalize contract set points, to validate and refine load calculations, to match equipment capability with application requirements, and to select and size equipment.

- When dehumidifier manufacturers determine equipment size, they consider load calculation output, owner preferences, space activity schedules, and the acceptable limits on space temperature and humidity excursions.

- The moisture removal capacity of the dehumidification equipment (space dehumidifier, or space dehumidifier and DOAS equipment) may be determined by the maximum moisture removal load, or a value that is adjusted for the frequency and intensity of space use.

- The sensible cooling capacity of the space conditioning system (dehumidifier only, or dehumidifier and DOAS equipment or supplemental cooling equipment) may be equal to or greater than the maximum sensible cooling load,

Dehumidifier Performance at Sea level [7]				
Attribute	**Model**			
See notes 1-6	**18**	**20**	**24**	**30**
Lb/Hr (82/60)	108	113	140	172
Total Mbtuh	242	250	312	383
Sens Mbtuh	137	140	176	216
Supply Cfm	8,200	8,200	11,000	13,800
OA Cfm	1,900	1,900	3,000	3,000
RA/EA Cfm	As applicable			

1) Pounds moisture removed per hour at 82 °F db and 60% RH
2) Total cooling capacity for 82 °F db and 60% RH entering coil (ambient condensing temperature is a default value that depends on conditions at the hot gas coil, water heating coil and remote condenser coil).
3) Sensible cooling capacity at total capacity conditions.
4) Design airflow rate for supply air blower.
5) Maximum outdoor air Cfm.
6) Return air or exhaust air Cfm for units with second blower.
7) Consult manufacturer for elevations above 2,500 Feet.

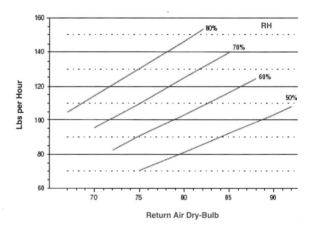

Figure 11-1

or a value that depends on the space temperature that the owner prefers, and the frequency and intensity of space use.

- The sensible heating capacity of the space conditioning system (dehumidifier only, or dehumidifier and supplemental heating equipment) may be equal to or greater than the maximum sensible heating load; or the heating load for a reduced space temperature (say 70°F to 75°F in the event that the dehumidifier is not able to provide heat on a design day).

- The minimum moisture removal load can be used to estimate the minimum value for space relative humidity during cold weather.

Capacity Control

Small dehumidifiers (say 15 Tons or less) cycle the compressor to maintain space air set point. For larger equipment, two or more stages of capacity may be used to track load change. Some applications may favor multiple units (single-stage and/or multiple stage), or some combination of dehumidifier equipment, DOAS equipment and/or supplemental sensible cooling equipment.

11-2 Dampers for the Outdoor Air Method

For the outdoor air method, a set of control dampers (outdoor air damper, exhaust air damper and return air damper) maintain the space humidity set point. For this duty, each damper must be able to incrementally adjust airflow from maximum Cfm to minimum Cfm. The dampers may have an opposed blade configuration or a parallel blade configuration (Figure 11-2).

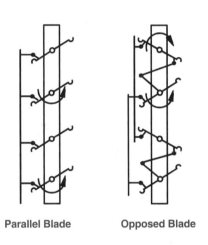

Parallel Blade   Opposed Blade

Figure 11-2

Response Curve

The authority of a damper at a given blade angle is summarized by its response curve, which relates Cfm to blade movement. This curve tends to be nonlinear, which means that the change in airflow is not proportional to the change in blade position. The distortion of the response curve depends on the damper design and on the pressure drop across a wide open damper.

A linear response curve is desirable because it provides predictable control, which means that compensation does not have to be built into the hardware or software that positions the damper. Figure 11-3 shows that the response curves for opposed blade and parallel blade dampers become more linear as the ratio of the open-damper pressure drop to the total system pressure drop increases. Note that the response curves are reasonably linear when the wide open damper pressure drop is equal to or greater than 15 percent of the total system pressure drop.

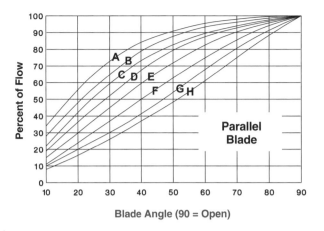

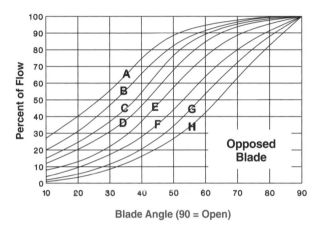

Parallel Blade		Opposed Blade	
Percent of System Resistance	Response Curve	Percent of System Resistance	Response Curve
1.5 to 2.5	A	0.3 to 0.5	A
2.5 to 3.5	B	0.5 to 0.8	B
3.5 to 5.5	C	0.8 to 1.5	C
5.5 to 9.0	D	1.5 to 2.5	D
9.0 to 15.0	E	2.5 to 5.5	E
15.0 to 20.0	F	5.5 to 13.5	F
20.0 to 30.0	G	13.5 to 25.5	G
30.0 to 50.0	H	25.5 to 37.5	H

Figure 11-3

■ Figure 11-3 does not show performance for a damper that is less than 10 percent open, but the response of an opposed blade damper is more linear than the parallel blade damper at these angles, especially if the damper pressure drop is small compared to the system resistance.

■ The opposed blade damper has another advantage in that it creates less distortion in the downstream flow.

For uniform authority over its entire operating range, a control damper should have a relatively large pressure drop when it is wide open. However, linear performance is not the only consideration.

■ Small dampers may increase the system resistance by 15 to 20 percent. This will result in an increase in the required fan pressure and fan power, and possibly an increase in the duct pressure class.

■ Transition fittings are required when the damper is smaller than the duct. These fittings occupy a significant amount of space.

■ High air velocity through a damper generates noise.

■ Control manufacturers may publish damper sizing guidelines in their product literature. Always follow the manufacturer's recommendations when available.

Damper Pressure Drop and Leakage

Damper pressure drop contributes to the system airflow resistance that produces a load on the blower or fan. Figure 11-4 shows that the pressure drop for an open damper depends on the velocity of the air flowing through the damper. Pressure drop information for a particular product is found in the manufacturer's engineering literature in the form of a graph or table that correlates pressure drop with air velocity.

The minimum value for outdoor air Cfm could be determined by the leakage through a closed damper. For this to be true, the closed damper leakage Cfm would have to be greater than the minimum outdoor air Cfm required for indoor air quality. If this is true, the leakage Cfm value is used for design calculations that apply to a minimum outdoor airflow scenario.

■ Leakage information for a particular product is found in the manufacturer's engineering literature in the form of a graph or a table that correlates leakage Cfm per SqFt of damper area with damper pressure drop.

■ Use low leakage dampers.

11-3 Desiccant Equipment

Desiccant equipment controls space temperature and humidity, and may have a water heating feature. Figure 11-5 shows the basic arrangement for equipment that uses hot compressor gas to reactivate the media (top), and the basic arrangement for equipment that uses a gas burner to reactivate the media (bottom). Note that the gas burner unit has a water heating feature. Also note that

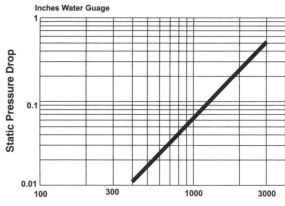

Figure 11-4

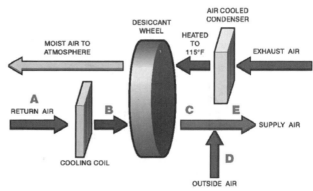

Figure 11-5

ventilation air is equivalent to infiltration because it is mixed with dehumidified supply air.

■ Desiccant equipment is better suited for DOAS service (see Section 8-3).

■ Equipment that uses hot gas for reactivation heat is compatible with moisture removal rates of 300 Lb/Hr or less.

■ Equipment that uses a gas burner for reactivation heat is compatible with moisture removal rates of 150 Lb/Hr or more. (Chemical laden air shall not pass though an open flame.)

■ There are different types of moisture absorbing media. The equipment manufacturer will select the best media for the climate and the application (consider moisture load, moisture levels, air temperatures, etc.).

■ It may be possible to dehumidify with outdoor air when outdoor air is dry enough.

■ An independent source of heat may be required during cold weather (in the equipment package, or external to the equipment package).

■ An independent source of sensible cooling provides space temperature control during warm weather (in the equipment package, or external to the equipment package).

■ An equipment package may have a pool water heating feature, and/or some type of air-side efficiency feature.

Performance Data

Figure 11-6 shows basic performance data published by a desiccant equipment manufacturer. Since this is a dehumidifier, the moisture removal rate is the primary issue of concern. However, this data does not address all the equipment selection and sizing issues.

■ Tons of cooling does not explain performance (ask for information about the sensible and latent capacity, and coil sensible heat ratio).

■ Ask for information about the reactivation heat requirement for hot refrigerant gas or gas burner.

■ Ask for information about reducing compressor capacity at part load (and simultaneously providing enough hot gas for reactivation heat).

■ Ask for information about the space heating capacity of discharge air (for cold weather heating).

■ For cooling, ask for information about the condition of the air leaving the desiccant wheel (hot gas type), or evaporator coil (gas burner type).

■ Sensible heating and cooling loads, latent load, and outdoor air Cfm depend on month, hour of day, occupancy and activity level. See if the equipment package controls humidity and temperature for all operating conditions.

■ There is a psychrometric process calculation for each component that modifies the condition of the air that flows through the component.

Desiccant Performance at Sea level [7]				
Attribute	Tons			
See notes 1-6	5	12	15	20
Lb/Hr (82/60)	40	90	115	160
Total Cfm	2,200	4,000	4,500	10,000
OA Cfm	1,000	2,250	2,800	3,600
RA Cfm	1,200	3,400	4,000	6,000
Min Exh Cfm	250	833	1,000	1,333
Max Exh Cfm	1,200	2,500	3,000	4,000

1) Pounds moisture removed per hour at 82 °F db and 60% RH
2) Maximum total supply air Cfm
3) Maximum outdoor air Cfm
4) Maximum return air Cfm
5) Minimum exhaust air Cfm.
6) Maximum exhaust air Cfm
7) Consult manufacturer for elevations above 2,500 Feet.

Figure 11-6

■ A set of conditional mathematical models (psychrometrics, heat flows, heat balances, heating and cooling capacities, operating temperatures, etc.) for this equipment must show adequate capacity for every operating condition.

■ Rely on selection and sizing guidance provided by the equipment manufacturer.

■ The practitioner must understand and approve the rationale for selecting, sizing and controlling equipment.

11-4 DOAS Equipment

Dedicated outdoor air system dehumidifiers are designed for the intended duty. Introduce yourself to a DOAS equipment manufacture and provide these values:

■ maximum outdoor air Cfm and the minimum outdoor air Cfm when the unit is in use

■ for heating, the 99.6% dry-bulb condition

■ for cooling, the 1% dew point condition, and the 1% dry-bulb condition

■ the desired leaving dew point temperature

■ the desired leaving dry-bulb temperature

The leaving dew point and leaving dry-bulb may, or may not be adjusted for the spectator load. If not adjusted, the sensible and latent loads for spectators go to the space dehumidifier. Discuss this issue.

Discuss variations in leaving dew point temperature and leaving dry-bulb temperature vs. the type of reheat system. Variable hot gas reheat provides close control, fixed reheat provides poor control, and there are methods that have intermediate performance. See Section 8-6.

Also discuss the performance benefits and economic benefits of exhaust air heat recovery. Compare the benefit for sensible recovery, and enthalpy recovery.

11-5 Heat Reclaim Equipment

Fixed plate heat exchangers, rotary heat wheels and heat pipe coils (see Section 9) recover sensible heat (or sensible and latent heat) from exhaust air. Performance is defined by the effectiveness rating of the device and the air-side pressure drop across the device.

Examples of performance data for a plate heat exchanger and a rotary wheel are provided by Figure 11-7. Effectiveness ratings depend on mass flow, so altitude and air temperature affect performance (manufacturers have protocols for using performance data).

Equipment selection and the anticipated effectiveness rating may be provided by the equipment manufacturer (practitioner requests assistance), or determined from manufacturer's performance data (practitioner reads guidance and follows instructions). Then, the effectiveness rating is used to find values for outdoor air temperature rise and reclaimed heat, per these equations:

$$LAT\ (°F) = OAT + TR$$
$$TR\ (°F) = SER \times M_{min} / M_{oa} \times (EAT - OAT)$$
$$RH\ (Btuh) = 1.1 \times 60 \times M_{oa} \times C \times TR$$

Where:
LAT = Temperature of outdoor air leaving unit (°F)
OAT = Temperature of outdoor air entering unit (°F)
TR = Temperature rise for outdoor air (°F)
EAT = Temperature of exhaust air entering unit (°F)
SER = Sensible effectiveness rating
Mass flow (M) depends on altitude and temperature
 M = Cfm × Air density in Lb/CuFt
  There is a mass flow for entering outdoor air (M_{oa})
  There is a mass flow for entering exhaust air (M_{ea})
M_{min} (Lbs/Min) = Minimum mass flow (M_{oa} or M_{ea})
RH = Reclaimed heat (Btuh)
C = Specific heat of air (default = 0.24 Btu/Lb)

11-6 Hot Gas Devices

When an evaporator coil is used to control space humidity, hot refrigerant-gas can heat pool water, or supply air, or both (see Section 11-1). Component hot gas loads and the net hot gas load vary from some minimum value to a maximum value. If the net hot gas load is less than

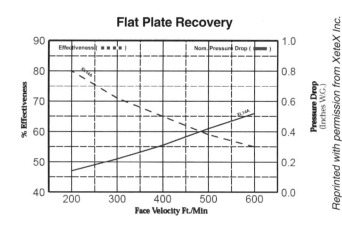

Flat Plate Recovery

Reprinted with permission from XeteX Inc.

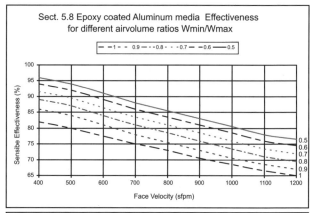

Sensible Heat Wheel Recovery

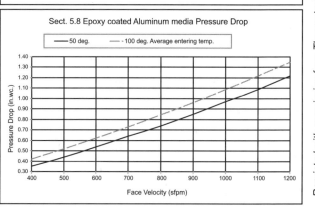

Figure 11-7

Reprinted with permission from Thermotech Enterprises.

maximum, some fraction of the hot gas heat is rejected at an external condenser.

Selecting, piping and controlling a hot gas coil requires specialized knowledge and experience. Dehumidifier manufacturers do this engineering for their products. Related guidance is provided by companies that manufacturer equipment that has hot gas reheat, and/or companies that manufacture devices and controls for refrigeration systems.

11-7 Heat Pump Pool Heater

A refrigerant-cycle equipment package that heats swimming pool water may be advertised as a heat pump pool heater, pool heating heat pump, swimming pool heat pump, etc., but it is not a reverse cycle heat pump unless it has a reversing valve.

- The common version of this equipment extracts heat from a source that may be colder or warmer than pool water, and adds heat to pool water.

- The reverse cycle version of this equipment can heat pool water for most of the year and cool pool water when outdoor conditions are sunny and hot (typically used for an outdoor pool).

- The heat source is usually outdoor air, but it could be ground water (essentially, an air to water heat pump, or water-to-water heat pump).

- Heating capacity depends on source temperature (air or water), sink temperature (water), fluid flow rates (Cfm and Gpm) and equipment size.

- Equipment size depends on duty (size for heating-only, or for heating and cooling).

- For heating, equipment size depends on climate (outdoor air temperature or ground water temperature affects heating capacity).

- For cooling an outdoor pool, equipment size depends on climate (outdoor temperature and outdoor humidity determines heat losses for evaporation, hot outdoor air adds heat to pool water, solar gain adds heat to pool water).

- The economics for heat pump equipment favors source temperature in the 45°F to 50°F range (a gas-fired pool heater is the competitive option).

11-8 Comfort Heating and Cooling Equipment

Under certain conditions, it may be possible to assemble a dehumidification system from comfort conditioning components. Appendix 8 and Appendix 9 discusses comfort conditioning equipment and equipment performance data.

Section 12

Air Distribution and Space Pressure

The possibility of surface condensation is reduced when supply air washes windows, skylights and exposed structural surfaces (this in no way diminishes the dew point requirement for fenestration and exposed panels, per Section 1-2). Air motion past spectators and near the water surface are additional considerations. Space pressures are adjusted to control the direction of moist airflow.

12-1 Supply Air Outlets

The primary issues for selecting and sizing supply air outlets (grilles, registers and diffusers) are supply air Cfm, location, style and outlet effectiveness. Engineering data published by air distribution hardware manufacturer's document outlet performance

Supply Air Cfm

Section 10 provides guidance pertaining to supply air Cfm for the space. This commentary focuses on mathematical models for determining supply air Cfm, but the final value for supply air blower Cfm is determined when manufacturer's performance data is used to select equipment. Section 11 provides guidance pertaining to equipment selection.

After the design value for supply air Cfm is determined, the practitioner decides on how many supply air outlets to use and where to place the hardware. It may be that some outlets flow more air than others, but the total flow through all outlets equals the blower Cfm.

Air Loading Factor

The air loading factor (ALF) for a space equals the ratio of supply air Cfm to floor area.

ALF = Supply Cfm / Floor Area in SqFt

Note that ALF values can vary from less than 0.5 to more than 10 (space load per SqFt of floor area depends on the envelope loads and internal loads for the application). In addition, the supply air Cfm for a desirable space air turn rate ranges from 4 to 8 changes per hour.

Air Loading Vs. Outlet Type

Supply air outlets are designed for specific ranges of air loading. This is a significant issue when selecting the type of outlet. Figure 12-1 summarizes this concept, but air loading is not the only criteria for selecting an outlet style because linear slot diffusers are the preferred way to wash windows with supply air.

Supply Outlet Type Vs. Air Loading	
Outlet Type	**ALF (Cfm / SqFt)**
Grilles and registers	0.5 to 1.2
Slot diffusers	0.8 to 2.0
Perforated plate	0.9 to 3.0
Ceiling diffuser	0.9 to 5.0
Perforated ceiling	1.0 to 10.0
ALF = Supply Air Cfm for space / Floor area for space	

Figure 12-1

Supply Outlet Location

If the methods and procedures for building design and construction are adequate, window glass, exterior doors and exposed walls are the most likely place for a condensation problem. In this regard, condensation will not occur if the R-value for any part of the window or wall assembly keeps the indoor surface temperature above the dew point temperature of the indoor air. This depends on component performance, and the winter design temperature for the location (see Section 1-2).

The possibility of condensation during severe weather is significantly reduced if a cold window or wall is continuously washed with supply air. For windows, performance depends on construction details, as summarized by Figure 12-2 (next page). Additional guidance is provided here:

- Dry supply air flowing over a surface shields the surface from moist room air. Supply-air patterns must cover the entire surface.

- Indoor glass should be flush with the indoor wall. The outdoor sill is sloped to shed rain and snow.

- For windows, the preferred location for the outlet is below the window, but adequate air washing is possible when the outlet is above the window.

- For windows, the supply outlet should be a linear diffuser that spans the width of the window. Supply air should blow straight up or straight down (sharp angles of projection are acceptable if the Coanda effect is maintained).

- Depending on the design value for winter outdoor air temperature, use 3 to 5 Cfm of supply air per SqFt of fenestration surface area (The lower value

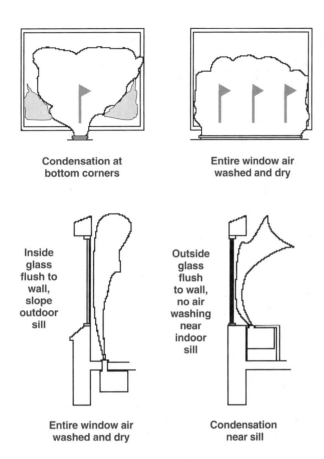

Condensation at bottom corners

Entire window air washed and dry

Inside glass flush to wall, slope outdoor sill

Outside glass flush to wall, no air washing near indoor sill

Entire window air washed and dry

Condensation near sill

Figure 12-2

is for a warm climate, and Cfm increases as the climate gets colder).

Washing all glass with a given amount of supply air is not possible if the total fenestration area is too large for the supply air Cfm for space conditioning.

- For walls the outlet should be at the floor (baseboard radiation produces the same effect).

There is uncertainty regarding the effectiveness of air washing because there is no procedure for evaluating the benefit as it relates to component R-values, the indoor air condition, outdoor temperature, supply air temperature and air velocity. All that can be said is that it helps prevent condensation.

- Install windows that will stay dry with no air washing (for condensation calculations based on the 99.6% outdoor condition).

- Air washing provides a margin of safety for weather that is colder than the winter design temperature.

Skylights

For cold, dry weather, skylights are just as prone to condensation as windows, and they are more prone to

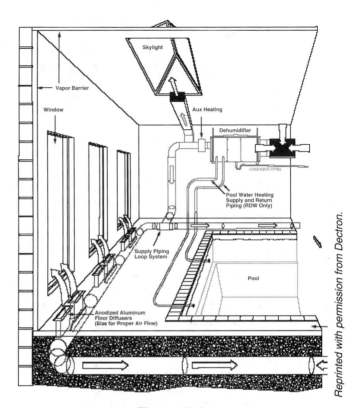

Figure 12-3

Reprinted with permission from Dectron.

condensation when falling precipitation contacts the glass. So, if air washing is appropriate for windows, it is more appropriate for skylights. This requires a duct run to the skylight, which creates an aesthetic problem, as demonstrated by Figure 12-3.

- A supply duct above the ceiling could feed a narrow slot diffuser plenum that runs along two sides of the skylight, or around the entire perimeter of the skylight. The bottom of the slot diffuser plenum can sit on the ceiling panel (like a curb). The bottom of the skylight frame is at the top of the curb. Slot vanes vector supply air at an upward angle toward skylight glass. Provide adequate structural support for the skylight frame. Provide trim panels or molding to hide slot diffuser plenum and ceiling edge.

- Supply air may not be required if heating elements are embedded in the glass (like the back window of an automobile).

- With some thought, it may be possible to heat the skylight with infrared light. The glass and frame should be designed to absorb as much of this spectrum as possible.

Other Supply Air Outlet Locations

The first priority is to wash glass with supply air. This is not relevant if the space has no glass, and this ceases to be relevant after the requirement is satisfied by some fraction of the supply air Cfm. In other words, there is just so much glass area (at 3 to 5 Cfm per square foot) for a given amount of supply air Cfm (at 4 to 8 air turnovers per hour), so some amount of supply air Cfm may not be used for glass washing.

If the supply air Cfm, or some portion of the supply air Cfm, is not used for glass washing, it can be introduced to the space at various locations. Since preventing condensation is important, the next priority after glass washing could be exposed wall washing, which would favor vertical discharge. In any case, there are a variety of reasons why a supply air outlet would be installed in a floor, a wall or a ceiling. Comments about these locations are provided here:

- If supply air outlets are in the floor, the air should blow straight up the wall or window glass. Floor outlets tend to collect moisture and dirt, so the floor should slope away from the wall so that water drains away from the outlet.

- Ceiling outlets may be in a ceiling or at the end of duct stubs that drop from a high supply trunk. The ceiling location produces better performance because the ceiling produces an airfoil effect that increases throw and reduces drop. Discharge is parallel to the ceiling (a jet of vertical discharge air impinging on an occupant is a draft).

- High wall outlets are installed somewhat below the ceiling so discharge air can be vectored up toward the ceiling (about a 20 degree angle). This increases throw and reduces drop.

- High wall outlets will cause a noticeable draft if cold primary discharge air drops into occupied space. This depends on mounting height, discharge velocity and the horizontal distance to a wall or partition.

- Ceiling and high wall outlets work better for cooling because cold supply air tends to drop. High outlets are less effective for heating because warm supply air tends to drift up (the buoyancy effect increases as supply air temperature increases).

Air Movement at Water Surface

Because chemicals are released from treated water, air moving across the water surface improves air quality for swimmers. However, the evaporation rate increases somewhat with air velocity.

There is no simple, cost effective way to fine tune air velocity at the water surface. Install supply outlets that provide good mixing, and at least 15 Fpm to 25 Fpm air velocity in the occupied zone. Then accept what happens at the water surface.

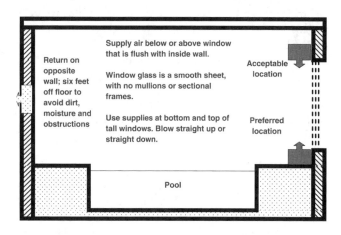

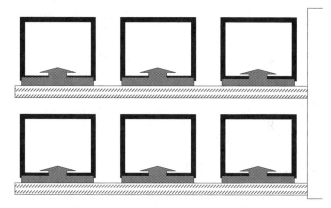

When windows are stacked two or three high, provide a supply duct below or above each level of windows.

Figure 12-4

- Computational investigations, based on computer models and observed behavior show that the air velocity across the pool surface tends to be adequate if supply outlets are at exterior walls, with a return on the opposite interior wall.

- Figure 12-4 shows air distribution arrangements that are known to have satisfactory performance.

Air Distribution Compromises

In a perfect world, windows and skylights would be washed with supply air, air motion through the deck and spectator areas would be about 25 Fpm, and air motion across the pool water surface would be about 25 Fpm.

In the real world, these goals conflict with each other because there is a limited amount of supply air Cfm and limited options for the number of supply air outlets. And, there are architectural constraints on possible outlet locations, which determines proximity to windows, skylights, deck areas, spectator areas and the water surface.

If tradeoffs are required, provide a design that reduces the likelihood of condensation (wash glass with air) and do the best you can with the rest of it (use a separate system for the spectator area, window condensation may not be a problem in a warm climate).

In any case, do not blow air directly down on the pool water surface with a supply air outlet. This has an undesirable effect on evaporation.

Mixing Effectiveness

It is important to understand that supply air outlets (grilles, diffusers, registers) are more than an entry point for supply air. To fulfill their mission, supply air outlets must thoroughly mix supply air with room air. This mixing action determines the mixing effectiveness of the hardware.

- Supply air outlets are designed for constant airflow or variable airflow.

- Variable air volume outlets are not an issue, because constant air volume systems are used for pool-spa applications (exceptions are uncommon, and beyond the scope of this manual).

Outlet Sizing

The mixing effectiveness of supply-air outlets depends on the type and style of the outlet, the Cfm flowing though the outlet, the nominal size of the outlet, how vanes are adjusted, and how the outlet is mounted. This boils down to using manufacturer's performance data to verify adequate throw and vectoring for a given scenario.

- The mixing ability of a jet of supply air increases with discharge velocity. Pool and spa spaces are noisy places, so noise produced by high discharge velocity is less of a problem. The acceptable noise criteria (NC) for supply outlets is 40 to 50.

- Deficient throw and/or incorrect vectoring can cause air distribution problems and may cause condensation problems.

- When properly designed and installed, a conventional duct system, or a fabric duct system, can provide appropriate throw and vectoring. In this regard, fabric duct systems tend to have some design-install uncertainly because of the lack of definitive generic guidance.

- See other sources of guidance for further instruction (ACCA *Manual T*, ASHRAE handbooks, engineering data published by hardware manufacturer's).

Continuous Circulation

Per commercial codes and standards, the supply air blower shall not cycle on and off during occupancy because a continuous supply of outdoor air and continuous air movement is required for indoor air quality. For residential applications, a continuous flow of supply air and ventilation air during occupancy is necessary (even if not required by code).

The outdoor air damper may be closed when the humid space is unoccupied (unless it is used to control the dew point of space air), but supply air Cfm must be continuous (maintenance interruptions should be twenty minutes or less, if possible). Supply air Cfm may be reduced when the space is unoccupied, providing the designer is confidant that this will not cause a condensation problem or air quality problem.

12-2 Returns

Returns that are properly sized and located optimize the air mixing effectiveness of the supply air outlets. However, returns do not correct design errors on the supply side of the air distribution system.

- The three dimensional flow area (SqFt) for approaching air increases with the square of the distance as this boundary moves away from the return (picture a set of hemispheres with an increasing radii).

- The velocity (Fpm) of air approaching a return decreases with the square of the distance from a return.

Velocity = Return Cfm / Flow Area

- Remote air may slowly drift toward the return (15 Fpm or less), but the effect can be overwhelmed by the movement of space air and/or buoyancy forces.

Preferred Location

Avoid having supplies and returns at the same level. Install one or more returns on the wall that is opposite of the wall that has the glass area (see Figure 12-4). If the glass is on two adjacent walls, the return can be on one of the opposite walls.

Return Size

Undersized returns may create objectionable noise, and/or have an undesirable effect on supply air Cfm or space air motion. Size returns so that the face velocity is about 400 Fpm.

Prevent Short Circuiting

The location of the return air grille for dehumidification equipment must be as far as possible from all supply air grilles (served by dehumidification equipment, and if applicable, outdoor air equipment). Supply grilles and return grilles should be at different levels.

Do Not Capture Spa Air

The air in the vicinity of a spa has oils, chemicals and particles that will harm equipment components (heating and cooling coils can be permanently fouled). The return air grille for the equipment that processes space air must be at least two spa widths away from the spa, based on the longest spa dimension.

Transfer Grilles and Transfer Ducts

Usually, the humid zone is one contiguous space. When there is an exception, provide a return path for every space that receives supply air (use a dedicated return or transfer path to a remote return).

- Locker rooms should have their own space conditioning system, the locker room should have tight doors, and the locker room pressure should be less negative than the pool-spa space.

- If a central return serves two or more spaces, there must be a low resistance flow path (0.05 IWC or less) from each space to the central return (via properly sized transfer grilles or transfer ducts).

- The pressure drop for a transfer path must be compatible with the pressure requirements for the various spaces (see Sections 12-3 and 12-4).

- A transfer grille shall not cross the boundaries of the humid zone.

- A transfer grille shall not cross the boundaries of the chemical storage area.

- A transfer grille shall not link a comfort conditioning space (at positive pressure) with a humid space (at negative pressure).

- The safest and most straightforward option is to provide at least one return for each separate space.

Return for Spa Space

Place return air grilles far away from the spa to keep chemical molecule capture and human skin-oil capture to a minimum (skin oil will plug the dehumidifier coil after a few years). Use a local exhaust grille to capture chemicals leaving the spa water surface.

Outlet and Return Materials

Grilles, registers and diffusers are exposed to humid air on a continuous basis. In addition, space air, return air and supply air have some concentration of airborne chemicals that have an adverse effect on metals. Supply air and return air hardware shall be suited for the environment, as far as material and/or finish is concerned.

12-3 Space Pressure and Exhaust Air

Continuous negative pressure in the humid zone must control airborne moisture flows, airborne chemicals and

odor. This can be a challenging requirement for a pool or spa area surrounded by other types of spaces.

- The adjacent spaces must be separated by partitions that have a vapor retarding membrane or surface, and an effective air barrier (seal cracks and use tightly gasketed doors).

- A spectator area is part of the pool area unless it conforms to the preceding requirements.

- Air must move toward the pool- spa area (except for air from a chemical storage space).

- The pool area and/or spa area shall have its own exhaust system.

- An exhaust grille placed above a spa tends to capture airborne chemicals and human skin-oil before they can diffuse into the space air.

- The pool- spa area must be maintained at a negative pressure with respect to the outdoors (0.05 to 0.15 IWC negative).

- An adjacent comfort conditioning space should be maintained at a slightly positive pressure with respect to the outdoors (about 0.05 IWC, positive).

- A food preparation space must be at a negative pressure with respect to the outdoors (0.05 to 0.10 IWC negative), but not be less negative than the pool or spa area. Provide an exhaust hood over cooking equipment and food service counters.

  Be careful about backflow. Be careful about combustion air being taken from the natatorium (chloramines).

- A locker room/dressing room area must be maintained at a negative pressure with respect to the outdoors (0.05 to 0.10 IWC negative), but not be less negative than the pool or spa area. Provide exhaust fans for shower and toilet areas.

- The pressure in the chemical storage space must be negative with respect to the pressure in the pool space and all other spaces.

- The chemical storage area shall have its own exhaust system (migrating moisture and airborne chemicals should not come in contact with each other).

- The pressure in a pool or spa space must be negative with respect to an unconditioned space.

- Appropriate pressure conditions must be maintained as space conditioning systems and exhaust systems adjust outdoor air Cfm, exhaust Cfm and supply air Cfm.

- Appropriate pressure conditions must be maintained during every hour of the year.

- Make air balance calculations for all spaces for all possible operating conditions.

- Space pressure sensors and airflow control devices should be used to control space pressures.

- Local pressure control may not be possible if the humid zone includes different types of spaces. For example, managing the pressure difference between a kitchen or food service area and the pool area, while simultaneously managing the pressure difference between these areas and an eating area or lounge area.

12-4 Controlling Space Pressure

Space pressure depends on the engineered airflow rate entering the space, the engineered airflow rate leaving the space, and the tightness of the space envelope. The net engineered flow rate for a space equals the difference between the supply air Cfm and the sum of the return air Cfm and exhaust air Cfm. The net engineered flow rate may be positive (for positive pressure), neutral, or negative (for negative pressure).

- Supply air Cfm is usually delivered by one piece of equipment (one supply air blower); but there can be a second system, or piece of equipment, that provides outdoor air for ventilation. In any case, supply air Cfm equals the total airflow rate entering the space.

- Return Cfm equals the total airflow rate leaving the space through return grilles. (What happens to this flow after it leaves the space is not relevant to space pressure. For example, some or all of the return Cfm may be exhausted to the outdoors at the equipment).

- Exhaust Cfm equals the total airflow rate leaving the space through one or more space exhaust systems. (A space exhaust system may be a simple exhaust fan in a roof or wall, an exhaust hood, or a ducted system that has multiple exhaust grilles and a remote exhaust fan.)

- Envelope leakage is an uncontrolled source of exfiltration or infiltration, depending on space pressure relative to the outdoors, or relative to an adjacent space. Tight construction benefits attempts to control space pressure.

- If space pressure causes a door to open, or makes it difficult to open a door, there is a space pressure problem. Find out why the space pressure on one or both sides of the door is out of control.

- If a pressure difference causes a door to open or close, the door moves toward the lower pressure. There is a pressure control problem if this is not consistent with the intended pressure difference.

- Gravity or mechanical vent dampers in a roof or exterior wall are an engineered source of envelope leakage. Normally, these are used to relieve positive space pressure, so they are of no use if a space is supposed to be at negative pressure.

- Someone may produce a roof or wall relief damper that opens to negative pressure (or someone might decide to install a positive pressure device in the wrong direction). Such installations are not acceptable.

- In general, roof and wall relief dampers must not be used because pressure control is too crude, and because such devices are susceptible to improper adjustment and/or poor maintenance.

Air Balance at Equipment

The air balance at equipment may depend on the flow rates through an outdoor air damper, an exhaust damper and a return air damper. This can affect space pressure, so airflow at the equipment must be balanced for every possible operating scenario. In other words, what happens to space pressure if exhaust air Cfm does not track a change in outdoor air Cfm.

- If the system has an air-side economizer cycle and just a supply fan, the system will try to deliver 100 percent outdoor air to the space (at some time), space pressure will be unacceptably high, supply Cfm will be less than design, and system performance will be generally unacceptable.

- Systems that have an air-side economizer shall have a return air fan or exhaust fan that is compatible with the maximum flow of outdoor air. The size of all inlet and exhaust openings shall be compatible with the maximum flow of outdoor air. The fans must work in tandem to control space pressure.

Constant Volume Systems, One Fan Speed

For constant volume systems operating at one speed, design procedures determine blower and/or fan Cfm for supply air, return air and exhaust air. Since system airflow rates do not change as controls match equipment performance to equipment loads, space pressure can be controlled by passive air balancing devices.

- Supply air, return air an exhaust air equipment operate simultaneously at constant fan speed (everything is switched on, or switched off).

- Damper settings in supply air ducts, return air ducts and exhaust air ducts determine space pressure.

- Damper positions are set manually and locked when air systems are balanced.

- Space pressure is maintained if everything is adjusted correctly, and if everything remains adjusted over time.

- There is a significant chance that system performance will change over time, because of human meddling (incompetent service, or owner tinkering); or due to normal wear and tear (filters get dirty, damper locks shake loose, and so forth).

- When designing the control system, include a space pressure sensor that reports on space pressure and activates a warning light when space pressure is out of range.

Constant Volume Systems with Fan Speed Change

For constant volume systems operating at more than one speed, design procedures determine maximum blower or fan Cfm for relevant supply air, return air and exhaust air equipment. This produces an operating scenario for air balancing if all fans operate at full capacity some of the time. A second operating scenario occurs if there is a supply fan speed change or an exhaust fan speed change.

There will be as many operating scenarios as there are combinations of supply fan speed and exhaust fan speed.

- Return fan performance must be adjusted to maintain space pressure as supply fan speed changes, and/or exhaust fan speed changes.

- Produce a table of possible operating scenarios, to determine the operating points for the return fan and the required range of adjustment.

- Select a return fan that can provide the required flow rates.

- Provide a control system that maintains space pressure as fan speeds change.

- Include a space pressure sensor that reports on space pressure and activates a warning light when space pressure is out of range.

Section 13

Duct Systems

Duct materials and construction details shall be suitable for a humid, wet, chemical laden environment. Condensation must not form on equipment cabinets, supply outlets, returns grilles or duct surfaces. Condensation must not wet duct insulation. Airway sizing and blower selection procedures are identical to the procedures used for comfort conditioning systems.

13-1 System Geometry

Duct system geometry depends on the locations of the air moving equipment, the supply air outlets and the return grilles. It also depends on how things are connected, which could feature trunk and branch routing with 90 degree turns, trunk and branch routing with spider geometry, radial geometry, and so forth.

System geometry also depends on available space (ceiling cavities, chases, floor cavities, below a slab floor, attics, etc.) and appearance (should duct runs be visible or hidden). The problem boils down to connecting air distribution system components with routing that is practical, economical and visually acceptable.

13-2 Equipment Location

Equipment may be located outdoors, or in a separate room for space conditioning equipment. The location must be compatible with the geometry of the duct system. In this regard, the first sections of supply and return trunk must be straight, and their lengths should not be less the minimum specified by AMCA-SMACNA 201-02, *Fans and Systems*. When applicable, an equipment room should be close to outdoor air (intake and exhaust duct runs should be direct and straight as possible).

13-3 Supply Outlet Location

The preferred location for supply outlets is below or above windows and exterior doors, and near skylights. Supply Cfm depends on surface area (see Section 12), but the total supply Cfm for fenestration will probably be different than the total supply Cfm for the space.

- Compromises are required if the total supply Cfm for glass exceeds the total supply Cfm for the space. Reduce window area, reduce the Cfm allotment for each window, or limit the number of windows that must be washed with air.

- Additional supply outlet locations are required if the total supply Cfm for the space exceeds the total supply Cfm for glass. Select locations that will

provide the most air mixing in the occupied zone with some air motion across pool water, considering space geometry, structural details, air handler location and duct routing geometry.

- If supply outlets cannot be placed at windows and at skylights, choose locations that will provide the most air mixing in the occupied zone, considering structural details and air handler location.

- If applicable, supply air locations must provide adequate air motion in the spectator area.

- Each application produces unique challenges. In general, supply air outlets must provide vigorous air mixing and appropriate air movement in the occupied zone.

- See Section 12-1 for additional guidance.

- Practitioners must be familiar with engineering guidance and application data published by hardware manufacturers, and guidance that appears in manuals, handbooks and standards.

13-4 Return Location

The concentration of airborne chemicals is greatest near the water, so air quality near the water surface is a concern. Ordinary return grilles in a wall next to a pool will not capture this contaminated air, because they are not capture devices (the design value for face velocity is too low, and the grille may be too far from the water surface).

- Some pool dehumidifier manufacturers say the return should be on the wall that is opposite from the wall that has a supply outlet that washes glass with supply air.

- Locate returns where they will not get wet or collect dirt.

- Locate returns in places that will not be blocked by spectator stands, pool furniture, pool equipment, or mischievous intent.

- Locate returns in places that minimize duct routing complexity.

- Supply air must not short circuit to a return. (Supply air vectored toward a return must slow to 50 Fpm or less before it gets near the return).

- Outdoor air introduced to the space must not short circuit to a return.

- A return must not capture the air near a spa.

- See Section 12-2 for additional guidance.

13-5 Exhaust Location

If the space has a spa, an exhaust opening should be located above the tub, as close to the tub as possible. If there is a pool, a general exhaust may be in the roof, high on a wall or at the space conditioning equipment.

- When properly designed and controlled, a general exhaust for an entire space maintains the desired space pressure. It may be too far from the water surface to improve the air quality near the water surface.

- If there is a pool and a spa, the spa exhaust Cfm must be part of the total exhaust Cfm.

- As mentioned above, the exhaust opening for a spa must be over the tub and close to the tub.

- Human skin-oil entrained in warm, humid air can plug a refrigerant coil (usually the hot gas reheat coil). Capture the air above the spa and exhaust it directly to the outdoors (there must be no contact with coils, heat exchangers, etc.).

- Duct runs are not required, or are minimized for roof and wall exhausts.

- Exhaust Cfm has to be synchronized with outdoor air Cfm to maintain space pressure. This is somewhat easier when the intake, return and exhaust dampers are at the dehumidification equipment.

13-6 Below Floor Duct

Below-grade duct, or duct runs below an above grade floor tend to collect water, dirt and debris. Water is less likely to drain to the duct if the natatorium floor slopes away from supply air outlets.

- Duct runs shall drain to an accessible low point that can be drained or pumped, and cleaned.

- Plastic duct is preferred. It is not affected by humidity, airborne chemicals or moisture. When properly glued, seams and joints are perfectly sealed.

- Plastic-coated, metal spiral duct is vulnerable at any point not protected by the coating. All seams, joints and jackets shall be sealed with mastic.

13-7 Traditional Materials

Ducts, grilles, registers, diffusers and equipment cabinets are subject to attack by moisture and chemicals. Use galvanized steel or aluminum for above grade duct. Use PVC for below grade duct. Use aluminum or plastic for grilles, registers and diffusers.

- High-build epoxy paint improves the corrosion resistance of galvanized steel, 316 stainless and aluminum ducts.

- Some authoritative guidance says that bare 300 series stainless steel is a suitable material, but the ASHRAE Handbook of HVAC Applications (2007, Page 4.7) does not recommend its use.

- 400 Series stainless steel shall not be used because it is vulnerable to corrosion.

- Use round plastic duct for below grade systems.

13-8 Fabric Ducts

Currently (2010), there is no ASHRAE or ANSI standard for designing and installing fabric duct systems. Application guidance for natatoriums is provided by fabric air dispersion system manufacturers and dehumidification equipment manufacturers.

If fabric duct is specified for a pool application, the manufacture of the fabric duct product is the authority for system design, installation practice and maintenance routines. A list of issues and questions to discuss and investigate is provided here:

- The fabric may be porous or non porous. Which material is best for washing glass with supply air, and for delivering supply air to this particular space?

  Supply air holes shall be appropriately placed to blow air across windows, skylights and exposed walls.

  Supply air jets should not be perpendicular to window and skylight glass (20 degree angle, or less).

- For porous fabric, what happens to air delivery, duct system pressure drop and the blower operating point if the fabric gets plugged with dust?

- Whether porous fabric or nonporous fabric, what are the filter requirements, the filter maintenance requirements and fabric washing-cleaning requirements?

- If fabric duct must be taken down and sent out for cleaning, how often is this done, where is this done, how much does it cost, how long does it take?

- What is the service life of fabric ducts that must be washed on a periodic basis?

- How do I operate the facility when the duct runs are out for cleaning?

- For the recommended filter, what is the pressure drop across a clean filter, and what is a pressure drop across a filter that needs to be cleaned or changed?

- Jets of air leaving fabric duct holes at relatively high velocity produce a reaction-torque that may cause the duct to rotate. Are there hangers, mounts and fixtures that will keep the supply air jets pointing in the desired direction?

- How are duct airways sized if the blower operates at one speed?

- How are duct airways sized if the blower operates at two or more speeds?

- What happens to duct fabric tension and duct system performance when the blower operates at reduced speed?

- What instruments, procedures and protocols are used for testing and balancing airflow?

- Are there additional installation and/or maintenance issues that need to be addressed for this specific application?

13-9 Duct Insulation

Fiberglass duct or fiberglass duct liner shall not be used when wetting due to condensation is a primary design issue. The entire duct may have to be replaced if the duct losses its structural integrity, or if the material is infested with mold and mildew.

If insulation is required to prevent condensation, it should be applied to the outside of a metal or plastic duct. The amount of insulation depends on the condition of the air in the duct and on the condition of the air outside the duct.

- This guidance applies to duct runs. Dehumidifer manufacturer's are responsible for appropriate cabinet insulation and gasketing.

- Condensation may form inside of the duct if the surrounding air is cold and the duct air is warm and humid (return or exhaust duct in a cold space).

- Condensation may form on the outside of the duct if the surrounding air is warm and humid and the duct air is cool (supply duct during cooling season, or cold outdoor air in an intake duct).

- The condition of the air outside the duct depends on location (in the humid zone, in a conditioned space outside the humid zone, in an unconditioned space, or outdoors).

- At the extreme, the condition of the air outside the duct can be as erratic as the condition of the outdoor air (a duct in a vented attic, or leaky unconditioned space, or outdoors, for example).

- The condition of the air entering a supply duct depends on the mode of operation (humid space heating, humid space cooling).

- At the extreme, the condition of the air in a supply duct can vary over a range for heating, and over a range for cooling (for a system that uses a variable supply air dry-bulb temperature, and/or variable supply air dew point temperature).

- The condition of the air entering a return duct or exhaust duct equals the condition of the air in the humid space (determined by contract set points).

- The condition of the air in the humid space is relatively constant, so operating conditions vary with weather patterns, mode of equipment operation (heating or cooling), and supply air set points.

- Investigate and determine the worst case operating condition for the whole year. This condition shall be used to determine the insulation R-value that will prevent condensation.

Insulation R-Value to Prevent Condensation

Duct insulation and a vapor retarding surface must prevent condensation on exterior and interior surfaces. The exposed surface of the insulating material is used for this calculation (the vapor membrane R-value is negligible).

Cold Air Inside the Duct

Condensation must not occur at any point on the outside of the duct perimeter. If cold air is inside the duct, this equation determines the minimum R-value for duct insulation (R_{ins}). It uses the worst case air film coefficient for still air (horizontal panel, heat flow down) to maximize the insulation R-value.

$$R_{ins} = 0.95 \times (T_a - T_f) / (T_a - T_s - 5) - 1.12$$

Where:
Air film resistance for still air (worst case) = 0.95
T_a = Dry-bulb air temperature outside the duct (ambient)
T_f = Dry-bulb air temperature inside the duct
T_s = Dew point temperature of humid air (ambient)
Safety factor for dew point temperature = 5 °F
Sum of outside and inside air film resistance = 1.12
(0.17 for 1,300 Fpm or less, plus 0.95 for still air)
R-value for duct material assumed to be negligible.
R-value for vapor retarder assumed to be negligible.

For example, a supply air duct runs through a pool space, the temperature of the duct air is 55°F, the ambient air is 80°F and 60% RH. The dew point temperature of the ambient air is 64.85 °F (not dependant on altitude). The insulation R-value has to be 1.22 or greater, to prevent condensation on the outside surface.

$$R_{ins} = 0.95 \times (80 - 55) / (80 - 64.85 - 5) - 1.12 = 1.22$$

If an outdoor air intake duct runs through the same pool space, and if the temperature of the duct air is 0°F, the insulation R-value has to be 6.37 or greater, to prevent condensation on the outside surface.

$$R_{ins} = 0.95 \times (80 - 0) / (80 - 64.85 - 5) - 1.12 = 6.37$$

Cold Air Outside the Duct

Condensation must not occur inside the duct. If the cold air is outside the duct, this equation determines the minimum R-value for duct insulation (R_{ins}). It uses the worst case air film coefficient for still air (0.68 for vertical panel, horizontal heat flow) to maximize the insulation R-value.

$$R_{ins} = 0.17 \times (T_f - T_a) / (T_f - T_s - 5) - 0.85$$

Where:
Negative values for Ri_{ns} translate to no insulation
Air film resistance for duct air = 0.17
T_a = Dry-bulb air temperature outside the duct (ambient)
T_f = Dry-bulb air temperature inside the duct
T_s = Dew point temperature of humid air (inside the duct)
Safety factor for dew point temperature = 5 °F
Sum of outside and inside air film resistance = 0.85
(0.17 for 1,300 Fpm or less plus 0.68 for still air)
R-value for duct material assumed to be negligible.

For example, a return duct runs through a 0°F space, the condition of the duct air is 80°F and 60% RH. The dew point temperature of the duct air is 64.85 °F. The insulation R-value has to be 0.49 or greater, to prevent condensation on the inside surface.

$$R_{ins} = 0.17 \times (80 - 0) / (80 - 64.85 - 5) - 0.85 = 0.49$$

For this scenario, the amount of insulation decreases as space temperature increases. At about 29°F duct insulation is not required to prevent condensation on the inside surface. This is demonstrated below. If the space temperature increases to 30°F or more, the equation will return a negative number for R_{ins}. When R_{ins} is negative, it means that insulation is not required to prevent condensation.

$$R_{ins} = 0.17 \times (80 - 29) / (80 - 64.85 - 5) - 0.85 = 0.0042$$

Insulation for Sensible Heat Transfer

When duct heat loss or heat gain is the issue, the duct insulation R-value should be at least R-6. If the unconditioned space is very hot or very cold, use R-8.

Design Value for Duct Insulation

The insulation R-value to prevent condensation is determined by the procedures described above; this may be different than the insulation R-value for sensible heat transfer. The design value for duct insulation equals the larger of the two values.

13-10 Duct Sealing

Approved methods and materials (per codes and industry standards) shall be used to completely seal duct runs. This optimizes duct system efficiency and minimizes the possibility of local condensation.

- Supply-side leakage wastes heating-cooling capacity, dehumidification capacity, and reduces delivered capacity at the supply outlets.

  There is no simple way to adjust for leakage effects when making supply air Cfm calculations for individual spaces.

- Cold supply air leakage to a hot humid space may cause condensation on space surfaces.

- For cold supply air, duct leakage produces cold spots within duct insulation and at the outside surface of duct insulation. Local condensation will occur if these surfaces are colder than the dew point temperature of the ambient air.

- Return leaks mix ambient air with return air. This changes the condition of the air entering the space conditioning equipment, which affects the performance of the equipment, which affects the condition of the supply air.

- If a return or exhaust duct is in a cold space, duct leakage produces cold spots within duct insulation and at the duct surface. Local condensation will occur if these surfaces are colder than the dew point temperature of the ambient air.

- Return or exhaust leaks may pull cold air into an unconditioned space. This may cause condensation on space surfaces.

- Duct leaks can have an undesirable effect on space pressure. This could degrade moisture containment and control, and could cause condensation on structural surfaces.

Seal all Leakage Points

A leak anywhere in the air distribution system may cause condensation, mold and mildew and material damage. Duct sealing must be comprehensive.

- All duct seams and joints must be sealed.

- All fitting joints and connections must be sealed.

- Seal duct to boots and necks, seal boots and necks to supply or return air outlet collars, seal outlet or return frames to vapor retarding membranes.

- Seal all connections, seams and joints on equipment cabinets and fans. Equipment access panels must be tightly clamped to compliant gaskets.

Quantifying Leakage

Duct sealing work or the lack of a sealing effort is quantified by the leakage lines on Figure 13-1 (next page). The Class 3 line (CL-3) shows that some leakage is associated with good practice (about 3 Cfm per 100 SqFt of duct surface area at one inch of pressure). The Class 6 and Class 12 lines are for sealed duct that have acceptable performance. The rest of the lines are for ducts that are partially sealed (CL-24), or unsealed duct that is increasingly deficient (CL-96 and CL-192).

- The consequences of condensation are critical, so the approved leakage class for sealed duct is CL-6 or less.

- Round plastic duct is relatively easy to seal, but fire codes limit it's use to below grade systems.

- Longitudinal seams in rectangular metal duct require considerable sealing work. Investigate the benefits of round spiral duct.

13-11 Vapor Retarding Jacket

Because of moisture migration, external insulation may not prevent condensation on cold duct walls. If cold air flows though a duct located in a humid space, provide insulation with external facings and wraps that have a perm rating of 0.50 or less .

- The humid space may be within the humid zone, or a space exposed to outdoor air. For outdoor air, Figure 13-2 roughly identifies locations that have extended periods of high humidity.

- The vapor retarding jacket must be completely sealed (no open seams, slits, cracks or penetrations).

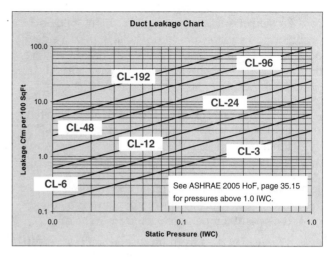

Figure 13-1

- These sealing and vapor jacket requirements also apply to equipment cabinets and cold air intake ducts installed in humid spaces.

13-12 Thermo Syphoning

Buoyancy forces cause air to circulate through the duct and equipment cabinet when there is no forced airflow through an overhead duct. This may cause condensation

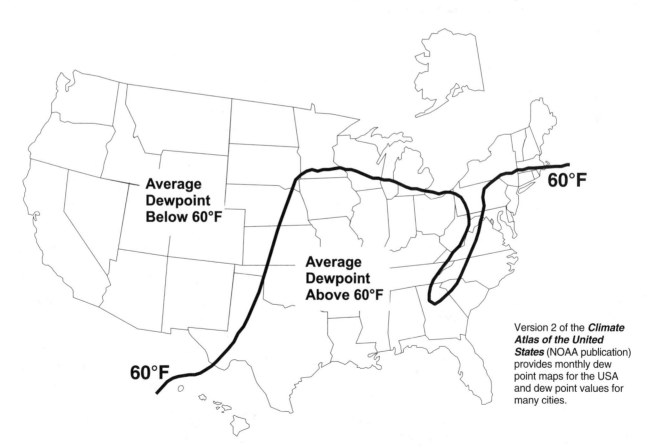

Figure 13-2

on the inside of duct walls. However, this should not be a problem for a natatorium, commercial pool or residential pool because space airflow should be continuous (every day of year and every hour of day). However, it could be a problem for a space that just has a spa.

- The humidity ratio of the air in the duct (and equipment cabinet) equals the humidity ratio in the humid space.

- The duct may be in a cold, unconditioned space.

- Condensation will form on the inside of a duct wall if the wall surface temperature is below the dew point temperature of the air in the duct.

- Water may drip from unsealed duct seams, supply air outlets and return grilles.

- The insulation R-value must be adequate to prevent condensation inside ducts and equipment cabinets.

- R-values are not effective at leakage points. Seal all duct runs and equipment cabinets.

13-13 Airway Shape

Round spiral duct is preferred because it is inherently tighter than rectangular duct. As far as aerodynamic efficiency is concerned, round duct is the most efficient shape. Airway shape may be dictated by available space.

- Square duct is more efficient than aspect ratio duct (aspect ratios of 4:1 or less are normal).

- Aspect ratios of more than 4:1 can be used to fit available space, but this should be minimized.

13-14 Fittings

Fittings usually produce most of the pressure drop for a duct run. Use efficient fittings that have a low pressure drop. Efficient fittings may have:

- Inside and outside radius for turns, with sweep sheets.

- Properly installed turning vanes in square elbows (single thickness vanes, not airflow shape).

- Gradual and smooth changes in airway shape or size.

- Branch take off with 45 degree knee on upstream side.

- See ACCA *Manual D* Third Edition, Appendix 3 for a quick comparison of fitting performance.

  Equivalent length represents pressure drop for a specified velocity and friction rate. Equivalent length is not applicable to commercial calculations that are based on fitting pressure drop. However, equivalent length is directly related to fitting efficiency. Use fitting styes that have a low equivalent length.

13-15 System Effect

Blower tables for air handlers, furnaces and duct mounted fans are for ideal entrance and exit conditions. In other words, when tested, air approached the inlet of the equipment in a straight, uniform manner, and exited the equipment in a straight, uniform manner.

Equipment airflow is significantly affected when blower test conditions are not duplicated in the field. Turbulent or stratified air entering equipment may cause inadequate heat transfer within the equipment, and may cause condensation at some point in the airstream.

- A fitting near the entrance or exit of a blower or air handler produces a system effect loss and a fitting pressure drop. The system effect loss accounts for degraded fan performance, and the fitting loss accounts for fitting pressure drop.

- The system effect loss can be much larger than the fitting loss. For example, an elbow right at the discharge of a blower collar could produce a total loss that is ten times larger than it would cause if it was well downstream from the blower.

- The reference length is the diameter of a round inlet or discharge collar, or the longest dimension of a rectangular inlet or discharge collar.

- A straight section of discharge duct must extend 5.0 reference lengths before discharge air passes through any type of fitting.

- A straight section of return duct must extend 2.5 reference lengths before return air passes through any type of fitting.

- The space required for equipment installation includes the space required for straight sections of entrance duct and exit duct.

- The equipment room must be large enough for the equipment and the entrance and exit ducts, or a straight duct may penetrate the equipment room wall and run the required distance before encountering a fitting located in an adjacent space.

- Fittings near the inlet or outlet of a blower or air handler must be efficient. Use elbows with generous inside and outside radiuses, plus sweep sheets. For square elbows, use single thickness turning vanes and make sure the leading and trailing edges point in the direction of airflow.

13-16 Supply Air Cfm and Return Air Cfm

The total supply air Cfm for a space depends on space loads (see Sections 10-1 through 10-3). The actual design value for duct airway sizing is determined when manufacturer's performance data is used to select and size equipment.

For a pool or spa space return Cfm depends on the method used to maintain negative space pressure. In this regard, the combination of return Cfm and the Cfm exhausted by a separate exhaust system (if applicable) will be five to ten percent more than the supply Cfm (compressors and heaters should be switched off for airflow measurements).

13-17 Airway Sizing

Commercial duct design procedures apply to swimming pool and spa applications regardless of the type of structure that surrounds the humid space. This includes institutional buildings, commercial buildings, and all types of residential buildings.

- Commercial airway sizing procedures shall be used for pool and spa applications.

- ACCA *Manual D* shall not be used for pool and spa applications.

- If a swimming pool and/or spa is in a residence, the commercial procedure mandate only applies to the mechanical system that serves the humid zone. Standard residential procedures (*Manual J, Manual S and Manual D*) apply to the HVAC system(s) that serve spaces outside the humid zone. (Separate systems are mandatory).

Equal Friction Method

The probability that a practitioner will decide to use the equal friction method for duct airway sizing is extremely high (compared to the static regain method or T-method). The equal fiction method is summarized here. See ACCA *Manual Q*, or information published by ASHRAE and SMACNA for comprehensive guidance.

- Perform a block load calculation (to determine equipment size).

- Use manufacturer's performance data to select equipment (to determine blower Cfm).

- Perform room load calculations (to determine room Cfm).

- Determine the design Cfm for each supply outlet and each return (considering local heating, cooling and humidification loads, and space pressure requirements).

- Locate central equipment, locate supply outlets and locate return inlets.

- For supply and return hardware, select style, make, model and size (for adequate throw and acceptable noise).

- Connect all components with duct routes (consider available space, penetrations, obstructions and appearance).

- Specify the exact type of fitting for each turn, tee, wye, branch take-off, transition, boot, equipment connection, etc. (use efficient fittings that have a low pressure drop).

- Select the maximum air velocity for the primary trunk ducts leaving and entering the air handler (see Figure 13-4, note 2, next page).

- Use the blower Cfm and the maximum air velocity to find the design value for the airway sizing friction rate (FR) in IWC/100 Ft.

  Read the friction rate from a duct slide rule or friction chart that summarizes the performance of the actual duct material.

- Start at the end of the supply runs and calculate the Cfm for each section of duct as the calculations move toward the air handler (branch Cfm is what it is, trunk Cfm increases upstream of each branch). Mark values on the drawing or sketch.

- Repeat the Cfm calculation for the return runs (branch Cfm is what it is, trunk Cfm increases downstream of each branch). Mark values on the drawing or sketch.

- Use the design friction rate and the Cfm flowing through a branch run or trunk duct section to determine round airway size. Mark values on the drawing or sketch.

- Use a duct slide rule to convert round sizes to rectangular sizes that have the same friction rate (as necessary, if round duct is not installed). Mark values on the drawing or sketch.

Example

A duct system that has a few supply runs and a few return runs is sufficient to demonstrate the airway sizing procedure. Figure 13-3 (next page) summarizes system geometry and system attributes, and Figure 13-4 summarizes the airway sizing calculations.

13-18 Duct Run Pressure Drop

Duct system pressure drop calculations are made after duct airways are sized. The goal is to determine the supply run that has the largest pressure drop and the return run that has the largest pressure drop. The procedure is summarized here:

- Determine the total straight line lengths (in feet) of all supply runs (start at the blower and work toward the outlets), then repeat for the returns. Mark values on the drawing or sketch.

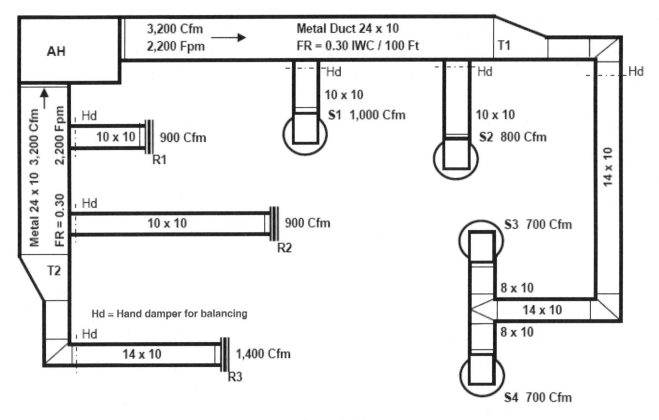

Figure 13-3

- Use the design friction rate and the total length of each supply path and each return path to find the straight duct pressure drops (IWC) for supply and return runs.

- Use fitting pressure drop tables (ACCA *Manual Q*, ASHRAE guide or SMACNA guide) to find the pressure drop for each fitting in a supply path or return path.

- Show the location of all air-side devices (supply air outlets, return grilles, hand dampers, reheat coils, etc.) on the drawing or sketch. Obtain pressure drop values from manufacturer's engineering data. Record the values.

- When applicable, use manufacturer's performance data to find the upstream pressure requirement for devices that operate by system pressure (a system powered VAV diffuser, for example). Record the values.

- For each supply run, add the total pressure drop for straight duct to the total pressure drop for fittings and devices to find the total pressure drop for the run. Then repeat for the return runs.

- The critical supply path is the path with the largest pressure drop. The critical return path is the path with the largest pressure drop. Identify these paths and record the pressure drop values.

Airway Sizing Calculations for Figure 13-3				
Design Friction Rate = 0.30				
Duct Run	Run Cfm	Round Size (In)	Rect. Size (In)	Rect. Vel. (Fpm)
AH to T1	3,200	17.3	24 x 10	2,200
S1	1,000	11.0	10 x 10	1,520
S2	800	10.2	10 x 10	1,230
T1 to Tee	1,400	12.5	14 x 10	1,570
S3	700	9.7	8 x 10	1,360
S4	700	9.7	8 x 10	1,360
AH to T2	3,200	17.3	24 x 10	2,200
R1	900	10.7	10 x 10	1,400
R2	900	10.7	10 x 10	1,400
R3	1,400	12.5	14 x 10	1,570

1) Design value for blower Cfm = 3,200 (from equipment selection)
2) 2,200 Fpm air velocity limit is based on acceptable noise level for a pool space. Figure A3-6 in ACCA *Manual Q* deals with this issue, but not for a pool space. Related choices are 1,800 Fpm for retail stores/cafeterias and 2,500 Fpm for industrial spaces.
3) Design friction rate (metal duct slide rule) = 0.28 IWC / 100 Ft (round to 0.30 for convenient slide rule use).

Figure 13-4

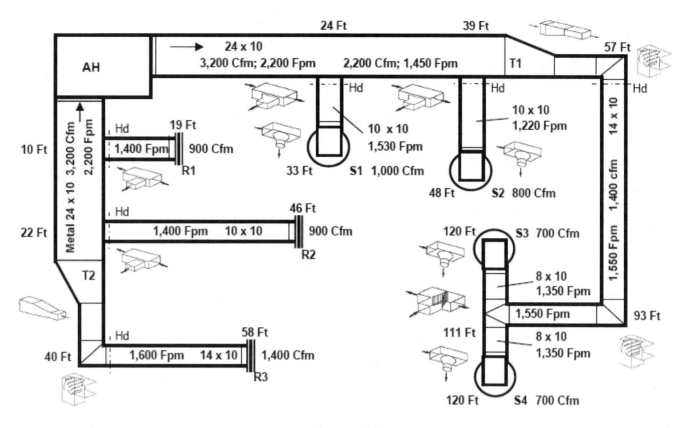

Figure 13-5

Figure 13-5 summarizes information for the pressure drop calculations. Note that pressure drops are produced by straight runs, fittings and devices. Guidance pertaining to particular aspects of the calculations is provided here:

Pressure Drop for Straight Duct

The pressure drop (PD) for straight duct depends on the design friction rate (FR) value and the duct length (Feet).

PD (IWC) = FR x (Length / 100)

For example
FR = 0.30
Duct length = 120 Feet
PD = 0.30 x (120 / 100) = 0.36 IWC

Fitting Pressure Drop

A fitting loss coefficient (C) table and a reference velocity determine fitting pressure drop (see Figure 13-6). Fitting pressure drop at sea level is determined by this equation.

PD (IWC) = C x (V$_{ref}$ / 4,005)^2

For example, evaluate supply branch take-off fitting for branch S1 on Figure 13-6.
Vb = 1,530 Fpm; Vu = 2,200 Fpm; Vb / Vu = 0.70
Qb = 1,000 Cfm; Qu = 3,200 Cfm; Qb / Qu = 0.31

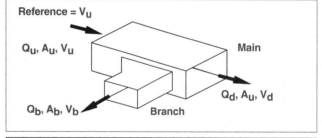

Reference = V$_u$

Q$_u$, A$_u$, V$_u$

Main

Q$_b$, A$_b$, V$_b$

Branch

Q$_d$, A$_u$, V$_d$

Branch Coefficient C$_b$						
	Q$_b$ / Q$_u$					
V$_b$ / V$_u$	0.10	0.20	0.30	0.40	0.50	0.60
0.2	0.91	0.89				
0.4	0.81	0.79	0.77			
0.6	0.77	0.72	0.70	0.69		
0.8	0.78	0.73	0.69	0.66	0.63	
1.0	0.78	0.98	0.85	0.79	0.74	0.70
1.2	0.90	1.11	1.16	1.23	1.03	0.86

Main Coefficient C$_m$						
V$_d$ / V$_u$	0.10	0.20	0.30	0.40	0.60	0.80
C$_m$	0.28	0.22	0.17	0.13	0.06	0.02

Figure 13-6

C_b = 0.70 (approximate)
Reference velocity = 2,200 Fpm
Branch PD = 0.70 x (2,200 / 4,005) ^{2}= 0.21 IWC
Pressure drop for air that flows past branch S1 (main PD)
Vd / Vu = 1,450 / 2,100 = 0.69
C_m = 0.04
Reference velocity = 2,200 Fpm
Main PD = 0.04 x (2,200 / 4,005) ^{2}= 0.01 IWC
Paths for main PD = AH to S2 and AH to S3

System Effect

When blower data is produced by laboratory test, much care is devoted to making sure air approaches and leaves the blower or blower cabinet as well ordered, uniform flow (no turbulence or distorted velocity profile near entrance and exit). In practice, blower performance is diminished if test conditions are not reproduced in the field (installing a 90 degree elbow close to the discharge opening of a blower or blower cabinet, for example). This reduction in performance is called the system effect.

The system effect is treated as an increase in system resistance (instead of derating blower performance). Therefore, tables similar to Figure 13-6 provide loss coefficient values (C_s) for entering geometry and discharge geometry that diminishes blower performance. The system effect is evaluated by this equation. Note that this procedure is identical to the fitting pressure drop procedure.

$$PD\ (IWC) = C_s \times (V_{ref}/4,005)^2$$

Note: A fitting near a blower or blower cabinet inlet, or discharge opening, produces two pressure drops. First, use a loss coefficient from a system effect table to calculate pressure drop one, then use a loss coefficient from a fitting loss table to calculate pressure drop two.

Device Pressure Drop

The pressure drop across a diffuser, return grill, open balancing damper, open VAV damper, coil, filter, etc., depends on the Cfm flowing through the device. Sea level pressure drop values are read from performance tables published by equipment manufacturers. Some air-side devices must have a minimum upstream pressure in order to operate. Minimum upstream pressure values are read from engineering data published by equipment manufacturers. For example:

- The pressure drop for a supply air outlet, return grill, fire damper, balancing damper or open VAV damper can range from 0.01 to more than 0.10 IWC.

- The pressure drop for a filter can range from about 0.10 to more than 1.0 IWC.

- The pressure drop for an electric coil can range from 0.05 to more than 0.20 IWC.

Supply Path Pressure Drop				
AH → S1	**Feet**	**F/100**	**Fpm**	**PD (IWC)**
Straight	33	0.30	~	0.10
BTO to S1	~	~	2,200	0.21
HD	~	~	1,530	0.07
Drop to S1	~	~	1,530	0.14
Diffuser	~	~	~	0.04
			Total	0.56
AH → S2	**Feet**	**F/100**	**Fpm**	**PD (IWC)**
Straight	48	0.30	~	0.14
BTO past S1	~	~	2,200	0.01
BTO to S2	~	~	1,450	0.08
HD	~	~	1,220	0.05
Drop to S2	~	~	1,220	0.10
Diffuser	~	~	~	0.04
			Total	0.42
AH → S3; S4	**Feet**	**F/100**	**Fpm**	**PD (IWC)**
Straight	120	0.30	~	0.36
BTO past S1	~	~	2,200	0.01
BTO past S2	~	~	1,450	0.01
T1	~	~	1,450	0.01
Ell	~	~	1,550	0.03
Ell	~	~	1,550	0.03
Tee	~	~	1,550	0.04
Drop to S3; S4	~	~	1,350	0.12
Diffuser	~	~	~	0.04
			Total	0.65

BTO = Branch Take Off; T1 = Transition fitting

Figure 13-7

- The pressure drop for a hot water coil, refrigerant coil or chilled water coil can range from about 0.15 to more than 0.30 IWC. (Component pressure drop can be ignored when the blower performance table is adjusted for cabinet items. Find a precise declaration in the blower table notes, or ask the manufacturer for this information.)

Example

Figure 13-5 shows duct system information for the pressure drop calculations. Figure 13-7 summarizes the pressured drop calculations for the supply runs and Figure 13-8 summarizes the pressured drop calculations for the return runs.

- Lengths of straight duct are installed at the inlet and discharge openings, so there are no system effect losses.

- Figure 13-7 shows that AH to S3 or S4 is the critical supply path and the largest supply-side pressure drop is 0.65 IWC.

- Figure 13-8 shows that R2 to AH to is the critical return path and the largest return-side pressure drop is 0.52 IWC.

13-19 Blower Selection

The practitioner shall use manufacturer's blower data (Figure 13-9, for example) to determine blower speed (RPM) and blower motor horsepower (HP). These values depend on the design value for blower Cfm and the total resistance that the blower has to work against. Blower RPM and motor horsepower are specified when equipment is ordered. All data is for sea level operation.

- The design Cfm for a supply fan is determined when the primary equipment (heating, cooling, humidification) is selected.

- The design Cfm for a return fan or exhaust fan is determined by the space air balance requirement (see Figure 13-10, next page).

- The external static pressure for a supply fan equals the resistance of the critical downstream path, the resistance of the critical upstream path, and any cabinet devices that were not in place when the blower was tested. Upstream resistance may be produced by an outdoor air intake hood, by an air-side economizer damper, by outdoor air damper and duct, or by a return air damper and duct (see Figure 13-10).

- The external static pressure for a return fan or exhaust fan equals the resistance of the critical upstream path plus the resistance of the downstream path.

Return Path Pressure drop				
R1 → AH	**Feet**	**F/100**	**Fpm**	**PD**
Straight	19	0.30	~	0.06
Return Grille	~	~	~	0.03
HD	~	~		0.05
BTO from R1	~	~	1,400	0.16
			Total	**0.30**
R2 → AH	**Feet**	**F/100**	**Fpm**	**PD**
Straight	46	0.30	~	0.14
Return Grille	~	~	~	0.03
HD	~	~	~	0.05
BTO from R2	~	~	1,400	0.16
BTO past R1	~	~	2,200	0.14
			Total	**0.52**
R3 → AH	**Feet**	**F/100**	**Fpm**	**PD**
Straight	58	0.30	~	0.17
Return Grille	~	~	~	0.03
HD	~	~	~	0.05
Ell	~	~	1,600	0.03
T2	~	~	1,600	0.04
BTO past R2	~	~	1,500	0.04
BTO past R1	~	~	2,200	0.14
			Total	**0.50**

BTO = Branch Take Off; T2 = Transition fitting

Figure 13-8

Figure 13-10 summarizes the issue for a fan that is external to the equipment cabinet.

- If the exhaust or return fan is located in the equipment cabinet, the external static pressure depends on the downstream resistance and the expected static pressure at the equipment return.

	External Static Pressure (Inches of Water)																			
	1.10		1.20		1.30		1.40		1.50		1.60		1.70		1.80		1.90		2.00	
CFM	RPM	BHP	RPM	BHP	RPM	BHP	RPM	BHP	RPM	BHP	RPM	BHP	RPM	BHP	RPM	BHP	RPM	BHP	RPM	BHP
	3-HP Standard Motor & Drive								3-HP Standard Motor & High Static Drive Accessory[ii]											
4000	799	1.75	829	1.87	856	1.99	884	2.11	911	2.24	937	2.35	962	2.47	987	2.59	1010	2.70	1034	2.82
4500	820	2.12	847	2.24	873	2.36	900	2.50	927	2.64	952	2.77	978	2.91	1003	3.05	1025	3.18	1049	3.32
5000	847	2.56	873	2.70	897	2.83	921	2.96	945	3.09	970	3.24	993	3.38	1017	3.53	1041	3.69	1064	3.85
5500	881	3.06	903	3.22	926	3.37	948	3.52	971	3.67	993	3.80	1015	3.95	1036	4.09	1058	4.25	1081	4.41
6000	916	3.61	938	3.78	959	3.96	980	4.13	1001	4.31	1021	4.46	1042	4.62	1062	4.78	1082	4.93	1103	5.09
	5-HP Oversized Motor & Drive[iii]									5-HP Oversized Motor & Field Supplied High Static Drive[iv]										

Figure 13-9

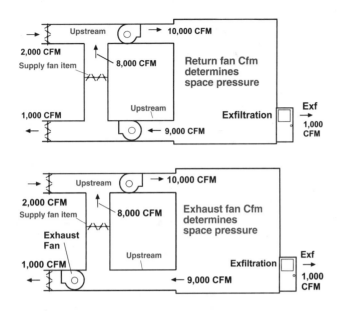

Figure 13-10

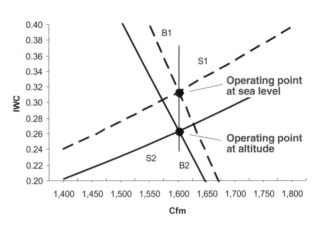

Figure 13-11

Example

For a 5,000 Cfm supply fan, the downstream resistance produced by the critical supply-side path is 0.80 IWC. The upstream path has an outdoor air damper and duct, and a return air damper and duct. The upstream resistance produced by the critical return-side path is 0.27 IWC. The equipment cabinet has a reheat coil that was not in place when the blower was tested. The pressure drop for the reheat coil is 0.13 IWC.

Blower Cfm = 5,000
External static pressure = 0.80 + 0.27 + 0.13 = 1.20 IWC
Blower table = Figure 13-9
Blower RPM = 873
Blower motor HP = 2.70 (use 3.0 HP standard size)

A similar procedure is used to select RPM and horsepower for an return fan or exhaust fan.

13-20 System Performance at Altitude

Flow-pressure relationships for the blower and the duct system are summarized by Figure 13-11. Note that the intersection of the blower curve and the duct system is the only possible operating point for the combined system (for a particular blower RPM, and a particular set of balancing damper positions).

- Duct system design procedures use sea level blower data, so bower performance is plotted as curve B1.

- Duct system design procedures use sea level data for duct system drops, so system performance is plotted as curve S1.

Approximate Altitude Correction Factor	
Elevation	**ACF**
Sea Level	1.00
1,000	0.97
2,000	0.93
3,000	0.89
4,000	0.87
5,000	0.84
6,000	0.80
7,000	0.77
8,000	0.75
9,000	0.72
10,000	0.69
11,000	0.66
12,000	0.63

This table provides approximate correction factors for the range of air temperatures associated with comfort heating and cooling processes. Accuracy is compatible with the accuracy of load calculation procedures, equipment selection procedures and duct design procedures.

Figure 13-12

- The intersection of the B1 and S1 curves is the sea level operating point.

- Blower pressure is proportional to air density, so all points on the blower curve are multiplied by an altitude correction factor. Curve B2 shows blower performance at altitude.

- System resistance is proportional to air density, so all points on the system curve are multiplied by an altitude correction factor. Curve S2 represents system performance at altitude.

- The intersection of the B2 and S2 curves is the altitude operating point.

- At altitude, the operating point Cfm equals the sea level operating point Cfm.

- A given amount of blower Cfm has more heating and cooling capacity at sea level than at altitude. Therefore altitude is an important issue when primary equipment is selected. The typical result is that the design value for blower Cfm is larger at altitude, compared to a sea level design. (Section 11 deals with equipment selection.)

- At altitude, operating pressure is reduced, therefore blower horsepower is reduced (multiply blower table horsepower by an altitude correction factor from Figure 13-12 (previous page).

13-21 Balancing Dampers

Duct systems designed by the equal friction method are not self balancing. This can produce serious problems if system airflow rates significantly deviate from the design values. Install a comprehensive set of balancing dampers at appropriate points in the supply runs and return runs.

Part 2

Example Problems

Section 14 — Design Example for a Pool and Spa in a Home

Section 15 — Design Example for a Pool and Spa in a Motel or Hotel

Section 16 — Design Example for a Competition Pool

Design Example for a Pool and Spa in a Home

This example evaluates the moisture loads, sensible cooling loads and sensible heating loads for a natatorium in a Boise, Idaho home. The humid zone has a 30 Ft by 18 Ft pool, a 6 Ft by 6 Ft spa, with no spectators.

14-1 Survey Data for Load Calculations

Figure 14-1 shows the plan view of the humid zone and the input values for items that are peculiar to this application. Inputs for the building envelope construction (roof, walls, floor, windows, skylights an doors) are not shown, but suitable values were used for load calculations (see Section 14-2).

- Pool water is 84°F and spa water is 102°F. For cooling calculations, space air is 86°F and 60% RH. For heating calculations, space air is 86°F and 50% RH. (Using 60% RH for summer reduces equipment size. Using 50% for winter anticipates that dry outdoor air for ventilation will cause space humidity to be closer to 50% RH.)

- Tables A5-4 and A5-5 are used to evaluate evaporation loads. Moisture release values depend on water temperature, and on the temperature and relative humidity of space air. The activity factor for a residential pool is 0.50, and 1.0 for the spa.

- The summer (60% RH) evaporation rates for pool water and spa water are 0.0426 and 0.1464 Lb/Hr·SqFt. The winter (50% RH) evaporation rates (not shown by Figure 14-1) for pool water and spa water are 0.0554 and 0.1570 Lb/Hr·SqFt.

- It is assumed that the wet deck area extends six feet from the edge of the pool and three feet for the spa (the practitioner investigates and decides what is reasonable for a particular application).

- Figure 14-1 shows the water surface areas and wet deck areas for the pool and spa.

- Figure 14-1 shows the length, width and height of the space, and the glass areas for each compass direction. There are no skylights.

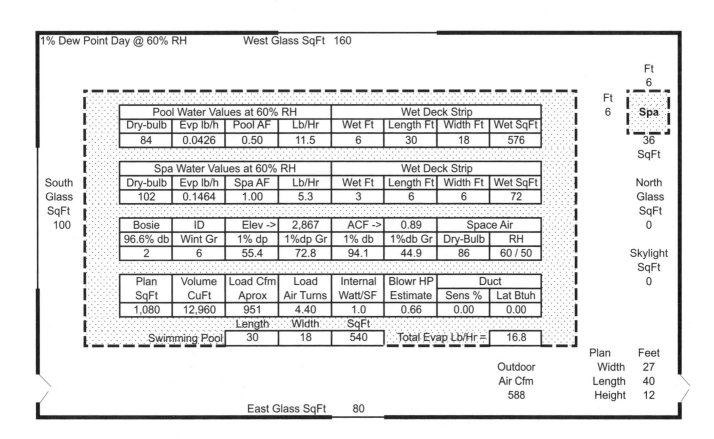

Figure 14-1

- Figure 14-1 shows that the internal load for lighting is 1.0 Watt per SqFt.

- Figure 14-1 shows the outdoor design conditions for Boise, ID (which has a dry climate).

  Grains values are for 2,867 feet elevation
  Winter (99.6%) = 2°F; and 6 grains for 90% RH
  Summer 1% DP = 55.4°F dp; 71.6°F db; 72.8 grains
  Summer 1% DB = 94°F db; 62.8°F wb; 44.9 grains

- Figure 14-1 also shows some output values. These are discussed later.

14-2 Check the Thermal Performance of the Structure

The R-values for the opaque panels and the U-values for fenestration have to be suitable for the application. Use the R-value equation from Section 3-5 to produce a rough estimate for the minimum R-value for a dry interior surface.

$$R_t = K \times (T_i - T_o) / (T_i - T_s)$$

Outdoor dry-bulb = T_o = 2 °F
Indoor dry-bulb = T_i = 86 °F
Indoor relative humidity = 50% and 60%
indoor air dew point = 65.2 °F and 70.5 °F
Safety factor = 5 °F
Surface temperature T_s = 70.2 °F and 75.5 °F
K = 0.68 (vertical surface)
R_t = 3.6 @ 50%; 5.4 @ 60% (includes air films)
U-value = 0.28 @ 50%; 0.18 @ 60% (includes air films)
K = 0.95 (horizontal surface)
R_t = 5.1 @ 50%; 7.6 @ 60% (includes air films)
U-value = 0.20 @ 50%; 0.13 @ 60% (includes air films)

Space humidity may vary from 50% RH to 60% RH, so 60% RH is a worst-case scenario. The preceding calculations show that the minimum R-value from outdoors to an indoor glass surface, or indoor surface of a vapor retarding membrane must be 7.6 or greater. This applies to any thermal bridge in a wall or ceiling and to any point on the fenestration assembly. This may not be a challenge for a wall or ceiling, but the corresponding U-value for windows (about 0.18) requires a high quality product (the U-value for a skylight is about 0.13).

This is a crude way to see if the construction may be suitable for the application. The architect or building designer is responsible for detailed condensation calculations (see Section 3-6).

14-3 Peak Dew Point Loads for Cooling

Figure 14-2 shows the load calculation for the 1% dew point condition. In addition there are ballpark values for the heat contained in hot compressor gas, the heat for water evaporation and the heat available for another use,

Boise Idaho — 1% Dew Point Day		
Space at 60% RH In use, OA damper open	Sensible Btuh	Latent Btuh
Windows	13,905	
Skylights	0	
Wall transmission	964	
Roof transmission	2,030	
Infiltration	0	0
Evaporation (16.8 Lb/Hr)rnd		17,611
Spectators		
Lights, etc	3,686	
Blower heat	2,376	
Supply duct	0	
OAcfm downstream (392)	- 8,283	- 18,561
Space load	14,660	- 950
Space load SHR	1.00	
Return fan	0	0
Return duct	0	0
Total load	14,660	- 9 50
Total load SHR	1.00	
- 0.9	Total moisture load (Lb/Hr)	
14,660	Total cooling load (Btuh)	
1.2	Load tons (884 SqFt/Ton)	
9.5	Default EER	
1.5	Estimated compressor KW	
19,927	Estimated Btuh in hot compressor gas	
17,611	Btuh for water evaporation	
2,316	Btuh for other use and/or rejection	

1) Outdoor air: Dry-bulb = 72°F; Wet-bulb = 61°F; Grains = 73
2) Indoor air: Dry-bulb = 86°F; RH = 60%; Grains = 125

Figure 14-2

and/or rejection. Comments pertaining to Figure 14-2 items are provided here:

- The weather data is for the hottest month of year and the load calculation is made for late in the day when glass loads peak (notice the West glass and South glass on Figure 14-1).

- The calculations for glass loads, wall loads and roof loads are equivalent to a comfort cooling calculation, but the outdoor and indoor design conditions are significantly different than what is used for a comfort calculation.

- It is assumed that non-operable fenestration, an infiltration barrier and a vapor retarding membrane prevent significant infiltration, so the infiltration loads are negligible.

- The latent load (Lb/Hr) for water evaporation is the sum of the loads for the pool and the spa. The evaporation load is the product of the values for the evaporation rate (Lb/Hr·SqFt), the activity factor and the water surface area (see Figure 14-1).

- The Lb/Hr load is multiplied by 1,050 Btuh/Lb to find the latent load in Btuh units.

- There are no spectators.

- A value of 1.0 watts per SqFt of floor area was used for the internal load. The practitioner must determine the appropriate internal load value for a particular application.

- Sensible heat from the supply air blower is based on a tentative horsepower value. This would be adjusted when load calculations are finalized during the equipment selection process.

- The sensible gain for the supply duct is a space load. For this example, it is assumed that the supply duct load is negligible because of some combination of location, insulation, surface area and tightness. In practice, the supply duct load is evaluated and added to the other sensible loads.

- For a dehumidifier, outdoor air enters downstream from the cooling coil so it is a space load. Outdoor air Cfm equals the Cfm for wet surfaces. Use 0.48 Cfm per SqFt of wet surface (water area and wet deck area). Figure 14-1 shows 588 outdoor air Cfm for wet surfaces.

- Figure 14-2 shows negative outdoor air loads (the space air is warmer and wetter than outdoor air at the 1% dew point condition).

- The total space load is 14,660 sensible Btuh and - 950 latent Btuh, and the sensible heat ratio for these loads is 1.00.

- The return fan is an equipment load. For this example, it is assumed that there is an exhaust fan, so the sensible load for the return fan is zero.

- The sensible and latent gain for a return duct is an equipment load. For this example, it is assumed that return duct loads are negligible because of some combination of location, insulation, surface area and tightness. In practice, return duct loads are evaluated and added to the other sensible and latent loads.

- Total loads equal the space loads because there are no equipment loads for this example. The equipment sizing loads for this scenario are:

Moisture = - 0.9 Lb/Hr

Sensible load Btuh = 14,660

Latent load Btuh = - 950

Total load Btuh = 14,660

- The total load is about 1.2 tons, which works out to about 884 SqFt per load ton.

- For estimating the amount of hot gas heat, the default value for EER is 9.5.

- The total load and the EER value provide a ballpark value for compressor heat (1.5 KW).

KW = Total Btuh / (1,000 x EER)

- 1.5 KW produces 19,927 Btuh of hot gas heat. The actual amount of hot gas heat is determined when the equipment is selected.

- The heat load for pool water evaporation is about 17,611 Btuh, so excess hot gas heat can be used for supply air and/or makeup water.

- If there is no use for some portion of the excess heat, it is rejected to an air cooled or water cooled condenser.

14-4 Peak Dry-Bulb Loads for Cooling

Figure 14-3 (next page) shows the dehumidifier loads for the 1% dry-bulb condition. Compared to the 1% dew point condition, outdoor dry-bulb increases and outdoor moisture decreases, so the latent loads that depend on outdoor moisture decrease and the sensible loads that depend on outdoor temperature increase.

- For 60% RH in the space, The moisture load goes from - 0.9 Lb/Hr to - 10.4 Lb/Hr.

- The latent cooling load goes from - 950 Btuh to - 10,870 Btuh.

- The sensible cooling load increases from 14,660 Btuh to 33,582 Btuh.

- Cooling load tons increases from 1.2 to 2.8.

- Assuming that air leaves the cooling coil at 50°F, 33,582 Btuh of sensible load translates to about 951 Cfm for the supply fan. This is a temporary value. The actual supply air Cfm is determined when equipment is selected.

- 951 Cfm provides 4.4 space air turns. This falls in the desired range (4.0 to 8.0), so bypass air is not required. (This is a tentative value that will change when the equipment is selected.)

- There is more than enough hot gas heat.

14-5 Other Cooling Loads

Similar calculations are made for a vacant space. Figure 14-4 (next page) summarizes the loads for the summer design conditions. Notice that the total moisture load is positive (about 12 to 13 Lb/Hr).

Boise Idaho — 1% Dry-Bulb Day		
Space at 60% RH In use, OA damper open	**Sensible Btuh**	**Latent Btuh**
Windows	15,809	
Skylights	0	
Wall transmission	3,804	
Roof transmission	3,240	
Infiltration	0	0
Evaporation (16.8 Lb/Hr)rnd		17,611
Spectators		
Lights, etc	3,686	
Blower heat	2,376	
Supply duct	0	
OA$_{cfm}$ downstream (392)	4,659	- 28,481
Space load	33,582	- 10,870
Space SHR	1.00	
Return fan	0	0
Return duct	0	0
Total load	33,582	- 10,870
Total SHR	1.00	
- 10.4	Total moisture load (Lb/Hr)	
33,582	Total cooling load (Btuh)	
2.8	Load tons (386 SqFt/Ton)	
951	Estimated supply air Cfm	
4.4	Estimated air turns for no bypass air	
9.5	Default EER	
3.5	Estimated compressor KW	
45,647	Estimated Btuh in hot compressor gas	
17,611	Btuh for water evaporation	
28,036	Btuh for other use and/or rejection	

1) Outdoor air: Dry-bulb = 94 °F; Wet-bulb = 63°F; Grains = 45
2) Indoor air: Dry-bulb = 86°F; RH = 60%; Grains = 125

Figure 14-3

- When the space is in use, the total moisture load is negative (- 1 to - 10 Lb/ Hr) because the negative outdoor air load is a larger than the evaporation load.

- The outdoor air damper closes when the space is vacant. This minimizes the drying effect of the outdoor air (there is some damper leakage), so the moisture load is + 12 to + 13 Lb/Hr when the space is vacant.

Cooling for Space in Use Outdoor Air Cfm = 588		
Issue	**1% Dew Point**	**1% Dry-Bulb**
Water evap (Lb/Hr)rnd	16.8	16.8
Total load (Btuh)	14,660	33,582
Sensible load (Btuh)	14,660	33,582
Latent load (Btuh)	- 950	- 10,870
Load SHR	1.00	1.00
Total moisture (Lb/Hr)	- 0.9	- 10.4

Cooling for Space Vacant Outdoor Air Cfm for Closed Damper = 48		
Issue	**1% Dew Point**	**1% Dry-Bulb**
Water evap (Lb/Hr)rnd	14.1	14.1
Total load (Btuh)	31,928	38,153
Sensible load (Btuh)	18,587	25,614
Latent load (Btuh)	13,342	12,539
Load SHR	0.58	0.67
Total moisture (Lb/Hr)	+ 12.7	+ 11.9

1) Space air at 86°F dry-bulb; 60% RH
2) Closed damper leakage = 5%

Figure 14-4

14-6 Heating Loads

Figure 14-5 (next page) shows the dehumidifier loads for the 99.6% dry-bulb condition. In addition, there is an assumed value for outdoor air preheat. Comments on Figure 14-5 items are provided here:

- The weather data is for the coldest month of year and there is no credit for solar gain.

- Glass, wall and roof loads are U x ΔT loads.

- Infiltration loads are negligible (as previously explained for cooling).

- The evaporation load and the corresponding latent load for the pool and spa are for 50% RH. Notice that this produces more evaporation than the summer condition.

  Summer at 60% RH, in use = 16.8 Lb/Hr
  Winter at 50% RH, in use = 20.6 Lb/Hr

- Lights and the supply air blower add sensible loads (same as summer).

- Supply duct load is zero (as previously explained for cooling)

- 588 Cfm of outdoor air produces a heating load and a negative latent load.

Boise Idaho — 99.6% Dry-Bulb Day		
Space at 50% RH In use, OA damper open	**Sensible Btuh**	**Latent Btuh**
Window transmission	- 7,140	
Skylights transmission	0	
Wall transmission	- 13,507	
Roof transmission	- 4,536	
Infiltration	0	0
Evaporation (20.6 Lb/Hr)$_{rnd}$		21,641
Spectators		
Lights, etc	3,686	
Blower heat	2,367	
Supply duct	0	
OA$_{cfm}$ downstream (392)	- 48,315	- 34,739
Load totals	- 67,436	- 13,098
Preheat outdoor air to 33°F	17,831	
Input at reheat coil	0	
Net space heating load	- 49,606	- 13,098
- 12.5 Total moisture load (Lb/Hr)		
1) Outdoor air: Dry-bulb = 2°F; Grains = 6 2) Indoor air: Dry-bulb = 86°F; RH = 50%; Grains = 103.7		

Figure 14-5

- Outdoor air is preheated to 33°F (or warmer) to prevent icing. This reduces the load on other heating equipment.

  Note: Equipment manufacturers have their own methods for dealing with cold outdoor air. Use their guidance for outdoor air calculations.

- With preheat, the total heating load for the space and outdoor air is -49,606 Btuh. The total latent load for the space and outdoor air is -13,098 Btuh.

- Heat input at the dehumidifier reheat coil requires compressor operation. For this feature, the default value for heating load calculations is zero Btuh.

  Note: Equipment manufacturers have their own methods for dealing with this issue. Use their guidance for reheat credit.

- The net space heating load could be for a heating coil in the equipment cabinet or supply air duct, or for separate space heating equipment.

- The moisture load is about -12.5 Lb/Hr, so space humidity may be less than 50% RH at some times.

- When the compressor operates there is a sensible and latent load on the evaporator (air enters at

Heating for Space in Use Outdoor Air Cfm = 588	
Issue	**Value**
Water evaporation (Lb/Hr)$_{rnd}$	20.6
Lights and blower (Btuh)	6,062
Outdoor air load (Btuh)	- 48,315
Total heating load (Btuh)	- 67,436
Preheat outdoor air to 33°F (Btuh)	17,831
Reheat (Btuh)	
Net space heating load (Btuh)	- 49,606
Total moisture (Lb/Hr)	- 12.5

Heating for Space Vacant Outdoor Air Cfm for Closed Damper = 48	
Issue	**Value**
Water evaporation (Lb/Hr)$_{rnd}$	17.8
Blower (Btuh)	2,367
Outdoor air load (Btuh)	- 3,910
Total heating load (Btuh)	- 26,718
Preheat outdoor air to 33°F (Btuh)	1,443
Reheat (Btuh)	
Net space heating load (Btuh)	- 25,274
Total moisture (Lb/Hr)	+ 15.1
1) Space air at 86°F dry-bulb; 50% RH 2) Closed damper leakage = 5%	

Figure 14-6

about 86°F and 50% RH (or lower) to 60% RH and leaves at about 50°F and 95% RH).

- If there are return duct loads and/or a return fan load, they affect the condition of the air entering the evaporator and the loads on the evaporator.

- The previous six bullets deal with issues that will be resolved by the dehumidifier manufacturer. The purpose of the discussion is to draw attention to these issues.

14-7 Other Heating Loads

Similar calculations were made for a vacant space. Figure 14-6 summarizes the loads for the winter design condition. Notice that the total moisture load varies from about -13 Lb/Hr when the space is in use to about +15 Lb/Hr when the space is vacant.

- For space in use, the total moisture load is negative (about -13 Lb/Hr) because the negative outdoor air load is larger than the evaporation load.

Load Summary				
Milwaukee, WI	In Use		Vacant	
	Lb/ Hr	Sen Btuh	Lb / Hr	Sen Btuh
1% Dew Point	19.2	22,678	14.3	22,383
1% Dry-Bulb	11.3	27,983	13.8	24,178
99.6% Heat	- 13.5	(79,250)	15.7	(28,848)

1) DP/DB = 72/80 °F; DB/WB = 86/72 °F; HDB= -7 °F; 723 Feet
2) Btuh heating values are for no outdoor air preheat.

Tucson, AZ	In Use		Vacant	
	Lb/ Hr	Sen Btuh	Lb / Hr	Sen Btuh
1% Dew Point	12.4	17,791	13.7	19,004
1% Dry-Bulb	- 10.8	40,078	11.5	27,393
99.6% Heat	- 5.8	(41,147)	15.3	(16,348)

1) DP/DB = 67/77 °F; DB/WB = 103/66 °F; HDB= 32 °F; 2,556 Feet
2) Btuh heating values are for no outdoor air preheat.

Boise, ID	In Use		Vacant	
	Lb / Hr	Sen Btuh	Lb / Hr	Sen Btuh
1% Dew Point	- 0.9	14,660	12.7	18,582
1% Dry-Bulb	- 10.4	33,582	11.9	25,614
99.6% Heat	- 12.5	(67,436)	15.1	(25,274)

1) DP/DB = 55/72 °F; DB/WB = 94/63 °F; HDB= -2 °F; 2,867 Feet
2) Btuh heating values are for no outdoor air preheat.

Miami, FL	In Use		Vacant	
	Lb / Hr	Sen Btuh	Lb / Hr	Sen Btuh
1% Dew Point	28.0	24,432	14.9	22,615
1% Dry-Bulb	20.1	31,273	14.4	24,934
99.6% Heat	1.0	(31,677)	16.5	(11,431)

1) DP/DB = 77/83 °F; DB/WB = 91/77 °F; HDB= 46 °F; 7 Feet
2) Btuh heating values are for no outdoor air preheat.

Figure 14-7

- When the space is vacant, a closed outdoor air damper minimizes the drying effect of the outdoor air (there is some damper leakage), so the moisture load is about +15 Lb/Hr.

14-8 Sensitivity to Climate

Climate has a large affect on the moisture load when the space is in use (outdoor air damper open). Figure 14-7 shows that the humid Miami climate produces the largest moisture load for summer. Milwaukee is second because it has a fair amount of summer humidity. Tucson is third

Grains Difference for Space at 60% RH				
Month	Tucson	Milwaukee	Boise	Miami
1	49.7	56.7	65.6	-27.5
2	53.8	55.7	62.1	-27.6
3	61.5	30.5	61.2	-31.5
4	58.3	21.0	55.6	-31.0
5	46.8	-6.6	48.1	-43.8
6	18.1	-24.6	37.7	-51.3
7	-4.9	-41.1	29.9	-50.5
8	-7.6	-37.4	36.5	-52.9
9	-2.1	-23.5	38.6	-52.0
10	16.3	8.1	59.6	-42.0
11	47.4	23.8	55.3	-42.7
12	47.5	39.7	62.7	-34.9

1) Grains Difference = Indoor grains - Outdoor grains for the month
2) Indoor grains based on 80°F dry-bulb and 60% RH
3) Outdoor grains based on the 1% wet-bulb value and the mean coincident dry-bulb value for the month.

Figure 14-8

because it has significant summer humidity during the rainy season. Boise has negative moisture load because it is a dry climate year-round (no negative values in Figure 14-8).

Climate does not have much affect on the moisture load when the space is vacant (outdoor air damper closed with 5% leakage). Figure 14-7 shows that the moisture loads are roughly the same for all four cities. (The winter loads are larger than the summer loads because the space humidity is 50% RH for winter and 60% RH for summer.)

14-9 Equipment Selection

Figure 14-8 shows that the Boise climate is dry enough to use outdoor air for dehumidification year-round. It also shows that outdoor air is not an option for Miami for any month of the year. For Milwaukee, outdoor air could be used for the seven coldest months, but not for May through October. For Tucson outdoor air cannot be used for July, August and September.

A packaged dehumidifier minimizes system design work. In this regard, sizing decisions and system attributes are based on the experience of the dehumidifier manufacturer. This should provide appropriate performance when loads peak, and at part load. In addition, water evaporation heat is recovered and used to heat pool water and/or supply air.

Section 15

Design Example for a Pool and Spa in a Motel-Hotel

This example evaluates the moisture loads, sensible cooling loads and sensible heating loads for a natatorium in a Miami, Fl motel or hotel. The humid zone has a 40 Ft by 24 Ft pool, an 8 Ft by 8 Ft spa, with no spectators.

15-1 Survey Data for Load Calculations

Figure 15-1 shows the plan view of the humid zone and the input values for items that are peculiar to this application. Inputs for the building envelope construction (roof, walls, floor, windows, skylights an doors) are not shown, but suitable values were used for load calculations (see Section 15-2).

- Pool water is 82°F and spa water is 102°F. For cooling calculations, space air is 84°F and 60% RH. For heating calculations, space air is 84°F and 50% RH. (Using 60% RH for summer reduces equipment size. Using 50% for winter anticipates that dry outdoor air for ventilation will cause space humidity to be closer to 50% RH.)

- Tables A5-4 and A5-5 are used to evaluate evaporation loads. Moisture release values depend on water temperature, and on the temperature and relative humidity of space air. The activity factor for a commercial pool is 0.65, and 1.0 for the spa.

- The summer (60% RH) evaporation rates for pool water and spa water are 0.0400 and 0.1464 Lb/Hr·SqFt. The winter (50% RH) evaporation rates (not shown by Figure 15-1) for pool water and spa water are 0.0520 and 0.1570 Lb/Hr·SqFt.

- It is assumed that the wet deck area extends six feet from the edge of the pool and three feet for the spa (the practitioner investigates and decides what is reasonable for a particular application).

- Figure 15-1 shows the water surface areas and wet deck areas for the pool and spa.

- Figure 15-1 shows the length, width and height of the space, and the glass areas for each compass direction. There is 300 SqFt of skylight area.

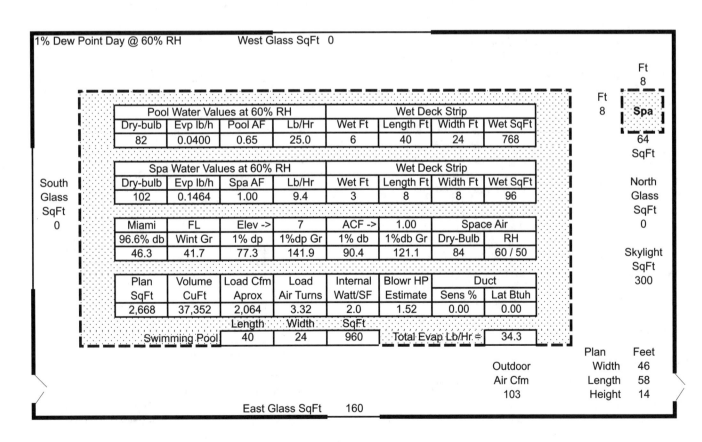

Figure 15-1

- Figure 15-1 shows that the internal load for lighting is 2.0 Watt per SqFt.

- Figure 15-1 shows the outdoor design conditions for Miami, Fl.

  Grains values are for 7 feet elevation
  Winter (99.6%) = 46°F; and 42 grains for 90% RH
  Summer 1% DP = 77°F dp; 83°F db; 142 grains
  Summer 1% DB = 90°F db; 77°F wb; 121 grains

- Figure 15-1 also shows some output values. These are discussed later.

15-2 Check the Thermal Performance of the Structure

The R-values for the opaque panels and the U-values for fenestration have to be suitable for the application. Use the R-value equation from Section 3-5 to produce a rough estimate for the minimum R-value for a dry interior surface.

$$R_t = K \times (T_i - T_o) / (T_i - T_s)$$

Outdoor dry-bulb = To = 46 °F
Indoor dry-bulb = Ti = 84 °F
Indoor relative humidity = 50% and 60%
indoor air dew point = 63.3 °F and 68.6 °F
Safety factor = 5 °F
Surface temperature T_s = 68.3 °F and 73.6 °F
K = 0.68 (vertical surface)
R_t = 1.63 @ 50%; 2.47 @ 60% (includes air films)
U-value = 0.61 @ 50%; 0.41 @ 60% (includes air films)
K = 0.95 (horizontal surface)
R_t = 2.28 @ 50%; 3.44 @ 60% (includes air films)
U-value = 0.44 @ 50%; 0.29 @ 60% (includes air films)

Space humidity may vary from 50% RH to 60% RH, so 60% RH is a worst-case scenario. The preceding calculations show that the minimum R-value from outdoors to an indoor glass surface, or the indoor surface of a vapor retarding membrane must be 3.44 or greater. This applies to any thermal bridge in a wall or ceiling, and to any point on the fenestration assembly. This may not be a challenge for a wall or ceiling, but the corresponding U-value for skylights (about 0.29) requires a high quality product (the U-value for a windows is about 0.41).

This is crude way to see if the construction may be suitable for the application. The architect or building designer is responsible for detailed condensation calculations (see Section 3-6).

15-3 Peak Dew Point Loads for Cooling

Figure 15-2 shows the load calculation for the 1% dew point condition. In addition there are ballpark values for the heat contained in hot compressor gas, the heat for

Miami Florida — 1% Dew Point Day		
Space at 60% RH In use, OA damper open	**Sensible Btuh**	**Latent Btuh**
Windows	8,492	
Skylights	32,670	
Wall transmission	688	
Roof transmission	1,480	
Infiltration	0	0
Evaporation (34.3 Lb/Hr)rnd		36,046
Spectators		
Lights, etc	18,212	
Blower heat	5,472	
Supply duct	0	
OAcfm downstream (906)	- 1,097	22,616
Space load	65,917	58,662
Space load SHR	0.53	
Return fan	0	0
Return duct	0	0
Total load	65,917	58,662
Total load SHR	0.53	
55.9	Total moisture load (Lb/Hr)	
124,579	Total cooling load (Btuh)	
10.4	Load tons (257 SqFt/Ton)	
9.5	Default EER	
13.1	Estimated compressor KW	
169,336	Estimated Btuh in hot compressor gas	
36,046	Btuh for water evaporation	
133,290	Btuh for other use and/or rejection	

1) Outdoor air: Dry-bulb = 83°F; Wet-bulb = 79°F; Grains = 142
2) Indoor air: Dry-bulb = 84°F; RH = 60%; Grains = 105

Figure 15-2

water evaporation and the heat available for another use, and/or rejection. Comments pertaining to Figure 15-2 items are provided here:

- The weather data is for the hottest month of year and the load calculation is made for late in the day when glass loads peak (notice the East glass and skylight glass on Figure 15-1).

- The calculations for glass loads, wall loads and roof loads are equivalent to a comfort cooling calculation, but the outdoor and indoor design conditions are significantly different than what is used for a comfort calculation.

- It is assumed that non-operable fenestration, an infiltration barrier and a vapor retarding membrane prevent significant infiltration, so the infiltration loads are negligible.

- The latent load (Lb/Hr) for water evaporation is the sum of the loads for the pool and the spa. The evaporation load is the product of the values for the evaporation rate (Lb/Hr·SqFt), the activity factor and the water surface area (see Figure 15-1).

- The Lb/Hr load is multiplied by 1,050 Btuh/Lb to find the latent load in Btuh units.

- There are no spectators.

- A value of 2.0 watts per SqFt of floor area was used for the internal load. The practitioner must determine the appropriate internal load value for a particular application.

- Sensible heat from the supply air blower is based on a tentative horsepower value. This would be adjusted when load calculations are finalized during the equipment selection process.

- The sensible gain for the supply duct is a space load. For this example, it is assumed that the supply duct load is negligible because of some combination of location, insulation, surface area and tightness. In practice, the supply duct load is evaluated and added to the other sensible loads.

- For a dehumidifier, outdoor air enters downstream from the cooling coil so it is a space load. Outdoor air Cfm equals the Cfm for wet surfaces. Use 0.48 Cfm per SqFt of wet surface(water area and wet deck area). Figure 15-1 shows 906 outdoor air Cfm for wet surfaces.

- Figure 15-2 shows a negative sensible load and a positive latent load for outdoor air (space air is a little warmer and significantly dryer than outdoor air at the 1% dew point condition).

- The total space load is 65,917 Sensible Btuh and 58,662 latent Btuh, and the corresponding sensible heat ratio is 0.53.

- The return fan is an equipment load. For this example, it is assumed that there is an exhaust fan, so the sensible load for the return fan is zero.

- The sensible and latent gain for a return duct is an equipment load. For this example, it is assumed that return duct loads are negligible because of some combination of location, insulation, surface area and tightness. In practice, return duct loads are evaluated and added to the other sensible and latent loads.

- Total loads equal the space loads because the are no equipment loads for this example. The loads for this scenario are:

Moisture = 55.9 Lb/Hr

Sensible load Btuh = 65,917

Latent load Btuh = 58,662

Total load Btuh = 124,579

- The total load is about 10.4 tons, which works out to about 254 SqFt per load ton.

- For estimating the amount of hot gas heat, the default value for EER is 9.5.

- The total load and the EER value provide a ballpark value for compressor heat (13.1 KW).

KW = Total Btuh / (1,000 x EER)

- 13.1 KW produces 169,336 Btuh of hot gas heat. The actual amount of hot gas heat is determined when the equipment is selected.

- The heat load for pool water evaporation is about 36,046 Btuh, so excess hot gas heat can be used for supply air and/or makeup water.

- If some portion of the excess heat has no use, it is rejected to an air or water cooled condenser.

15-4 Peak Dry-Bulb Loads for Cooling

Figure 15-3 (next page) shows the dehumidifier loads for the 1% dry-bulb condition. Compared to the 1% dew point condition, outdoor dry-bulb increases and outdoor moisture decreases, so the sensible cooling loads that depend on outdoor temperature increase and the latent cooling loads that depend on outdoor moisture decrease.

- The total moisture load drops from 56 Lb/Hr to 44 Lb/Hr.

- The sensible cooling load increases from 65,917 Btuh to 77,208 Btuh.

- The latent cooling load drops from 58,662 Btuh to 45,844 Btuh.

- Cooling load tons is about the same (10.4).

- Assuming that air leaves the cooling coil at 50°F, 77,208 Btuh of sensible load translates to about 2,064 Cfm for the supply fan. This is a temporary value. The actual supply air Cfm is determined when equipment is selected.

- 2,064 Cfm provides 3.3 space air turns. This is somewhat less than desired. Bypass air will be required to obtain 4.0 or more air turns. This is an equipment selection issue.

- There is more than enough hot gas heat.

15-5 Other Cooling Loads

Similar calculations were made for a vacant space. Figure 15-4 (next page) summarizes the loads for the

Miami Florida — 1% Dry-Bulb Day		
Space at 60% RH In use, OA damper open	Sensible Btuh	Latent Btuh
Windows	8,792	
Skylights	33,232	
Wall transmission	2,752	
Roof transmission	2,368	
Infiltration	0	0
Evaporation (34.3 Lb/Hr)$_{rnd}$		36,046
Spectators		
Lights, etc	18,212	
Blower heat	5,472	
Supply duct	0	
OA$_{cfm}$ downstream (906)	6,380	9,798
Space load	77,208	45,844
Space SHR	0.63	
Return fan	0	0
Return duct	0	0
Total load	77,208	45,844
Total SHR	0.63	

43.7	Total moisture load (Lb/Hr)
123,053	Total cooling load (Btuh)
10.3	Load tons (260 SqFt/Ton)
2,064	Estimated supply air Cfm
3.3	Estimated air turns for no bypass air
9.5	Default EER
13.0	Estimated compressor KW
167,261	Estimated Btuh in hot compressor gas
36,046	Btuh for water evaporation
131,215	Btuh for other use and/or rejection

1) Outdoor air: Dry-bulb = 90 °F; Wet-bulb = 77°F; Grains = 121
2) Indoor air: Dry-bulb = 84°F; RH = 60%; Grains = 105

Figure 15-3

Cooling for Space in Use Outdoor Air Cfm = 906		
Issue	1% Dew Point	1% Dry-Bulb
Water evap (Lb/Hr)$_{rnd}$	34.3	34.3
Total load (Btuh)	124,579	123,053
Sensible load (Btuh)	65,917	77,208
Latent load (Btuh)	58,622	45,844
Load SHR	0.53	0.63
Total moisture (Lb/Hr)	55.9	43.7

Cooling for Space Vacant Outdoor Air Cfm for Closed Damper = 48		
Issue	1% Dew Point	1% Dry-Bulb
Water evap (Lb/Hr)$_{rnd}$	23.9	23.9
Total load (Btuh)	76,332	79,538
Sensible load (Btuh)	48,677	53,343
Latent load (Btuh)	27,654	26,195
Load SHR	0.64	0.67
Total moisture (Lb/Hr)	26.3	24.9

1) Space air at 84°F dry-bulb; 60% RH
2) Closed damper leakage = 5%

Figure 15-4

the total moisture load is about 25 to 26 Lb/Hr when the space is vacant.

15-6 Heating Loads

Figure 15-5 (next page) shows the dehumidifier loads for the 99.6% dry-bulb condition. In addition, there is an assumed value for outdoor air preheat. Comments on Figure 15-5 items are provided here:

- The weather data is for the coldest month of year and there is no credit for solar gain.
- Glass, wall and roof loads are U x ΔT loads.
- Infiltration loads are negligible (as previously explained for cooling).
- The evaporation load and the corresponding latent load for the pool and spa are for 50% RH. Notice that this produces more evaporation than the summer condition.

  Summer at 60% RH = 34.3 Lb/Hr
  Winter at 50% RH = 42.5 Lb/Hr

- Lights and the supply air blower add sensible loads (same as summer).
- Supply duct load is zero (as previously explained for cooling)

summer design conditions. Notice that the total moisture load varies from about 56 Lb/Hr to 25 Lb/Hr.

- When the space is in use, the humid climate produces a large moisture load for outdoor air. This affect is larger for the 1% dew point condition (55.9 Lb/Hr total load) than for the 1% dry-bulb condition (43.7 Lb/Hr total load).
- The outdoor air damper closes when the space is vacant. This almost eliminates the outdoor air moisture load (there is some damper leakage), so

Miami Florida — 99.6% Dry-Bulb Day		
Space at 50% RH In use, OA damper open	Sensible Btuh	Latent Btuh
Window transmission	- 1,508	
Skylights transmission	- 2,828	
Wall transmission	- 10,987	
Roof transmission	- 4,464	
Infiltration	0	0
Evaporation (42.5 Lb/Hr)$_{rnd}$		44,621
Spectators		
Lights, etc	18,212	
Blower heat	5,472	
Supply duct	0	
OA$_{cfm}$ downstream (906)	- 37,582	- 28,101
Load totals	- 33,675	16,520
Preheat outdoor air to 33°F	0	
Input at reheat coil	0	
Net space heating load	- 33,675	16,520
15.7 Total moisture load (Lb/Hr)		

1) Outdoor air: Dry-bulb = 46°F; Grains = 42
2) Indoor air: Dry-bulb = 84°F; RH = 50%; Grains = 87

Figure 15-5

- 906 Cfm of outdoor air produces a heating load and a negative latent load.

- Outdoor air is warmer than 33°F, so preheat is not required.

  Note: Equipment manufacturers have their own methods for dealing with cold outdoor air. Use their guidance for outdoor air calculations.

- The total heating load for the space and outdoor air is 33,675 Btuh. The total latent load for the space and outdoor air is 16,520 Btuh.

- Heat input at the dehumidifier reheat coil requires compressor operation. If this feature is available, the default value for heating load calculations is zero.

  Note: Equipment manufacturers have their own methods for dealing with this issue. Use their guidance for reheat credit.

- The net space heating load could be a load on a heating coil in the equipment cabinet, in the supply duct, or a load on separate space heating equipment.

- The moisture load is about 15.7 Lb/Hr, so the compressor will operate to control humidity.

Heating for Space in Use Outdoor Air Cfm = 906	
Issue	Value
Water evaporation (Lb/Hr)$_{rnd}$	42.5
Lights and blower (Btuh)	23,684
Outdoor air load (Btuh)	- 37,582
Total heating load (Btuh)	- 33,675
Preheat outdoor air to 33°F (Btuh)	0
Reheat (Btuh)	
Net space heating load (btuh)	- 33,675
Total moisture (Lb/Hr)	15.7

Heating for Space Vacant Outdoor Air Cfm for Closed Damper = 103	
Issue	Value
Water evaporation (Lb/Hr)$_{rnd}$	30.0
Blower (Btuh)	5,472
Outdoor air load (Btuh)	- 4,280
Total heating load (Btuh)	- 18,585
Preheat outdoor air to 33°F (Btuh)	0
Reheat (Btuh)	
Net space heating load (Btuh)	- 18,585
Total moisture (Lb/Hr)	26.9

1) Space air at 84°F dry-bulb; 50% RH
2) Closed damper leakage = 5%

Figure 15-6

- When the compressor operates there is a sensible and latent load on the evaporator (air enters at about 84°F and 50% to 60% RH and leaves at about 50°F and 95% RH).

- If there are return duct loads and/or a return fan load, they affect the condition of the air entering the evaporator and the loads on the evaporator.

- The previous six bullets deal with issues that will be resolved by the dehumidifier manufacturer. The purpose of the discussion is to draw attention to these issues.

15-7 Other Heating Loads

Similar calculations were made for a vacant space. Figure 15-6 summarizes the loads for the winter design condition. Notice that the total moisture load varies from about 16 Lb/Hr when the space is in use to about 27 Lb/Hr when the space is vacant.

Load Summary				
Milwaukee, WI	**In Use**		**Vacant**	
	Lb/ Hr	Sen Btuh	Lb / Hr	Sen Btuh
1% Dew Point	42.3	63,730	24.8	48,721
1% Dry-Bulb	30.1	72,495	23.4	52,378
99.6% Heat	- 6.7	(109,952)	24.4	(51,119)

1) DP/DB = 72/80 °F; DB/WB = 86/72 °F; HDB= -7 °F; 723 Feet
2) Btuh heating values are for no outdoor air preheat.

Tucson, AZ	**In Use**		**Vacant**	
	Lb/ Hr	Sen Btuh	Lb / Hr	Sen Btuh
1% Dew Point	31.8	52,466	23.6	40,036
1% Dry-Bulb	- 4.0	89,411	19.5	56,006
99.6% Heat	5.2	(50,767)	25.7	(27,179)

1) DP/DB = 67/77 °F; DB/WB = 103/66 °F; HDB= 32 °F; 2,556 Feet
2) Btuh heating values are for no outdoor air preheat.

Boise, ID	**In Use**		**Vacant**	
	Lb / Hr	Sen Btuh	Lb / Hr	Sen Btuh
1% Dew Point	11.2	48,809	21.2	40,346
1% Dry-Bulb	- 3.4	80,215	19.6	54,062
99.6% Heat	- 5.1	(92,085)	24.6	45,830

1) DP/DB = 55/72 °F; DB/WB = 94/63 °F; HDB= -2 °F; 2,867 Feet
2) Btuh heating values are for no outdoor air preheat.

Miami, FL	**In Use**		**Vacant**	
	Lb / Hr	Sen Btuh	Lb / Hr	Sen Btuh
1% Dew Point	55.9	65,917	26.3	48,677
1% Dry-Bulb	43.7	77,208	24.9	53,343
99.6% Heat	15.7	(46,934)	26.9	(18,585)

1) DP/DB = 77/83 °F; DB/WB = 91/77 °F; HDB= 46 °F; 7 Feet
2) Btuh heating values are for no outdoor air preheat.

Figure 15-7

- The evaporation load is greater for space use (0.65 activity factor) than for a vacant space (0.50 activity factor).

- For space in use, the moisture load is less than the vacant space load because the negative outdoor air load is larger when the damper is open (906 Cfm vs. 101 Cfm).

15-8 Sensitivity to Climate

Climate has a large affect on the moisture load when the space is in use (outdoor air damper open). Figure 15-7 shows that the humid Miami climate produces the largest

Grains Difference for Space at 60% RH				
Month	**Tucson**	**Milwaukee**	**Boise**	**Miami**
1	49.7	56.7	65.6	-27.5
2	53.8	55.7	62.1	-27.6
3	61.5	30.5	61.2	-31.5
4	58.3	21.0	55.6	-31.0
5	46.8	-6.6	48.1	-43.8
6	18.1	-24.6	37.7	-51.3
7	-4.9	-41.1	29.9	-50.5
8	-7.6	-37.4	36.5	-52.9
9	-2.1	-23.5	38.6	-52.0
10	16.3	8.1	59.6	-42.0
11	47.4	23.8	55.3	-42.7
12	47.5	39.7	62.7	-34.9

1) Grains Difference = Indoor grains - Outdoor grains for the month
2) Indoor grains based on 80°F dry-bulb and 60% RH
3) Outdoor grains based on the 1% wet-bulb value and the mean coincident dry-bulb value for the month.

Figure 15-8

moisture load for summer. Milwaukee is second because it has a fair amount of summer humidity. Tucson is third because it has significant summer humidity during the rainy season. Boise has the smallest summer load because it is a dry climate. Boise and Milwaukee have negative winter loads because they have cold climates

Climate does not have much affect on the moisture load when the space is vacant (outdoor air damper closed with 5% leakage). Figure 15-7 shows that the moisture loads are roughly the same for all four cities. (The winter loads are larger than the summer loads because the space humidity is 50% RH for winter and 60% RH for summer.)

15-9 Equipment Selection

Figure 15-8 shows that the Boise climate is dry enough to use outdoor air for dehumidification year-round. It also shows that outdoor air is not an option for Miami for any month of the year. For Milwaukee, outdoor air could be used for the seven coldest months, but not for May through October. For Tucson outdoor air cannot be used for July, August and September.

A packaged dehumidifier minimizes system design work. In this regard, sizing decisions and system attributes are based on the experience of the dehumidifier manufacturer. This should provide appropriate performance when loads peak, and at part load. In addition, water evaporation heat is recovered and used to heat pool water and/or supply air.

Section 16

Design Example for a Competition Pool

This example evaluates the moisture loads, sensible cooling loads and sensible heating loads for a Milwaukee, Wisconsin natatorium. The facility has an Olympic size swimming pool and seating for 740 spectators.

16-1 Survey Data for Load Calculations

Figure 16-1 shows the plan view of the natatorium and the input values for items that are peculiar to this application. Inputs for the building envelope construction (roof, walls, floor, windows, skylights and doors) are not shown, but suitable values were used for load calculations (see Section 16-2).

- Pool water is 80°F and spa water is 102°F. For cooling calculations, space air is 82°F and 60% RH. For heating calculations, space air is 82°F and 50% RH. (Using 60% RH for summer reduces equipment size. Using 50% for winter anticipates that dry

outdoor air for ventilation will cause space humidity to be closer to 50%.)

- Table A5-4 and Table A5-5 are used to evaluate evaporation loads. Moisture release values depend on water temperature, and on the temperature and relative humidity of space air. The activity factor for the pool and the spa is 1.0.

- The summer (60% RH) evaporation rates for pool water and spa water are 0.0374 and 0.1422 Lb/Hr·SqFt. The winter (50% RH) evaporation rates (not shown by Figure 16-1) for pool water and spa water are 0.0486 and 0.1534 Lb/Hr·SqFt.

- It is assumed that the wet deck area extends six feet from the edge of the pool and three feet from the edge of the spa (the practitioner investigates and decides what is reasonable for a particular application).

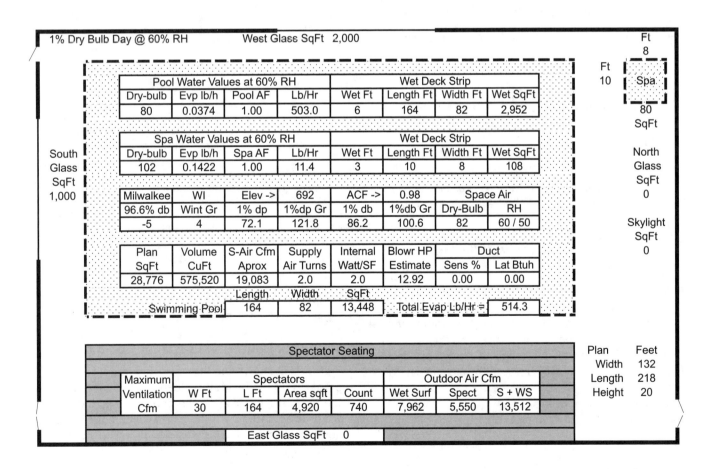

Figure 16-1

- Figure 16-1 shows the water surface areas and wet deck areas for the pool and spa.

- Figure 16-1 shows the length, width and height of the space, and the glass areas for each compass direction. There are no skylights.

- Figure 16-1 shows the dimensions of the spectator area and provides design value for spectator seating (740); it also shows that the internal load for lighting is 2.0 Watts per SqFt.

- Figure 16-1 shows the outdoor design conditions for Milwaukee, WI.

  Grains values are for 692 feet elevation
  Winter (99.6%) = -5°F; and 4 grains for 90% RH
  Summer 1% DP = 72°F dp; 80°F db; 122 grains
  Summer 1% DB = 86°F db; 72°F wb; 101 grains

- Figure 16-1 also shows some output values. These are discussed later.

16-2 Check the Thermal Performance of the Structure

The R-values for the opaque panels and the U-values for fenestration have to be suitable for the application. Use the R-value equation from Section 3-5 to produce a rough estimate for the minimum R-value for a dry interior surface.

$$R_t = K \times (T_i - T_o) / (T_i - T_s)$$

Outdoor dry-bulb = T_o = -5 °F
Indoor dry-bulb = T_i = 82 °F
Indoor relative humidity = 50% and 60%
indoor air dew point = 61.5 °F and 66.7 °F
Safety factor = 5 °F
Surface temperature T_s = 66.5 °F and 71.7 °F
K = 0.68 (vertical surface)
R_t = 3.82 @ 50%; 5.74 @ 60% (includes air films)
U-value = 0.26 @ 50%; 0.17 @ 60% (includes air films)
K = 0.95 (horizontal surface)
R_t = 5.33 @ 50%; 8.02 @ 60% (includes air films)
U-value = 0.19 a@ 50%; 0.12 @ 60% (includes air films)

Space humidity may vary from 50% RH to 60% RH, so 60% RH is a worst-case scenario. The preceding calculations show that the minimum R-value from outdoors to an indoor glass surface, or indoor surface of a vapor retarding membrane must be 5.74 or greater. This applies to any thermal bridge in a wall or ceiling and to any point on the fenestration assembly. This may not be a challenge for a wall or ceiling, but the corresponding U-value for windows (about 0.17) requires a high quality product (the U-value for a skylight is about 0.12).

This is crude way to see if the construction may be suitable for the application. The architect or building

Milwaukee, Wisconsin — 1% Dew Point Day Event with 740 Spectators		
Space at 60% RH In use, OA damper open	**Sensible Btuh**	**Latent Btuh**
Windows	128,673	
Skylights		
Wall transmission	4,,510	
Roof transmission	20,287	
Infiltration	0	0
Evaporation (514.3 Lb/Hr)$_{rnd}$		540,048
Spectators	181,300	140,600
Lights, etc	196,425	
Blower heat	46,512	
Supply duct	0	
OA$_{cfm}$ downstream (13,512)	- 24,763	187,295
Space load	552,495	867,943
Space load SHR	0.39	
Return fan	0	0
Return duct	0	0
Total load	552,495	867,943
Total load SHR	0.39	
826.6	Total moisture load (Lb/Hr)	
1,420,887	Total cooling load (Btuh)	
118.4	Load tons (243 SqFt/Ton)	
9.5	Default EER	
149.6	Estimated compressor KW	
1,931,359	Estimated Btuh in hot compressor gas	
540,048	Btuh for water evaporation	
1,391,312	Btuh for other use and/or rejection	

1) Outdoor air: Dry-bulb = 80°F; Wet-bulb = 72°F; Grains = 123
2) Indoor air: Dry-bulb = 82°F; RH = 60%; Grains = 101

Figure 16-2

designer is responsible for detailed condensation calculations (see Section 3-6).

16-3 Peak Dew Point Loads for Cooling

Figure 16-2 shows the load calculation for the 1% dew point condition. In addition there are ballpark values for the heat contained in hot compressor gas, the heat for water evaporation and the heat available for other use, and/or rejection. Comments pertaining to Figure 16-2 items are provided here:

- The weather data is for the hottest month of the year and the load calculation is made for late in the day when glass loads peak (notice the West glass and South glass on Figure 16-1). It is assumed that a spectator event may occur at this time (for an actual application the event schedule may affect the month and hour for the load calculation).

- The calculations for glass loads, wall loads and roof loads are equivalent to a comfort cooling calculation, but the outdoor and indoor design conditions are significantly different than what is used for a comfort calculation.

- It is assumed that non-operable fenestration, an infiltration barrier and a vapor retarding membrane prevent significant infiltration, so the infiltration loads are negligible.

- The latent load (Lb/Hr) for water evaporation is the sum of the loads for the pool and the spa. The evaporation load is the product of the values for the evaporation rate (Lb/Hr·SqFt), the activity factor and the water surface area (see Figure 16-1).

- The Lb/Hr load is multiplied by 1,050 Btuh/Lb to find the latent load in Btuh units.

- There are 740 spectators. Each spectator produces 245 sensible Btuh and 190 latent Btuh.

- A value of 2.0 watts per SqFt of floor area was used for the internal load. The practitioner must determine the appropriate internal load value for a particular application.

- Sensible heat from the supply air blower is based on a tentative horsepower value. This would be adjusted when load calculations are finalized during the equipment selection process.

- The sensible gain for the supply duct is a space load. For this example, it is assumed that the supply duct load is negligible because of some combination of location, insulation, surface area and tightness. In practice, the supply duct load is evaluated and added to the other sensible loads.

- For a dehumidifier, outdoor air enters downstream from the cooling coil so it is a space load. Outdoor air Cfm equals the Cfm for wet surfaces. Use 0.48 Cfm per SqFt of wet surface (water area and wet deck area). Figure 16-1 shows 7,962 outdoor air Cfm for wet surfaces.

- Figure 16-2 shows a negative sensible load and a positive latent load for outdoor air (space air is a little warmer and significantly dryer than outdoor air at the 1% dew point condition).

- The total space load is 552,495 sensible Btuh and 876,943 latent Btuh, and the corresponding sensible heat ratio is 0.39.

- There is an exhaust fan, so there is no sensible load for a return fan.

- The sensible and latent gain for a return duct is an equipment load. For this example, it is assumed that return duct loads are negligible because of some combination of location, insulation, surface area and tightness. In practice, return duct loads are evaluated and added to the other sensible and latent loads.

- Total loads equal the space loads because there are no equipment loads for this example. The loads for this scenario are:

  Moisture = 826.6 Lb/Hr

  Sensible load Btuh = 552,495

  Latent load Btuh = 876,943

  Total load Btuh = 1,420,887

- The total load is about 118 tons, which works out to about 243 SqFt per load ton.

- For estimating the amount of hot gas heat, the default value for EER is 9.5.

- The total load and the EER value provide a ballpark value for compressor heat (150 KW).

  KW = Total Btuh / (1,000 x EER)

- 150 KW produces 1,931,359 Btuh of hot gas heat. The actual amount of hot gas heat is determined when the equipment is selected.

- The heat load for pool water evaporation is about 540,048 Btuh, so excess hot gas heat can be used for makeup water and/or supply air.

- If there is no use for some portion of the excess heat, it is rejected to an air cooled or water cooled condenser.

16-4 Peak Dry-Bulb Loads for Cooling

Figure 16-3 (next page) shows the dehumidifier loads for the 1% dry-bulb condition. Compared to the 1% dew point condition, outdoor dry-bulb increases and outdoor moisture decreases, so the sensible cooling loads that depend on outdoor temperature increase and the latent cooling loads that depend on outdoor moisture decrease.

- The total moisture load drops from 826.6 Lb/Hr to 644.8 Lb/Hr.

- The sensible cooling load increases from 525,945 Btuh to 658,289 Btuh.

- The latent cooling load drops from 867,943 Btuh to 677,046 Btuh.

- Cooling load tons is somewhat less 118.4 to 111.3.

- Assuming that air leaves the cooling coil at 50°F, 658,289 Btuh of sensible load translates to about

Milwaukee, Wisconsin — 1% Dry-Bulb Day Event with 740 Spectators		
Space at 60% RH In use, OA damper open	**Sensible Btuh**	**Latent Btuh**
Windows	133,098	
Skylights		
Wall transmission	11,000	
Roof transmission	28,776	
Infiltration	0	0
Evaporation (514.3 Lb/Hr)$_{rnd}$		540,048
Spectators	181,300	140,600
Lights, etc	196,425	
Blower heat	46,512	
Supply duct	0	
OA$_{cfm}$ downstream (13,512)	61,178	-3,602
Space load	658,289	67,7046
Space SHR	0.49	
Return fan	0	0
Return duct	0	0
Total load	61,178	67,7046
Total SHR	0.49	
644.8	Total moisture load (Lb/Hr)	
1,335,335	Total cooling load (Btuh)	
111.3	Load tons (259 SqFt/Ton)	
19,083	Estimated supply air Cfm	
1.99	Estimated air turns for no bypass air	
9.5	Default EER	
140.6	Estimated compressor KW	
1,815,072	Estimated Btuh in hot compressor gas	
540,048	Btuh for water evaporation	
1,275,024	Btuh for other use and/or rejection	

1) Outdoor air: Dry-bulb = 86 °F; Wet-bulb = 72°F; Grains = 102
2) Indoor air: Dry-bulb = 82°F; RH = 60%; Grains = 101

Figure 16-3

19,083 Cfm for the supply fan. This is a temporary value. The actual supply air Cfm is determined when equipment is selected.

- 19,083 Cfm provides 1.99 space air turns. This is somewhat less than desired. Bypass air will be required to obtain 4.0 or more air turns. This is an equipment selection issue.

Cooling for Space in Use with Spectators Outdoor Air Cfm = 13,512		
Issue	**1% Dew Point**	**1% Dry-Bulb**
Water evap (Lb/Hr)$_{rnd}$	514.3	514.3
Total load (Btuh)	1,420,887	1,335,335
Sensible load (Btuh)	552,945	658,289
Latent load (Btuh)	876,943	667,046
SHR	0.39	0.49
Total moisture (Lb/Hr)	826.6	644.8

Cooling for Space in Use with No Spectators Outdoor Air Cfm = 7,962		
Issue	**1% Dew Point**	**1% Dry-Bulb**
Water evap (Lb/Hr)$_{rnd}$	514.3	514.3
Total load (Btuh)	1,032,229	989,786
Sensible load (Btuh)	379,161	446,711
Latent load (Btuh)	650,413	537,925
SHR	0.37	0.46
Total moisture (Lb/Hr)	619.4	512.3

Cooling for Space Vacant (activity factor = 0.50) Outdoor Air Cfm for Closed Damper = 954		
Issue	**1% Dew Point**	**1% Dry-Bulb**
Water evap (Lb/Hr)$_{rnd}$	257.2	257.2
Total load (Btuh)	481,483	493,476
Sensible load (Btuh)	198,234	233,706
Latent load (Btuh)	281,737	268,197
SHR	0.41	0.45
Total moisture (Lb/Hr)	269.8	256.9

1) Space air at 82°F dry-bulb; 60% RH
2) Closed damper leakage = 5%

Figure 16-4

- The water evaporation load is 540,024 Btuh and compressor gas has 1,815,072 Btuh, so there is more than enough hot gas heat.

16-5 Other Cooling Loads

Similar calculations are made for space in use with no spectators and space vacant. Figure 16-4 summarizes the loads for the summer design conditions. Notice that the total moisture load varies from about 257 Lb/Hr to 827 Lb/Hr, and that this difference is even larger when outdoor air grains are less than the 1% dry-bulb value. Peak loads, load variations, outdoor air Cfm and space air turns are equipment selection issues (see Section 16-9).

Milwaukee, Wisconsin — 99.6% Dry-Bulb Day Event with 740 Spectators		
Space at 50% RH In use, OA damper open	**Sensible Btuh**	**Latent Btuh**
Window transmission	- 65,250	
Skylights transmission	0	
Wall transmission	- 121,800	
Roof transmission	-125,176	
Infiltration	0	0
Evaporation (665.8 Lb/Hr)		699,137
Spectators	181,300	140,600
Lights, etc	196,425	
Blower heat	46,512	
Supply duct	0	
OA$_{cfm}$ downstream (392)	- 1,267,259	- 718,564
Load totals	- 1,155,248	121,173
Preheat outdoor air to 33°F	553,515	
Input at reheat coil	0	
Net space heating load	- 601,732	121,173
115.4 Total moisture load (Lb/Hr)		

1) Outdoor air: Dry-bulb = -5°F; Grains = 4
2) Indoor air: Dry-bulb = 82°F; RH = 50%; Grains = 83.8

Figure 16-5

16-6 Heating Loads

Figure 16-5 (next page) shows the dehumidifier loads for the 99.6% dry-bulb condition. In addition, there is an assumed value for outdoor air preheat. Comments on Figure 16-5 items are provided here:

- The weather data is for the coldest month of year and there is no credit for solar gain.

- Glass, wall and roof loads are U x ΔT loads.

- Infiltration loads are negligible (as previously explained for cooling).

- The evaporation load and the corresponding latent load for the pool and spa are for 50% RH. Notice that this produces more evaporation than the summer condition.

  Summer at 60% RH = 514 Lb/Hr
  Winter at 50% RH = 666 Lb/Hr

- Spectators, lights and the supply air blower add sensible and latent loads (same as summer).

- Supply duct load is zero (as previously explained for cooling)

- 13,512 Cfm of outdoor air produces a large heating load and a large negative latent load.

- Outdoor air is preheated to 33°F to prevent icing. This reduces the load on other heating equipment.

  Note: Equipment manufacturers have their own methods for dealing with cold outdoor air. Use their guidance for outdoor air calculations.

- With preheat, the total heating load for the space and outdoor air is 601,732 Btuh. The total latent load for the space and outdoor air is 121,173 Btuh.

- Heat input at the dehumidifier reheat coil requires compressor operation. If this feature is available, the default value for the heating load calculation is zero.

  Note: Equipment manufacturers have their own methods for dealing with this issue. Use their guidance for reheat credit.

- The net space heating load could be a load on a heating coil in the equipment cabinet, in the supply duct, or a load on separate space heating equipment.

- The moisture load is about 115 Lb/Hr, so the compressor will operate to control humidity.

- When the compressor operates there is a sensible and latent load on the evaporator (air enters at about 82°F and 50% to 60% RH and leaves at about 50°F and 95% RH).

- If there are return duct loads and/or a return fan load, they affect the condition of the air entering the evaporator and the loads on the evaporator.

- The previous six bullets deal with issues that will be resolved by the dehumidifier manufacturer. The purpose of the discussion is to draw attention to these issues.

16-7 Other Heating Loads

Similar calculations are made for space in use with no spectators and space vacant. Figure 16-6 (next page) summarizes the loads for the winter design condition. Notice that the total moisture load varies from about 115 Lb/Hr during an event to about 285 Lb/Hr when the space is vacant.

- The evaporation load is greater for in space use (1.00 activity factor) than for a vacant space (0.50 activity factor).

- For space in use, the moisture load is less than the vacant space load because the negative outdoor air load is larger when the damper is open (13,512 Cfm or 7,962 Cfm vs. 954 Cfm).

Heating for Space in Use with Spectators
Outdoor Air Cfm = 13,512

Issue	Value
Water evaporation (Lb/Hr)	665.8
Spectators, lights and blower (Btuh)	424,237
Outdoor air load (Btuh)	-1,267,259
Total heating load (Btuh)	-1,155,248
Preheat outdoor air to 33°F (Btuh)	553,515
Reheat (Btuh)	
Net space heating load (btuh)	- 601,732
Total moisture (Lb/Hr)	115.4

Heating for Space in Use with No Spectators
Outdoor Air Cfm = 7,254

Issue	Value
Water evaporation (Lb/Hr)	665.8
Lights and blower (Btuh)	242,937
Outdoor air load (Btuh)	- 746,747
Total heating load (Btuh)	- 816,035
Preheat outdoor air to 33°F (Btuh)	326,165
Reheat (Btuh)	
Net space heating load (Btuh)	- 489,870
Total moisture (Lb/Hr)	262.6

Heating for Space Vacant
Outdoor Air Cfm for Closed Damper = 945

Issue	Value
Water evaporation (Lb/Hr)	332.9
Blower (Btuh)	46,512
Outdoor air load (Btuh)	- 89,486
Total heating load (Btuh)	- 335,200
Preheat outdoor air to 33°F (Btuh)	39,086
Reheat (Btuh)	
Net space heating load (Btuh)	- 316,114
Total moisture (Lb/Hr)	284.6

1) Space air at 82°F dry-bulb; 50% RH
2) Closed damper leakage = 5%

Figure 16-6

Load Summary

Milwaukee, WI	In Use [2]		Vacant	
	Lb/ Hr	Sen Btuh	Lb / Hr	Sen Btuh
1% Dew Point	827 / 619	522,945 / 381,815	270	198,234
1% Dry-Bulb	645 / 512	658,289 / 451,861	257	223,706
99.6% Heat	115 / 263	(1,155,248) / (816,035)	285	(355,200)

DP/DB = 72/80 °F; DB/WB = 86/72 °F; HDB= -7 °F; 723 Feet

Tucson, AZ	In Use [2]		Vacant	
	Lb/ Hr	Sen Btuh	Lb / Hr	Sen Btuh
1% Dew Point	669 / 136	453,464 / 301,053	259	141,107
1% Dry-Bulb	527 / 213	892,324 / 594,913	221	251,873
99.6% Heat	292 / 367	(431,491) / (335,013)	297	(180,683)

DP/DB = 67/77 °F; DB/WB = 103/66 °F; HDB= 32 °F; 2,556 Feet

Boise, ID	In Use [2]		Vacant	
	Lb / Hr	Sen Btuh	Lb / Hr	Sen Btuh
1% Dew Point	362 / 345	391,462 / 266,670	237	141,598
1% Dry-Bulb	144 / 217	763,101 / 516,056	222	236,614
99.6% Heat	139 / 276	(921,146) / (667,770)	286	(315,321)

DP/DB = 55/72 °F; DB/WB = 94/63 °F; HDB= -2 °F; 2,867 Feet

Miami, FL	In Use [2]		Vacant	
	Lb / Hr	Sen Btuh	Lb / Hr	Sen Btuh
1% Dew Point	1,028 / 738	588,972 / 402,178	284	198,815
1% Dry-Bulb	846 / 630	725,114 / 492,532	271	231,352
99.6% Heat	450 / 460	(234,509) / (197,860)	308	(119,078)

DP/DB = 77/83 °F; DB/WB = 91/77 °F; HDB= 46 °F; 7 Feet

1) Btuh heating values are for no outdoor air preheat.
2) Upper value = Event; Lower value = No spectators

Figure 16-7

16-8 Sensitivity to Climate

Climate has a large affect on the moisture load when the space is in use (outdoor air damper open). Figure 16-7 (next page) shows that the humid Miami climate produces the largest moisture loads for summer. Milwaukee is second because it has a fair amount of summer humidity. Tucson is third because it has significant summer humidity during the rainy season. Boise has the smallest summer loads because it is a dry climate. Also notice that outdoor air for spectators tends to cause a large swing in the moisture load during summer (Bosie is the exception).

Climate does not have much affect on the moisture load when the space is vacant (outdoor air damper closed with 5% leakage). Figure 16-7 shows that the moisture loads are roughly the same for all four cities. (The winter loads are larger than the summer loads because the space humidity is 50% RH for winter and 60% RH for summer.)

16-9 Equipment Selection

Figure 16-8 shows that the Boise climate is dry enough to use outdoor air for dehumidification year-round. It also shows that outdoor air is not an option for Miami for any month of the year. For Milwaukee, outdoor air could be used for the seven coldest months, but not for May through October. For Tucson outdoor air cannot be used for July, August and September.

A packaged dehumidifier minimizes system design work. In this regard, sizing decisions and system attributes are based on the experience of the dehumidifier manufacturer. This should provide appropriate performance when loads peak, and at part load. In addition, water evaporation heat is recovered and used to heat pool water and/or supply air.

The outdoor air Cfm for spectators is a system concept issue. Two or more dehumidifier units make it easier for equipment to track load changes. One unit may be a DOAS unit that only operates during and event. Such decisions are based on the experience of the dehumidifier manufacturer.

	Grains Difference for Space at 60% RH			
Month	**Tucson**	**Milwaukee**	**Boise**	**Miami**
1	49.7	56.7	65.6	-27.5
2	53.8	55.7	62.1	-27.6
3	61.5	30.5	61.2	-31.5
4	58.3	21.0	55.6	-31.0
5	46.8	-6.6	48.1	-43.8
6	18.1	-24.6	37.7	-51.3
7	-4.9	-41.1	29.9	-50.5
8	-7.6	-37.4	36.5	-52.9
9	-2.1	-23.5	38.6	-52.0
10	16.3	8.1	59.6	-42.0
11	47.4	23.8	55.3	-42.7
12	47.5	39.7	62.7	-34.9

1) Grains Difference = Indoor grains - Outdoor grains for the month
2) Indoor grains based on 80°F dry-bulb and 60% RH
3) Outdoor grains based on the 1% wet-bulb value and the mean coincident dry-bulb value for the month.

Figure 16-8

Part 3

Related Guidance and Procedures

Good Practice

Swimming pool and spa projects have more than the normal amount of risk as far as undesirable consequences are concerned. The intent of this appendix is to provide guidance for architects and builders, and to inform mechanical designers-installers about individual and joint responsibilities.

- System designers and installers shall scrutinize the architectural plans and specifications.

- If potential condensation, moisture control and air quality problems are identified, they should be brought to the attention of the architect or builder, and all issues must be resolved to the satisfaction of all parties (including the client) before proceeding with the mechanical design.

- System designers and installers should not commit to a project if the structure is not suited to the application, in concept or in detail.

A1-1 Humid Zone

The entire space subject to moisture evaporating from wet surfaces is a humid zone. Zone boundaries should be limited to the space that contains the moisture generating surfaces (i.e., a swimming pool or spa). However, desires to create a water scene environment, or to make an esthetic statement, may cause the boundary of a humid zone to include spaces that have nothing in common with the space that has the wet surfaces. For example, a bar, eating space or guest room that is not isolated from the swimming pool space.

The first step for defining the architectural and mechanical requirements for a building that has a swimming pool, fountain, reflection pool or spa is to identify the boundaries of the humid zone. In this regard, the mechanical system designer must insist that the humid zone be limited to the space that contains the wet surfaces, even if the owner or architect has other ideas.

- The mechanical system designer must convince the architect and owner that it is not possible to maintain comfort conditioning spaces and wet surface spaces at different conditions when all spaces are in the humid zone. For example, keep the wet space at 82°F and 60% RH and simultaneously maintain another non-isolated space at 75°F and 50% RH.

- All parties must agree that this is true and all parties shall jointly identify and acknowledge the limited boundaries of the humid zone.

Indoor Air Conditions			
Application	Dry-Bulb Temp °F	Relative Humidity	Dew Point Temp °F
Residential Pool	78 to 86	50% to 60%	57.8 to 70.5
Hotel or Motel Pool			
Public, Institutional or Recreation Pool			
Competition Swimming Pool			
Diving Pool	82 to 86		61.5 to 70.5
Water Fitness Class	84 to 86		63.3 to 70.5
Elderly Swimmers	86		61.2 to 70.5
Therapeutic Pool			
spa or Whirlpool			

1) Preferred air temperature 2 °F to 4 °F warmer than the design value for water temperature.
2) Maximum air temperature = 86° F.
3) Maximum relative humidity = 60% (prevent mold and mildew).
5) Dew point temperature does not change with altitude.

Abridged Copy of Table A5-2

- Once the boundaries of the humid zone are identified, the architect or building designer must assure that the construction details of these boundaries are compatible with the moisture in the humid zone (Sections A1-2 and A1-3).

- The mechanical system designer is responsible for controlling temperature and humidity in the humid zone space (Sections A1-2. A1-4 and A1-6).

A1-2 Approved Contract Set Points

Contract set points for indoor temperature and relative humidity for the humid zone are jointly determined by the owner, architect or builder, and the mechanical system designer. These set points may only apply to the heating season (no summer cooling) or to all twelve months (year- round conditioning). Contract set points shall be determined before proceeding with the architectural design.

- Table A5-2 summarizes the possibilities for the space that encloses a swimming pool or spa and Section 2 provides comprehensive guidance.

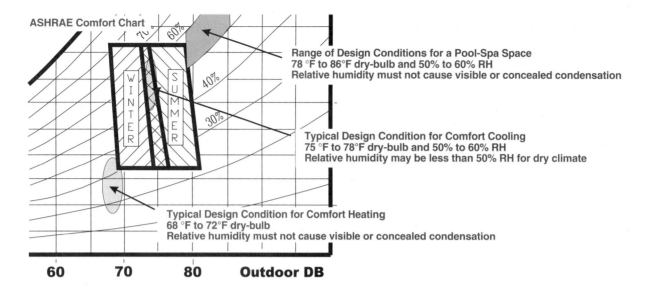

Figure A1-1

- Indoor conditions for common comfort conditioning have nothing in common with indoor conditions for a humid space (Figure A1-1, next page).

- A legal document that summarizes contract set points (with appropriate bands and tolerances) for all humid zone spaces shall be signed by all parties, notarized, and distributed to all parties.

A1-3 Architectural Mission

Condensation and wetting issues, and related construction requirements tend to conflict with desire for esthetic architecture and space ambiance. Moisture issues will increase budgets for building cost, equipment installation cost, equipment operating cost and maintenance cost.

The laws of physics are merciless, so the probability of serious building damage, air quality problems, mold, mildew, litigation, and so forth, is very high if the structure is not designed and built for the intended use. This means that all aspects of the architectural plans and specifications must be compatible with the demands of the application.

- There must be no condensation on exposed building surfaces when the air in the humid zone is maintained at approved contract set points and the outdoor air condition is at a design condition, or a less severe condition.

- There must be no condensation on partition surfaces when the air in the humid zone is maintained at approved contract set points and the air in adjacent rooms or zones is maintained at a design condition for common comfort heating and cooling.

- Building surfaces and partition surfaces include all visible and concealed surfaces for opaque panels and fenestration assemblies (windows, skylights, glass doors and opaque doors).

A1-4 Architectural Check List

Infiltration must be blocked and moisture migration must be controlled. Surfaces and building materials that will be exposed to humid indoor air must be compatible with the specified indoor humidity levels, and with relevant airborne gases and chemical molecules.

Humid Zone

Define the boundaries of the humid zone.

- The indoor air condition for a humid space is not compatible with the indoor air condition for an ordinary comfort conditioning space.

- If people in adjacent spaces are to view the pool area, use sealed glass panels to separate the humid zone from adjacent conditioned spaces.

- Identify humid zone boundaries that will be subjected to a significant moisture difference.

  a roof, ceiling, wall, or floor that separates indoor air from outdoor air (plus relevant fenestration)

  a vertical or horizontal partition that separates humid indoor air from drier indoor air (plus relevant fenestration)

Air Tightness Requirements

The humid zone must be exceptionally tight. Windows, skylights and doors must be extremely tight. All frame gaps must be tightly sealed.

- Use an exterior finish that blocks air leakage, or install a continuous air barrier.

- The exterior finish or air barrier must be comprehensively sealed over its surfaces.

Vapor Membrane Requirements

Moisture must not migrate into or through the opaque boundaries of the humid zone. Provide a low-perm membrane near inside finish or provide a suitable interior finish.

- This manual defines low-perm as 0.10 Grains/Hr · SqFt per InHg, or less.

- An effective infiltration barrier keeps dry air from flowing through a wall or ceiling sandwich. Moisture that condenses inside a shielded cavity is likely to stay there, so the vapor membrane must do its job.

- Membranes that control moisture migration must be continuous. There must be no unsealed seams, cuts, cracks, penetrations, and so forth.

  All vertical and horizontal seams must be overlapped and taped. Seal seams at ceiling-wall interface and floor-wall interface.

  Electrical outlets should not be installed in walls, roofs, ceiling or floors that are exposed to outdoor air, or make sure the penetration is completely sealed.

- A ground slab has default requirements for ground preparation, bedding material, drainage and a vapor retarding membrane (normally installed to keep moisture on the ground side of the slab). Ground temperatures are usually moderate, but the possibility for condensation should be checked (especially when there is permafrost).

  Insulation beneath the slab may be required to prevent condensation on a slab surface (perform dew point and surface temperature calculations).

  Condensation may not be a problem if the slab covers radiant heating coils.

Fenestration Tightness

Windows and skylights must be very tight, closed doors must have minimum leakage.

- Air and moisture must not pass though cracks in widow and skylight assemblies; or through cracks between rough opening framing and the window or skylight frame.

- Door frames and sashes must be very tight.

- Doors must have tight seals and automatic closing devices.

- An air-lock vestibule is preferable for exterior doors and desirable for interior doors.

Opaque Panel Insulation

Opaque panel insulation levels (R-values) must be compatible with contract set points for indoor air and all outdoor air conditions.

- The R-value for any heat transmission path from outdoor air to a vapor membrane surface must be large enough to prevent condensation on the vapor retarding surface.

- The R-value for any heat transmission path from a cold unconditioned space to a vapor membrane surface must be large enough to prevent condensation on the interior of the retarding surface.

- The R-value for any heat transmission path from an ordinary comfort conditioned space to a vapor membrane surface must be large enough to prevent condensation on the interior of the retarding surface.

- The vapor membrane surface should be 5°F warmer than the dew point of the humid zone.

- Evaluate all possible transmission paths (i.e., investigate thermal bridging). For example, a steel beam that goes all the way through the wall above an exit door can be very cold in winter. More than one credible witness has seen an exit door with ice on it.

Suspended Ceilings

Suspended ceilings are not suitable for humid spaces. T-bar framing tends to rust and ceiling tiles tends to sag or drop out. Ceiling performance is significantly improved if moisture-resistant tiles are supported by framing that is not affected by moisture or chemical action, but this does not keep moisture out of the ceiling cavity.

- For a suspended ceiling, the humidity ratio in the ceiling cavity is at least equal to the humidity ratio in the pool or spa space, and may be significantly higher due to stagnant air.

- The cavity walls and cavity ceiling must have a continuous vapor membrane, with all seams and cracks thoroughly sealed.

- The R-value for any heat transmission path from outdoors or a cold unconditioned space to the vapor membrane surface in the ceiling cavity must be large enough to prevent condensation on the interior of the retarding surface. Evaluate all possible paths (i.e., investigate thermal bridging).

- If cold cavity surfaces have large R-values and the ceiling has a low R-value, cavity temperature will be relatively warm during cold weather. Condensation on the inside face of the suspended ceiling will not occur if the surface temperature is warmer than the dew point temperature of the cavity air.

- Preferred construction features a ceiling that is, or has, a vapor retarding membrane with an adequate insulation above the ceiling (no general or local condensation in the ceiling cavity, no general or local dripping from the ceiling).

Fenestration Performance

The R-values for any transmission path through a window, skylight and door assembly must be large enough to prevent condensation on the interior surface.

- Evaluate all possible paths (i.e., consider glass, sash, frame, etc.). Fire doors may have construction that produces a thermal bridge.

- If fenestration has thermal break framing, the indoor glass surface will be the coldest surface. For cold climates, triple pane, high performance glass may not prevent surface condensation without adequate supply air.

- If a closed drape or blind covers a window, glass temperature will be colder and condensation more likely. Supply air should be provided between the window and any drapes or blinds.

- Washing interior fenestration surfaces with a flow of supply air reduces condensation potential. However, this does not reduce the R-value requirement for a piece of fenestration that is exposed to a given set of design conditions.

Washing Fenestration with Air

Condensation calculations (see Section 3) should conclude that windows, exterior doors and skylights will be dry. Air washing provides a margin of safety for unusually cold weather, and compensates for minor errors in the design procedure, product manufacturing, and product installation.

- The architect may have to provide (or approve) space to duct supply air to the bottom or top of each window, and to discharge supply air up the window or down the window.

- The interior surfaces of the window should be flush with the interior wall surface so that all window surfaces are bathed with supply air (air will slide past recessed corners).

- Flow over glass surfaces should not be interrupted by mullions and muntins that are not flush.

Skylights Should be Avoided

Skylights tend to create condensation problems. Make sure everyone understands the issues.

- Cold rain and snow increase heat transfer.

- Thermal bridging and condensation is a problem.

- Dripping condensation is unsanitary and causes stains.

- Condensation calculations must show that the installed product performance is adequate.

- Air washing is highly recommended. This may require visible duct work that may not be aesthetically pleasing.

- Bathing a skylight with supply air is a challenging problem. (Supply air will slide past recessed corners, and airflow will be disrupted by mullions and muntins that are not flush.)

Space for Equipment and Chemicals

There must be dedicated space for mechanical dehumidification equipment, a separate dedicated space for pool water equipment, and a separate dedicated space for chemical storage.

- Space requirements for mechanical equipment are determined by the system designer.

- Space requirements for pool equipment are determined by the water-chemical system designer.

- Water treatment chemicals shall be stored in an appropriate space. Applicable code may provide explicit requirements, if not use these guidelines.

  Provide a separate space with exhaust fan, with no air coupling to a pool space, any type of equipment room, a locker room, or any other space.

  The envelope of the storage space shall be sealed, use a tight low-leakage door or outside door; space pressure must be negative with respect to adjacent spaces.

Altitude

For condensation calculations (minimum R-value requirement), the humidity ratio of indoor air and outdoor air shall be adjusted for altitude.

Materials and Finishes

All interior surfaces are subject to harsh conditions. Consider the potential for rust, corrosion, staining, mold, mildew, peeling, etc., and use suitable materials and finishes.

- There will be direct wetting around the pool deck or spa perimeter.

- A spa may be near a wall or partition, splashing can wet wall surfaces.

- All surfaces subject to direct wetting, splashing or dripping must be suitable for the duty.

- Airborne chemicals from water sanitation must be identified.

- All interior surface materials and finishes must be compatible with airborne chemicals.

Carpets and Fabrics

Avoid carpets and fabric, even if treated to resist biological attack.

- Materials that are continuously exposed to humid air do not dry out.
- There is no solar irradiation to sanitize fabric.
- Carpets and fabrics are a breading ground for mold, mildew, fungi, bacteria.
- Carpets collect dirt.

Duct Runs Below the Floor

Duct runs under a floor tend to collect dirt, debris and moisture, but this may be the only way to get supply air to the bottom of the windows.

- Provide grading that allows duct runs to drain to a low point.
- Floors that slope away from supply air openings reduce or eliminate moisture in below floor duct.
- Provide access for cleaning duct runs.
- Do not install return openings in the floor.

A1-5 Water Treatment

The mechanical system designer must verify that the project has appropriate water treatment equipment and programs before participating in the project.

- Pool designers, water treatment equipment vendors and facility maintenance people are responsible for water treatment.
- Ventilation Cfm requirements for indoor air quality are for proper water treatment on a day-to-day basis.
- Water shocking (adding a lot of chlorine) is normally required to neutralize chloramine build up.
- Purge airborne contaminants with outdoor air after water shocking.

A1-6 Mechanical System Mission

The mechanical system must control the dew point of the humid space air. The mechanical system must provide appropriate engineered ventilation (outdoor air Cfm) for relevant operating conditions. The mechanical system must provide appropriate ventilation effectiveness and air movement for occupied space. The mechanical system must maintain the appropriate amount of positive or negative pressure in relevant conditioned spaces and unconditioned spaces. The mechanical system should wash exposed glass with air and should induce air movement across the pool water surface.

- Maintain space humidity and temperature set points for every hour of the year (subject to differentials that apply to control systems).
- Provide ASHRAE Standard 62.1 ventilation rates for all occupied operating conditions (winter, summer, day, night, fully occupied, partially occupied, unoccupied, etc.).
- Maintain negative space pressure for all possible operating conditions. (Provide appropriate exhaust fan or return air fan, dampers and controls.)
- Provide continuous (24 hours, every day of year) air circulation in the pool or spa space. (The amount of supply air Cfm may vary, depending on space use and spectator count).
- During occupancy, space air circulation must be equivalent to 4 to 8 air changes per hour (space air turns).

A1-7 Preconditions for Mechanical Design Work

Verify that the concepts and details of architectural plans and specifications, or existing conditions, are compatible with the boundaries of the humid zone, the contract set points, and local weather patterns.

- Be familiar with Section 1 and Sections A1-1 through A1-5 of this manual.
- Get a set of architectural plans and specifications.
- Obtain a written, signed document that specifies the boundaries of the humid zone.
- Obtain a written, signed document that specifies the contract set points for all spaces in the humid zone.
- Obtain a copy of the architect's or owner's condensation calculations.
- Obtain a written statement, signed and stamped by the architect, or project authority signature, that states the building construction details are compatible with the intended use and the contract set points.
- The mechanical designer-installer must be indemnified for visible or concealed condensation on structural surfaces, providing all humid-zone spaces are maintained at contract set points.
- Verify that adequate space is reserved for mechanical equipment and distribution systems. Determine locations for relevant air intake and air exhaust openings.

A1-8 Survey for Mechanical Design Work

Relevant information must be collected for mechanical system design work.

- Obtain local weather data (dry-bulb and wet-bulb temperature, humidity ratio, etc.). for each winter month for heating only systems, or for all twelve months for heating-cooling systems.

- Architectural plans and specifications provide dimensional information and thermal performance information for the surfaces and components of the building envelope.

- The boundaries of humid zone are provided by a contract document.

- Set points for humid zone temperature, humidity and/or dew point are provided by a contract document.

- The contract document must specify the seasonal requirement for space dehumidification (maintain space set points year-round, or let space conditions drift during warm weather).

- Determine design values for temperature and moisture in all unconditioned spaces that share a boundary with the humid zone.

- Obtain pool and/or spa dimensions, calculate water surface areas and estimate wet deck areas.

- Determine the maximum value for spectator seating.

- Determine how water use and spectator count vary with the week of year, day of week and hour of day (produce operating and attendance schedules).

- Ask about the chemicals for pool water treatment, and gasses or chemical molecules that will be released to indoor air.

- Determine if there is a purge cycle requirement. If there is a purge cycle, ask about frequency and duration

- Determine if there is a bar, an eating space, or a food preparation space in the humid zone, or in a space that shares a boundary with the humid zone.

- Determine pressure requirements for humid zone spaces, and for spaces that share boundaries with the humid zone.

A1-9 Check List for Mechanical Design Work

This check list includes all issues and tasks that apply to swimming pool and spa applications. Some items may not apply to a particular solution. Practitioners should study this list and find the items that are relevant to the project at hand.

1) Indoor Conditions

Figure A1-1 shows that the indoor design condition for a pool-spa space is warmer and more humid than a normal comfort conditioning space during warm weather, and that it is way out of range for cold weather. This makes dehumidification systems fundamentally different than comfort systems.

2) Outdoor Conditions

The local climate can make space dew point control easier or more difficult. The moisture in the outdoor air affects the latent ventilation load on the equipment and determines when outdoor air can be used to control the moisture in space air. The temperature of the outdoor air affects the sensible load on the equipment, but the more important issue is how it affects the dew point calculations for structural surfaces (the possibility of surface condensation increases as it get colder outdoors).

- During cold weather, outdoor air is dryer than indoor air, regardless of climate (outdoor air produces a negative latent load).

- During warm weather, outdoor air may be wetter or dryer than indoor air, depending on climate (outdoor air produces a positive or negative latent load).

- Dehumidification system features and economics are sensitive to climate.

3) Facility Use

The activity in the humid space affects the outdoor air requirement and equipment loads.

- Water activity has a significant effect on evaporation rate and the outdoor air Cfm requirement.

- Spectator count has a significant effect on the outdoor air Cfm requirement.

- Outdoor air damper may be closed when the space is vacant.

- The space is not in use during water shocking and the associated purge cycle.

4) Altitude

Altitude adjustments must be made for elevations above 2,500 feet.

- Psychrometric state points, mixed air calculations and other psychrometric processes, and load calculations are sensitive to altitude.

- Equipment performance is sensitive to altitude.

5) Water Evaporation Load

The water evaporation load depends on water temperature, water surface area, activity level, space temperature and space humidity.

- Calculate the water evaporation load for water surfaces and wet deck areas for the maximum activity level.

- Calculate the water evaporation load for water surfaces and wet deck areas for a normal activity level.

- For a vacant facility, calculate the water evaporation load for still water and no wet deck area.

- Evaporation load values are used in related load calculation scenarios.

6) Outdoor Air Cfm for Engineered Ventilation

Outdoor air ventilation rates for indoor air quality can range from significant to robust, depending on spectator count and wet surface area.

- Ventilation rates shall conform to the current version of ASHRAE Standard 62.1.

- Calculate ASHRAE 62.1 Cfm requirement for water surface area.

- Calculate ASHRAE 62.1 Cfm requirement for wet deck area.

- Calculate ASHRAE 62.1 Cfm requirement for spectators.

- Use outdoor air Cfm values in related load calculation scenarios.

7) Load Calculations

Load calculations are used to select and size equipment. Use a procedure that complies with ASHRAE/ACCA/ANSI Standard 183-2007.

- Note that engineered ventilation may be a system load or a space load. (If outdoor air enters the system down stream from an evaporator coil, it is equivalent to an infiltration load; i.e., space load).

- Use the procedures in this manual to calculate the water evaporation load (latent load to the space).

- For a humid climate, the maximum moisture removal load occurs with full occupancy.

  Outdoor air at the 1% dew point condition has more moisture than space air; space has maximum water activity; all spectator seats occupied; outdoor air Cfm per ASHRAE 62.1. Also calculate the coincident sensible cooling load.

- For a dry climate, the maximum moisture removal load occurs when there are no spectators.

  Outdoor air at the 1% dew point condition has less moisture than space air; space has maximum water activity; spectator seats empty; outdoor air Cfm per ASHRAE 62.1. Also calculate the coincident sensible cooling load.

- For all climates, calculate the maximum sensible cooling load for full occupancy.

  Outdoor air at the 1% dry-bulb condition; space has maximum water activity; all spectator seats occupied; outdoor air Cfm per ASHRAE 62.1. Also calculate the coincident moisture removal load.

- For all climates, calculate the sensible heating load for space use with full occupancy.

  Outdoor air at the 99.6% dry-bulb condition; all spectator seats occupied; outdoor air Cfm per ASHRAE 62.1; option to deduct internal loads.

- For all climates, calculate the sensible heating load for space use with no spectators.

  Outdoor air at the 99.6% dry-bulb condition; all spectator seats empty; outdoor air Cfm per ASHRAE 62.1; option to deduct internal loads.

- For all climates, calculate the sensible heating load for a vacant space.

- Outdoor air at the 99.6% dry-bulb condition; outdoor air Cfm for damper leakage; no deduction for internal loads.

- For all climates, calculate the minimum moisture removal load.

  Outdoor air at the 99.6% dry-bulb condition; all spectator seats occupied; outdoor air Cfm per ASHRAE 62.1.

- Additional load calculations may be required if equipment operates in a purge cycle after water shocking.

8) Equipment Selection

Equipment can range from a set of blowers and dampers to a complex combination of mechanical components that act on two or more fluids. Equipment may be in one self-contained package, multiple self-contained packages, or a piggy-back package. Supplemental and ancillary components may be external to an equipment package. Equipment shall have appropriate and adequate air filters.

- Year-round moisture removal is a mandatory requirement.

  Maximum moisture removal capacity must satisfy the maximum moisture load (Lb/Hr).

  If the moisture load has significant variations, equipment capacity should vary to track the load.

- Adequate sensible cooling must be provided, when required.

  Maintain space dry-bulb set point when there is a net sensible cooling load.

If the sensible cooling load has significant variations, sensible cooling capacity should be adjusted to track the load.

■ Adequate sensible heating must be provided, when required.

Maintain space dry-bulb set point when there is a net sensible heating load.

If the sensible heating load has significant variations, heating capacity should be adjusted to track the load.

■ Provide outdoor air Cfm for ASHRAE 62.1 ventilation.

Equipment shall process the outdoor air Cfm for the maximum ventilation rate (maximum Cfm value from ASHRAE 62.1 calculations).

All the outdoor air may be processed by dehumidification equipment.

All the outdoor air may be processed by a dedicated outdoor air system (DOAS).

Some outdoor air may be processed by dehumidification equipment, and some by DOAS equipment (typically for spectators).

If the outdoor air Cfm for indoor air quality has significant variations, Cfm must be adjusted to track the load (efficiency issue)

Outdoor air dampers can be closed when the facility is vacant (consider damper leakage).

Outdoor air dampers may be wide open during a purge cycle after water shocking.

■ Supply air Cfm for space air turns.

Provide four to eight space air turns.

If the supply air Cfm for space air turns is deficient, a dedicated air circulating system is acceptable.

9) Entering Conditions for Equipment Selection

By design, the face velocity for a dehumidification coil is substantially lower than the face velocity for comfort cooling coil. And, the face velocity for a reheat coil is much higher than the face velocity for a dehumidification coil. Dehumidifiers use bypass air to reconcile this difference.

■ If a cold dehumidification coil processes 100% return air, entering conditions are relatively constant year-round (something like 82°F dry-bulb; 50% to 60% RH).

■ For 100% return air and negligible return duct load, the condition of space air determines the condition of entering air.

■ Significant return-side duct leakage and heat transmission are unacceptable (seal super tight,

provide vapor membrane, install duct in a benign space, or use a lot of insulation).

■ If outdoor air is provided by dedicated equipment, discharge air must not short circuit to the return side of the dehumidification equipment.

■ Supply air from dehumidification equipment must not short circuit to the return side of the dehumidification equipment.

■ When a dehumidification coil processes 100% return air, heat should not be added to return air.

■ Some dehumidification systems use a comfort cooling coil.

An enthalpy wheel partially dehumidifies outdoor air before it is mixed with return air, then mixed air is further dehumidified by a comfort cooling coil.

Output air from desiccant dehumidification equipment can be input air for an comfort cooling coil.

Rely on manufacture's guidance pertaining to the condition of the air entering and leaving components and devices.

■ Desiccant equipment has multiple entering conditions as two air streams flow though components in both sides of the equipment. (Rely on manufacture's guidance pertaining to the condition of the air entering and leaving components and devices.)

■ A DOAS dehumidification coil processes 100% outdoor air.

Entering conditions vary with outdoor conditions.

The equipment is designed for this service, follow manufacturer's guidance.

10) Bypass air

Bypass air means that a fraction of the humid return air flows through a dehumidifying coil, and the remaining fraction flows around the coil. Bypass air provides two important benefits.

■ If a reheat coil is downstream from a dehumidification coil, the face velocity for the dehumidification coil can be low, and the reheat coil face velocity can be much higher.

■ Bypass air increases system airflow, which increases space air turns, which makes four or more air turns possible when dehumidification coil airflow produces less than four air turns.

■ ome dehumidification system arrangements do not provide bypass air, so four or more air turns may not be possible with supply air Cfm. (If space air turns are deficient, a dedicated air circulating system is acceptable.)

11) Outdoor Air Insertion Point

For dehumidification equipment, outdoor air enters the system after return air has been dehumidified.

- This stabilizes the environment for the evaporator coil (the entering air condition and coil sensible heat ratio are relatively constant all the time).

- This maximizes the heat reclaim opportunity provided by evaporating water (latent load on evaporator coil is not diminished by dry outside air).

12) Preheat for Downstream Outdoor Air

Mixing cold outdoor air with dehumidifier air (dehumidifier with downstream insertion) can cause saturated air (100% RH or supersaturated).

- Mixing bypass air at something like 82°F and 50% to 60% RH with cold outdoor air can cause condensation.

- Mixing air discharged from a dehumidifying coil at something like 40°F to 50°F and 95% RH with cold outdoor air can cause condensation.

- Condensation between the refrigerant coil and the reheat coil is not a problem if captured by a drip pan (no moisture on reheat coil).

- Ice can form on the refrigerant coil if the local air temperature is below freezing (preheat outdoor air to prevent freezing mixed air temperature).

- The need for preheat, or the amount of preheat depends on the dehumidification product.

- Preheat requirements are specified by the people that manufacturer a dehumidifier product.

13) Preheat for Upstream Outdoor Air

Mixing cold outdoor air with return air upstream from the equipment (normal comfort cooling configuration) can cause saturated air (100% RH or supersaturated).

- Mixing return air at something like 82°F and 50% to 60% RH with cold outdoor air can cause condensation.

- he system designer is responsible for unintended or undesirable consequence of condensation (do not use this arrangement if there is a possibility of a problem).

- The system designer could be an equipment package manufacturer, or a practitioner that builds a system from standard components.

14) Preheat for Air-to-Air Heat Exchangers

Air to air heat exchangers can freeze up during cold weather.

- Preheat can prevent frost and icing.

- Discuss preheat requirements with the people that manufacturer a heat recovery product.

15) Post Heat

Dehumidification systems need an auxiliary source of heat.

- Heat supplied by dehumidification equipment is not available if the equipment is not operating (cycles off on a humidity control, equipment failure, or pool drained, for example).

- Dehumidification equipment can heat supply air (if so configured), but this may not satisfy the net heating load during cold weather.

- Downstream heat may be in an dehumidifier package, or supply air duct, in a space, or provided by a separate air heating system.

16) Post Cooling

A dehumidification system may need help when the sensible load peaks.

- When warm-dry outdoor air is used for dehumidification, additional equipment is required for sensible cooling.

- Desiccant dehumidification wheels discharge warm air, so additional equipment is required for sensible cooling.

- Mechanical dehumidification equipment provides adequate sensible cooling for most applications.

- Supplemental cooling by ancillary system may be required if a facility has an unusually large glass load (this depends on the capabilities and attributes of the product).

- Auxiliary space cooling equipment must have its own duct system.

    If auxiliary cooling air and dehumidifier air share a duct system, back flow may occur when one equipment package stops.

    Supply air may get too cold, causing fog and dripping from supply air outlets.

17) Purge Cycle

For water shocking, supply air Cfm may be 100% outdoor air for several minutes to several hours. This is a special operating condition that may require additional load calculations and equipment capacity.

- The desired outdoor air Cfm for the purge cycle is usually larger than the Cfm for indoor air quality.

- Space temperature may fall below set point during a purge cycle. Space humidity will drift during the purge cycle.

- Visible or concealed condensation is possible if the condition of the space air gets out of range.

  Water evaporation rate and water chemical release depend on space temperature and space humidity.

  A dehumidifier is ineffective during a purge cycle (no return air Cfm, 100% outdoor air enters down stream from the refrigerant coil).

  Dry outdoor air reduces space humidity during a purge cycle. Humid outdoor air increases space humidity during a purge cycle.

  Maintaining space temperature requires sensible cooling and sensible heating for 100% outdoor air.

18) Winter Humidification

When a large amount of dry outdoor air provides engineered ventilation, the net latent load on the dehumidification system can be negative.

- If moisture removal equipment cycles on and off, space humidity stabilizes at some value less than 50% RH (this can be calculated).

- Space humidification is not normally used for pool and spa applications (this is a wet person comfort issue).

- Space humidification may be required if 50% RH or more is a mandatory requirement for health reasons (unusual).

19) Water Heat

Evaporation produces a heating load for pool water, and a significant amount of heat is required for make-up water (cold fill load).

- Provide dedicated water heating equipment that can satisfy the largest water heating load.

- Using reclaimed heat for pool water heat is appropriate and desirable.

- Dedicated water heating equipment provides supplemental heat, emergency heat and cold fill heat.

20) Heat Recovery

Heat recovery opportunities and concept viability depend on the type of system and the type of equipment. The practitioner must investigate relevant options and issues.

- Hot compressor gas can be used to heat supply air or pool water.

The heat of evaporation for pool water is relatively constant and available year-round.

Pool water is a relatively constant load for recovered heat, year-round.

Supply air needs heat or reheat most of the time.

Using an independent fuel source for reheat air may be prohibited by standards and codes. (See the latest versions of ASHRAE Standards 90.1 and 90.2 and local code.)

- Various types of equipment extract sensible heat, or sensible and latent heat from exhaust air.

21) Capacity Control

Capacity control may be required to hold excursion tolerances for contract set points, and/or to prevent undesirable operating conditions (shut-down by a safety control, or a mechanical problem).

- It is possible for the net moisture removal load to vary from maximum to zero, or this load can be negative (drying effect).

  The water evaporation load and the associated outdoor air Cfm value depends on activity level (still water with dry deck vs. maximum water churning, splashing and dripping).

  Outdoor air may be relatively humid or relative dry.

  Facilities that have events have significant changes in the latent gain from spectators and the latent outdoor air load for spectators (no spectators to a full house).

- The sensible load varies from the maximum heating load to the maximum cooling load.

  For mechanical dehumidification, reheat is required when the moisture removal load causes excess sensible cooling when the sensible cooling load is reduced.

  For mechanical dehumidification during cold weather, the reheat load is part of the net heating load.

- Dehumidifying coils may operate at temperatures as low as 40°F, so frosting and freezing are possible. Hot gas bypass and other methods can be used to prevent coil freezing, while maintaining moisture removal capacity.

- For mechanical dehumidifier, the heat in compressor discharge gas may flow to one or two reclaim coils, and/or to a heat rejection coil. This has to be properly managed.

  Hot-gas reheat coil heats supply air.

  Hot-gas to water heat exchanger heats pool water.

  Hot-gas heat rejected at an outdoor condenser coil, or water equivalent.

- For desiccant equipment, some of the heat in compressor discharge gas may be used to regenerate the media, and some may flow to a heat rejection coil. This has to be properly managed.

- Large variations in supply air temperature are possible when outdoor air mixes with dehumidified air downstream from an evaporator coil. This has to be properly managed.

- System components and controls may have to deal with large variations in outdoor air Cfm.

  Outdoor air for the water evaporation load depends on activity level (still water with dry deck vs. maximum water churning, splashing and dripping).

  Facilities that have spectator seating for events have significant changes in the ventilation.

  Outdoor air damper fully open during a purge cycle, or economizer cycle.

  Outdoor air damper can be closed when the facility is not in use.

- Provide adequate capacity control for heating equipment, dehumidification equipment, cooling equipment and outdoor air Cfm.

  Strategies depend on the application, the type of system and the type of equipment.

  Consider using a combination of DOAS equipment and dehumidification equipment if the facility accommodates a significant number of spectators.

  Discuss capacity control issues with equipment manufacturers.

  A practitioner that builds a system from standard components is responsible for the capacity control strategy.

22) Energy Use and Economics

The dehumidification load, heating load and sensible cooling load may be satisfied by more than one type of system, but suitable candidates usually have different efficiencies, different installed costs and different operating costs. In this regard, there are no definitive guidelines for estimating and comparing energy use and operating cost.

- There are too many conditional variables. Calculations must consider climate, building envelope attributes, space use, the attributes of the basic dehumidification method, the effect of standard and optional recovery devices, equipment cost, local installation cost, local utility cost, available and future funds, and so forth.

- Pool-spa economics are sensitive to exposed glass area and the design condition for space air (which depends on the design value for water temperature).

- In general, take advantage of energy recovery opportunities that can be applied to the method that is used to control space moisture.

- The final system concept is jointly determined by the owner, architect or builder, and the mechanical system designer (which may be the dehumidification equipment provider).

23) Supply Air

Do not blow supply air directly on pool water. Robust impingement increases evaporation and reduces swimmer comfort. Provide continuous air circulation.

Wash fenestration with dehumidified supply air. For exposed windows, air should flow straight up the window, or straight down the window (air must not strike the window at a large angle).

- The width of the supply air pattern must cover the width of the fenestration assembly.

- If two or more windows are vertically stacked and separated by a strip of wall, provide slot diffusers for each window level.

- Duct air to skylights and wash glass with air.

- Encourage moderate airflow across the water surface.

  Use vertical supply air discharge at outside walls.

  A return air grille on the wall opposite of outlets that wash windows with air encourages some air motion over pool water. (A return that is six to fifteen feet above the floor avoids exposure to dirt, moisture, towels, people and objects).

- Use a separate air distribution system for DOAS equipment.(Supply air may be 1°F to 2°F cooler than space air for spectator comfort.)

- The condition of the space air may drift out of the desired range when supply air is disrupted for a significant period of time (say twenty minutes or more). This may cause condensation.

- There must be a continuous flow of air though duct systems to prevent condensation in duct runs.

  The duct may be in a cold, unconditioned space.

  When there is no forced airflow through the duct, buoyancy forces may cause humid air to circulate through the duct.

  Duct air may go from 60% RH to 90% RH in about 20 minutes.

  Condensation will form on the inside of a duct wall if the wall surface temperature is below the dew point temperature of the air in the duct.

  Water may drip from duct seams, supply air outlets and return grilles.

24) Duct Systems

Duct airways may be sized by standard procedures (typically, the equal friction method). Materials, insulation, vapor retarders and construction methods must be compatible with a humid, chemical laden environment.

- Performance requirements apply to supply ducts, return ducts, outdoor air intake ducts and exhaust air ducts.

- Duct runs must be extremely tight.

  Seal supply and return ducts. Seal air intake ducts and exhaust ducts.

  Seal all seams, joints, connections and penetrations with mastic.

  Seal duct to boot fitting, seal the boot to the frame of the supply air diffuser-register-grille, or return air grille, or exhaust air grille. Then, seal frames to the vapor retarding membrane.

  Seal all equipment cabinet leaks, and verify tight seals at access panels.

- Condensation must not form on the outside or inside of duct walls, or cause wet duct insulation; likewise for equipment cabinets.

  Insulate cold air ducts that run through a humid or unconditioned space.

  The insulation R-value must be adequate to prevent condensation.

  Protect insulation with a vapor retarding jacket that is completely sealed (no opens seams, slits, cracks or penetrations).

- Duct materials may be exposed to humidity, moisture and chemicals.

  Painted (epoxy) galvanized steel or 316-series stainless steel has adequate corrosion resistance.

  400-series stainless steel is vulnerable to corrosion from airborne chlorides.

- Duct runs under a floor tend to collect dirt, debris and moisture.

  The floor should slope away from the diffuser, so that water is less likely to drain into the duct work.

  Duct runs should drain to a low point that has a gravity drain or pump.

  Provide access for cleaning duct runs.

  Use sealed plastic duct for duct runs beneath a ground slab.

  Verify compliance with ground preparation, fill and vapor membrane requirements for duct embedded in a ground slab.

- Fabric duct has its own set of issues, see Section 13-8.

25) Installation Issues

This list of issues is provided by dehumidifier manufacturers that have extensive experience with pool-spa applications. Always conform to comprehensive installation instructions and guidance provided by the equipment manufacturer.

- Water treatment chemicals shall be stored in a separate, sealed and ventilated space (architectural requirement).

- Chemical laden air shall not pass though an open flame.

  There shall be no open flame in the chemical storage room.

  Some space heaters and water heaters have an open flame. Where such devices have sealed combustion, the seals must be checked for leaks.

- Do not assume that dehumidification equipment, or any other type of equipment, can be installed in the pool or spa space.

  Equipment must be internally designed to process humid, chemical laden air.

  Equipment may not be externally designed for installation in a humid, chemical laden environment (this can add significant cost).

  The equipment manufacturer specifies acceptable locations and provides installation details.

- Define the space requirements for the equipment room.

  Provide adequate space for space conditioning equipment and water equipment.

  For space conditioning equipment, provide space for discharge and entry duct runs that do not produce a system effect.

  Provide room for servicing equipment components.

  Provide room for removing and replacing equipment and equipment components.

- Provide an approved equipment platform for overhead installation.

  The platform must provide enough space for scheduled maintenance, enough space for dealing with all equipment problems and enough space for removing and replacing components.

  Provide adequate space for discharge duct geometry and return duct geometry that does not degrade blower performance (no system effect).

  The minimum platform dimensions for installation and servicing are specified by the equipment manufacturer.

  Provide appropriate guard rails and safe access, etc.

- Provide adequate distance between a dehumidifying coil and a hot gas reheat coil.

For a purchased dehumidifier package, this distance is determined by the equipment manufacturer.

This minimizes rehumidification effects.

This captures mixed air condensation and dehumidifying coil condensation.

This may prevent sizzling sounds.

- There are reasons for installing a long drip pan behind a dehumidification coil.

This maximizes carry-over capture.

This is a safety feature for outdoor air mixing (should condensation occur).

- Prevent short circuiting.

Outdoor air intakes must not capture exhaust air, vent or flue discharge, or sewer stack discharge.

Outdoor air intakes must not capture cooling tower air or outdoor condenser air.

Outdoor air supplied to the space by DOAS equipment must not short circuit to the dehumidifier return air grille.

Supply air must not short circuit to a return air grille.

- Block entry of rain and snow.

Air intake openings and exhaust air openings shall have suitable protection (hoods, penthouses, goose-necks and caps).

Air intake openings and exhaust air openings shall have a mesh screen.

- Provide adequate vibration isolation and equipment pads.

  • *Use appropriate vibration devices for equipment and equipment cabinets.*

  • *Use flexible duct connections at equipment collars.*

- Investigate and satisfy piping requirements.

Provide ports for temperature and pressure gauges; provide an appropriate collection of shut-off and operating valves.

Do not exceed allowable limits for refrigerant line length or riser height; provide suitable traps and valves.

Condensate lines shall have appropriate drains and traps; and ambient pressure must not cause backflow.

Water piping is usually by others, but someone has to verify appropriate installation details and practices.

- All electrical, piping and duct penetrations must be properly sealed to the vapor retarding membrane with either tape or mastic.

- Fuel burning equipment shall have appropriate vents and stacks.

Observe code requirements and/or manufacturer's instructions.

Structural arrangements must allow direct routing for vents and stacks.

- Do not install a control element or ancillary device in a location that may cause condensation.

For example, destructive condensation may form in a smoke detector that is in a return air duct.

If a control or component is a potential point of condensation, the control shall be impervious to moisture or shall have its own source of heat.

Equipment manufacturers have seen many unfortunate scenarios, seek their guidance.

- Protect outdoor condensing units.

The condenser must be in an open space, or a space that is approved by the equipment manufacturer. (New air must continuously flow though the condenser.)

Provide adequate distance between the condenser and any nearby surfaces. (Condenser airflow must not be restricted.)

Do not install condensing equipment in a pit. Protect against damage by vehicles, vandals and falling ice.

Protect against leaves, branches, litter and debris.

Keep airways clear if necessary airflow goes under, over or though a fence.

A1-10 Consequences of Poor Practice

There probably is an unlimited supply of stories pertaining to pool and spa problems. Common examples of the consequences of poor practice are provided here:

- Window fogging; wet glass, sash or frame; sash or frame shows rot or corrosion.

- Visible condensation on indoor fenestration surfaces or opaque surfaces.

- Wet ceiling tiles, or soaked insulation; corroded T-bars and hangers.

- Sagging ceiling tile in pool area, or in related spaces.

- Wet tiles and/or ceiling insulation falls from the ceiling; entire ceiling collapses.

- Visible mold and mildew, on carpets, behind walls or above ceiling.

- Corroded fixtures, metal finishes, metal trim and wiring.

- Ice dams and/or water in building materials freezes and expands.

- Fractured masonry, chipping or splitting (exfoliates), and/or stains on exterior cladding.

- Structural fasteners show corrosion making structural framing vulnerable to failure under normal wind, rain and snow loads.

Equipment Capacity at Altitude

Expanded equipment performance data published by equipment manufacturers shall be used to select and size heating equipment, air conditioning equipment and heat pumps. However, published performance data applies to sea-level locations (may be used for locations 2,500 Feet or less). This appendix offers procedures for estimating equipment capacity at altitude.

A2-1 Why Altitude Matters

Altitude reduces air density, which affects the performance of indoor and outdoor fin-tube refrigerant coils, furnace heat exchangers, electric heating coils, gas burners, air-to-air heat exchangers, desiccant wheels, equipment blowers, air-side components and duct runs.

- Refrigerant coils, air-to-air heat exchangers, desiccant wheels and furnace heat exchangers are affected because surface to air heat transfer depends on air mass-flow (pounds or air per minute), which depends on volume flow (cubic feet of air per minute) and air density (pounds or air per cubic foot).

  Mass flow also depends on entering air temperature. This is ignored for most HVAC equipment, because entering air temperature falls into a narrow band of temperatures. Entering temperature is a consideration for air-to-air heat exchangers and desiccant wheels, because there can be large variations in entering air temperature.

- Heat-rejection refrigerant coils are affected because altitude affects condensing temperature and head pressure.

- The relationships between gauge pressures and condenser or evaporator temperatures depend on altitude (refrigerant-side performance is not affected if absolute pressures at altitude equal absolute pressures at sea level).

- Expansion valves, capillary tubes and orifices selected for air mass flow and refrigerant-side pressure drop at sea level may be too large for reduced air mass flow at altitude (metering pressure drop and refrigerant flow increase, with possible refrigerant slugging at part load).

- For constant volume airflow, the temperature rise across electric heating coils increases with altitude, because heat input is constant and mass flow decreases.

- Gas burner heating capacity is reduced because a fuel orifice sized for a sea level mass flow, oxygen content and orifice pressure drop is not compatible with air mass flow at altitude.

- If RPM is constant, blower Cfm is not affected by altitude, but mass flow and external pressure decrease with altitude, and input horsepower decreases with decreasing mass flow.

- The aerodynamic resistance of duct airways decreases with altitude because velocity pressure and duct friction depend on air density.

- For a given air volume flow (supply Cfm), supply grille, register and air diffuser performance is affected by altitude, because pressure drop and discharge momentum depend on air density.

Altitude also affects psychrometric calculations, heating and cooling load calculations, air balancing instruments and air balancing procedures.

- Use psychrometric software that adjusts for altitude (see Appendix A3).

- Altitude affects infiltration loads and engineered ventilation loads. ACCA *Manual N* Fifth Edition accounts for this effect.

- Use test and balance manuals, handbooks, standards, and adhere to engineering guidance published by testing equipment manufacturers.

A2-2 Psychrometric Calculations

Moisture is the primary design issue for swimming pool and spa applications. Relevant psychrometric calculations must be adjusted for altitude because moisture and humidity are so sensitive to altitude. The effects of increasing altitude are summarized here:

For a set of dry-bulb and wet-bulb values

- Grains of moisture increases
- Relative humidity increases
- Dew point increases
- Specific volume increases

For a set of dry-bulb and relative humidity values

- Wet-bulb decreases (slightly)
- Grains of moisture increases
- Dew point does not change
- Specific volume increases

A2-3 Air-Cooled Cooling Equipment

Figure A2-1 provides an example of expanded performance data for air cooling equipment that has a refrigerant coil (all components may be in the same cabinet, or it may be a split system). Such performance summaries are for sea level operation. Performance at altitude is obtained by applying Table A5-8 factors to sea level data.

For example, load calculations for Denver, CO show that the state point of return air for a swimming pool space is about 67°F wet-bulb and 80°F dry-bulb. Outdoor air will be introduced downstream from the evaporator coil, so it has no effect on the condition of the air entering the evaporator (dehumidifier configuration).

Figure A2-1 provides cooling performance values for 67°F entering wet-bulb, 80°F entering dry-bulb 7,000 Cfm, 95°F outdoor dry-bulb. (Denver's 1% db temperature is 90°F; but using 95°F avoids interpolation.)

> Total capacity (Btuh) = 281,000
> SHR = 0.72
> Sensible capacity (Btuh) = 0.72 x 281,000 = 202,320
> Latent capacity (Btuh) = 281,000 - 202,320 = 78,680.

Table A5-8 factors are used to adjust performance for Denver, CO (about 5,000 feet). Since 67°F wet-bulb and 80°F dry-bulb is a wet-coil condition, the equipment will have this performance for 7,000 Cfm:

> Total capacity (Btuh) = 0.96 x 281,000 = 269,760
> Sensible capacity (btuh) = 0.85 x 202,320 = 171,972
> Latent capacity (Btuh) = 269,760 - 171,972 = 97,788

Altitude Adjustment Factors				
Cooling Evaporator with Air-Cooled Condenser				
Altitude (Feet)	**Total Capacity**		**Sensible Capacity**	
	Wet Coil	**Dry Coil**	**Wet Coil**	**Dry Coil**
Sea Level	1.00	1.00	1.00	1.00
1,000	0.99	0.98	0.97	0.98
2,000	0.98	0.97	0.94	0.97
3,000	0.98	0.95	0.91	0.95
4,000	0.97	0.94	0.88	0.94
5,000	0.96	0.92	0.85	0.92
6,000	0.95	0.90	0.82	0.90
7,000	0.94	0.89	0.80	0.89
8,000	0.94	0.87	0.77	0.87
9,000	0.93	0.86	0.74	0.86
10,000	0.92	0.84	0.71	0.84
11,000	0.91	0.82	0.68	0.82
12,000	0.90	0.81	0.65	0.81

1) Interpolation and extrapolation of values published by the Carrier Corp (*Engineering Guide for Altitude Effects*, 1967).
2) Use wet coil values for sensible heat ratios (SHR) less than 0.95.

Copy of Table A5-8

Cfm	Ent Dry Bulb (°F)	Outdoor Temperature (°F)																
		85						95						105				
		Entering Wet-Bulb (°F)																
		61		67		73		61		67		73		61		67		73	
		Mbh	SHR	Mbh	SHR	Mbh	SHR	Mbh	SHR	Mbh	SHR	Mbh	SHR	Mbh	SHR	Mbh	SHR	Mbh	SHR
	75	246	77	276	58	309	42	233	78	261	58	293	42	218	79	246	59	276	42
5,000	80	246	87	276	67	309	50	233	88	262	68	293	47	218	88	246	69	276	52
	85	248	96	276	76	303	58	235	98	262	77	293	59	221	100	246	79	276	60
	75	266	81	298	60	331	42	251	83	282	60	314	41	234	85	264	61	295	41
7,000	80	267	93	298	67	331	51	253	95	281	72	314	52	237	98	263	73	295	52
	85	273	100	297	82	331	61	260	100	281	84	314	62	247	100	263	86	295	63
	75	278	86	310	61	344	41	262	87	292	63	325	41	244	90	273	64	305	41
8,750	80	280	100	309	74	344	53	266	100	292	78	325	53	250	100	273	78	305	54
	85	292	100	310	87	343	64	279	100	293	89	325	65	264	100	274	81	305	67

Cooling Performance for Air Cooled Equipment

1) Capacities not adjusted for indoor fan heat. To obtain effective cooling capacity, subtract indoor fan heat.
2) Mbh—Total cooling capacity (1,000 Btuh), SHR—Sensible heat ratio (percent of total capacity)
3) Sensible cooling capacity = MBh x SHR, Latent capacity = Total capacity—Sensible capacity

Figure A2-1

If the adjusted equipment capacity values are compatible with the cooling loads, the air distribution system is designed for 7,000 cfm. If capacity values are deficient, capacity is evaluated at a higher Cfm, or investigate the next larger unit. In any case, the Cfm used to determine cooling capacity at altitude is the design Cfm for the air distribution system.

For comfort conditioning, cooling coils tend to be dry when the altitude is 3,000 Feet or higher (because of dry infiltration, dry outdoor air for ventilation, and relatively low latent internal gain). This is obviously not the case when a cooling coil is used to dehumidify a humid pool space. If an application does have a dry coil, use the dry-coil factors provided by Table A5-8.

A2-3 Water-Cooled Cooling Equipment

The water-side of water cooled air conditioning equipment is not affected by altitude. Sea level cooling capacity is maintained if the air mass flow rate through the indoor refrigerant coil at altitude equals the air mass flow rate at sea level. This also applies to water-source heat pumps.

- Obtain values for blower Cfm, total capacity, sensible capacity, latent capacity and sensible heat ratio from manufacturer's expanded performance data for sea level operation. (This data is similar to Figure A2-1, but entering water temperature replaces outdoor air temperature.)

- Use an ACF value (Table A5-6) to find the blower Cfm that will produce an equivalent mass flow rate at altitude (sea level performance is maintained and sea level capacity data applies at altitude).

- The limit for coil face velocity may determine the maximum blower Cfm value.

For example, the ACF value for 5,000 Feet is 0.84, so 1,600 Cfm at sea level is about 1,900 Cfm at altitude. Design the air distribution system for 1,900 Cfm.

Blower Cfm at altitude = 1,600 / 0.84 = 1,905 Cfm
Capacity at altitude = Sea level capacity

A2-4 Chilled Water Coil or Hot Water Coil

Sea level cooling capacity or heating capacity is maintained at altitude if the air mass flow rate through the water coil at altitude equals the air mass flow rate at sea level. Use the Section A2-3 procedure.

A2-5 Electric Heating Coil

The output heating capacity of an electric resistance heating coil is not affected by altitude, but the temperature rise (TR) across the coil depends on air mass-flow trough the

Approximate Altitude Correction Factor [1, 2]	
Feet	**ACF**
0	1.00
1,000	0.97
2,000	0.93
3,000	0.89
4,000	0.87
5,000	0.84
6,000	0.80
7,000	0.77
8,000	0.75
9,000	0.72
10,000	0.69
11,000	0.66
12,000	0.63

1) Approximate adjustment factors for entering air temperatures associated with comfort heating and cooling processes.
2) Calculations for air-to-air heat exchangers, desiccant wheels heat industrial process equipment, and special heating and cooling applications may require adjustment factors that include the effect of air temperature (see Table A5-7).

Copy of Table A5-6

coil. If Cfm is held constant, the temperature rise at altitude is larger than at sea level. If temperature rise is held constant, the air mass flow rate must increase at altitude.

Temperature rise (TR) is evaluated by applying an air density adjustment to the psychrometric equation for sensible heat. Table A5-6 provides the approximate altitude correction factor (ACF).

$$TR \text{ }°F = (Kilowatts \text{ } x \text{ } 3.413) / (1.1 \text{ } x \text{ } ACF \text{ } x \text{ } Cfm)$$

For example, suppose 1,500 Cfm flows through a 10 KW coil in Denver, CO (approximately 5,000 Feet).

Sea level TR = (10.0 x 3.413) / (1.1 x 1.00 x 1,500) = 20.7 °F
Denver TR = (10.0 x 3.413) / (1.1 x 0.84 x 1,500) = 24.6 °F
Denver Cfm for 20.7 °F rise = 1,500 x 24.6 / 20.7 = 1,786

A2-5 Gas Burner

The input heating capacity of a gas burner depends on the mass flow of the gas-air mixture that flows to the burner, which depends on the pressure drop across the metering orifice, the density of the combustion air and the oxygen content of the combustion air. This is affected by altitude. Refer to original equipment manufacturer's (OEM) guidance on this matter.

- OEM specifications have derating tables or charts (for input capacity) for burner assemblies at altitude. This guidance may call for a replacement burner orifice or burner kit for altitudes above 4,000 Feet. These kits reduce gas flow to match the reduced oxygen content of the air. Such kits are based on National Fuel Gas Code ANSI Z223.1, which calls for a reduction of input capacity for each 1,000 Feet above sea level.

- Many OEMs use the derating from the National Fuel Gas Code (2% to 4 % less input capacity per 1,000 Feet of elevation, depending on furnace efficiency). To determine output capacity, adjust input capacity and multiply the adjusted input capacity by the sea level steady-state efficiency (not the AFUE) of the furnace.

For example, a sea level furnace that has 100,000 Btuh of input capacity and a 86% steady state efficiency is installed in Denver, CO (5,000 Feet). The derate factor is 0.04 per 1,000 Feet of elevation.

Input adjustment factor = 0.04 x (5,000 / 1,000) = 0.20
Input Btuh at altitude = 100,000 x (1.00- 0.20) = 80,000
Output Btuh = 0.86 x 80,000 = 68,600

The temperature rise across the furnace heat exchanger is affected by altitude. This behavior is evaluated by applying an air density adjustment to the psychrometric equation for sensible heat (as demonstrated for an electric heating coil).

For example, evaluate Denver, CO performance if 1,600 Cfm flows through a furnace that has 80,000 input Btuh and 86% SS efficiency at sea level.

Sea level output Btuh = 80,000 x 0.86 = 68,800
Sea level TR = (68,800) / (1.1 x 1.00 x 1,600) = 39.1 °F
Denver adjustment factor = 0.04 x (5,000 / 1,000) = 0.20
Denver input Btuh = 80,000 x (1.00 - 0.20) = 64,000
Denver output Btuh = 0.86 x 64,000 = 55,040
ACF for Denver = 0.84
Denver TR = (55,040) / (1.1 x 0.84 x 1,600) = 37.2 °F

A2-6 Oil Burner

The input heating capacity of an oil burner depends on the mass flow of oil that is pumped to the burner. This is not affected by altitude, but the amount of oxygen in a cubic foot of combustion air is reduced at altitude. Refer to original equipment manufacturer's (OEM) guidance on this matter

- The fueling rate and input capacity of an oil furnace are reduced at altitude if the volume flow rate (Cfm) of combustion air equals the sea level flow rate.

Altitude Adjustment Factors			
Air-Cooled Condenser Capacity			
Altitude	**Factor**	**Altitude**	**Factor**
1,000	0.98	7,000	0.86
2,000	0.96	8,000	0.84
3,000	0.94	9,000	0.82
4,000	0.92	10,000	0.80
5,000	0.90	11,000	0.78
6,000	0.88	12,000	0.76

1) Sea level adjustment = 1.0
2) Interpolation and extrapolation of values published by the Carrier Corp (***Engineering Guide for Altitude Effects***, 1967).

Copy of Table A5-9

- For natural draft furnaces, sea level input capacity is maintained at altitude by increasing the chimney height (to maintain the sea level mass flow rate for combustion air).

- For forced draft furnaces, sea level input capacity is maintained at altitude by increasing the combustion air Cfm (to maintain the sea level mass flow rate for combustion air).

- The temperature rise calculation for gas furnaces applies to oil furnaces. Determine output Btuh and apply the an air density adjustment to the psychrometric equation for sensible heat (as demonstrated by Section A2-5.)

A2-7 Air Cooled Condenser

If an air cooled condenser at altitude is operated at the sea level Cfm (SLCfm) for its capacity rating, air mass flow rate is reduced and condenser capacity is reduced. Table A5-9 provides capacity reduction factors for operation at sea level Cfm. If condenser fan speed can be adjusted, Table A5-7 factors are used to determine equivalent mass flow at altitude.

Capacity at altitude for the sea Level Cfm:
Capacity = Sea level capacity x Table A5-9 Factor

Altitude Cfm for sea level Capacity:
Altitude Cfm = Sea Level Cfm / Table A5-7 Factor

A2-8 Hot Gas Coil

If the pressure and temperature for the refrigerant side of a hot gas coil is the same at altitude as for sea level, heating capacity depends on air mass flow rate. If Cfm is held constant, the temperature rise at altitude is larger than at sea level. If temperature rise is held constant, the air mass flow rate must increase at altitude.

Temperature rise (TR) is evaluated by applying an air density adjustment to the psychrometric equation for sensible heat. Table A5-6 provides the approximate altitude correction factor (ACF).

TR (°F) = Btuh Capacity / (1.1 x ACF x Cfm)

For example, suppose 1,500 Cfm flows through a 24,000 Btuh coil in Denver, CO (approximately 5,000 Feet).

Sea level TR = 24,000 / (1.1 x 1.00 x 1,500) = 14.5 °F
Denver TR = 24,000 / (1.1 x 0.84 x 1,500) = 17.3 °F
Denver Cfm for 20.7 °F rise = 1,500 x 17.3 / 14.5 = 1,791

A2-9 Air-to-Air Heat Exchangers and Desiccant Wheels

The performance of air-to-air heat exchangers and desiccant wheels (and the hot gas coil or gas burner for a desiccant wheel) depends on altitude and entering air temperatures. Refer to published engineering guidance provided by the product manufacturer, or use performance data provided by the product manufacturer's engineering department or technical representative.

A2-10 Heat Pump Heating

Air source heat pump manufacturers publish heating capacity tables for refrigerant cycle heating at sea level. Figure A2-2 shows that heating capacity is very sensitive to outdoor temperature and marginally sensitive to indoor temperature ("integrated capacity" means that the data has been adjusted for minimal operation of the defrost cycle, which is appropriate for a dry climate).

For a heat pump at altitude, the dry-coil adjustment factors for a cooling evaporator with an air-cooled condenser may be used for heat pump heating (Table A5-8). However, this is not a critical issue.

- Integrated heating capacities are used to draw balance point diagrams for heat pump heating.

- Because air source (and water source) heat pumps are sized for cooling, the balance point diagram for heating need not be perfect.

- An approximate balance point value is sufficient for selecting the set-point of a control that deactivates supplemental electric resistance heat when outdoor temperature is above the balance point.

- Balance point diagrams are used to size electric resistance heaters used for supplemental heat. Because of standard sizes, the installed wattage of supplemental heat is usually more than adequate.

Integrated Heating Capacity (MBtuh)				
Outdoor DB (F)	Entering Dry-Bulb (°F)			
	60	70	75	80
-5	78.1	75.8	74.9	74.0
0	86.8	84.4	83.4	82.5
5	96.0	93.6	92.4	91.4
10	106.4	103.8	102.0	100.9
15	119.9	117.1	115.0	114.0
20	131.0	120.6	120.0	119.5
25	142.5	139.4	137.9	136.4
30	154.5	151.2	149.6	148.0
35	167.2	163.6	161.7	160.0
40	180.8	176.9	174.8	172.9
45	194.0	189.8	187.5	185.3
50	213.9	209.0	206.6	204.3
55	243.4	237.4	234.5	231.7
60	262.1	255.5	252.3	249.1
70	278.3	271.2	267.7	264.1
75	295.6	286.3	284.3	280.5

Figure A2-2

- If heating coils are sized for 100 percent back-up heat, installed heating capacity is excessive for normal operation.

A2-11 Blower Performance

If blower speed (RPM) is constant, blower Cfm is not affected by altitude. However for a given RPM, air mass flow is reduced at altitude, and reduced mass flow translates to less fan pressure, less air horsepower power and less motor horsepower.

A2-12 Duct System Performance

If duct system airflow rates (Cfm values) are the same at altitude as for sea level, system resistance to airflow (external static pressure) is less than at sea level. And, because a given Cfm value has less mass flow at altitude, the heating or cooling capacity for a supply air Cfm value is less than sea level capacity.

A2-13 Duct System Design

Duct sizing procedures are not affected by altitude. Use sea level blower data, sea level friction charts, and sea level pressure drop data for air side components and duct fittings to size duct runs.

- The duct system is designed for the blower Cfm value that was used to select equipment. (This Cfm tends to be larger than the value that would be used for a sea level application because heating and cooling capacity depends on mass flow.)

- The fraction of blower Cfm flowing through a supply outlet or return grille is the same at altitude as for sea level.

A2-14 Effect on Duct System Operating Point

Flow-pressure relationships for the blower and the duct system are summarized by two curves on a pressure vs. volume flow rate graph (Figure A2-3). The intersection of these two curves is the only possible operating point for the blower (for a particular blower RPM and a particular set of damper positions).

- Duct system design procedures use sea level blower data, so blower performance is plotted as curve B1.

- Duct system design procedures use sea level values for component pressure drops and fitting pressure drops, so system performance is plotted as curve S1.

- If duct sizing procedures are correctly applied, the operating point Cfm equals the design value for blower Cfm (as dictated by the equipment selection procedure).

- The system operating point is affected by altitude because blower pressure and system flow resistance are reduced by altitude.

- Blower pressure is proportional to air density, so all points on the blower curve are multiplied by an ACF value from Table A5-6. This produces curve B2, which represents blower performance at altitude.

- System resistance is proportional to air density, so all points on the system curve are multiplied by an ACF value from Table A5-6. This produces curve S2, which represents system performance at altitude.

- At altitude, the operating point Cfm is equal to the sea level operating point Cfm, and the operating pressure is reduced (therefore blower power is reduced).

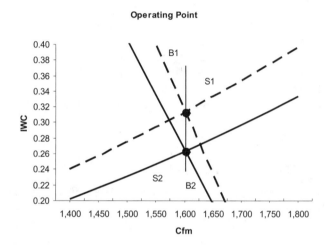

Figure A2-3

Appendix 3

State Point Psychrometrics

Grains values are provided by altitude sensitive, psychrometric software that may be packaged with ACCA-logo products such as **Manual J** or **Manual N**, or by stand-alone products advertised in trade journals, or on the web. Alternatively, grains values at altitude may be calculated by spreadsheet implementation of the equations provided here:

Reference:
2005 ASHRAE Handbook of Fundamentals, Chapter 6

A3-1 Outdoor Grains from Outdoor Dry-Bulb and Wet-Bulb

Use the following equations to convert outdoor dry-bulb temperature and wet-bulb temperature to an humidity ratio value (in grains per pound of air units).

Step 1: Calculate the atmospheric pressure (P) at the desired feet (Z) of altitude in Psia.

ASHRAE Equation 3, page 6.1

$P \ (Psia) = 14.696 \times (1 - 6.8754 \times 10^{-6} \times Z)^{5.2559}$

Example: For 5,100 feet
P = 12.18 Psia

Step 2: Convert the outdoor wet-bulb temperature (Od WB) to degrees Rankine (Od WBR) and calculate the natural log of Od WBR.

Od WBR = Od WB + 459.67
Natural log of Od WBR = Ln (Od WBR)

Example: For 62 wet-bulb
od WBR = 521.67 and Ln (od WBR) = 6.25704

Step 3: Calculate the natural log of the saturation pressure at the outdoor wet-bulb temperature (odwb Pws).

ASHRAE Equation 6, page 6.2

$Ln \ (odwb \ Pws) = - (1.0440397 \times 10^{4} / WBR) - (1.129465 \times 10^{1}) - (WBR \times 2.7022355 \times 10^{-2}) + (WBR^{2} \times 1.289036 \times 10^{-5}) - (WBR^{3} \times 2.4780681 \times 10^{-9}) + (6.5459673 \times Ln \ (od \ WBR))$

Example: For 62 wet-bulb
Ln (odwb Pws) = -1.2903

Step 4: Calculate the inverse of the natural log of the outdoor wet-bulb saturation pressure to obtain the saturation pressure value (odwb Pws)

odwb Pws = Exp (Ln (odwb Pws))

Example: For 62 wet-bulb: odwb Pws = 0.2752

Step 5: Calculate the humidity ratio of saturated air at the outdoor wet-bulb temperature (odwb Ws) and the desired elevation (Lb water per Lb air).

ASHRAE Equation 23, page 6.12

odwb Ws = 0.62198 x odwb Pws / (P - odwb Pws)

Example: For 62 wet-bulb
odwb Ws = 0.01438

Step 6: Calculate the absolute outdoor humidity ratio (od W) for the desired outdoor dry-bulb (od DB) and wet-bulb (od WB) temperatures (°F) at the desired elevation (Lb water per Lb air) .

ASHRAE Equation 35, page 6.13

od W = ((1093 - 0.556 x od WB) x odwb Ws - 0.24 x (od DB - od WB)) / (1093 + 0.444 x od DB - od WB)

Example: For 62 wet-bulb and 97 dry-bulb:
od W = 0.00635

Step 7: Convert the humidity ratio value for the desired state-point to grains of water per pound or air

od Grains = 7004 x od W

Example: For 5,100 feet, 62 wet-bulb and 97 dry-bulb
od Grains = 44.45

A3-2 Indoor Grains from Indoor Dry-Bulb and Relative Humidity

Use the following equations to convert indoor dry-bulb temperature and relative humidity to an humidity ratio value (in grains of moisture per pound of air units).

Step 1: Calculate the atmospheric pressure (P) at the desired feet (Z) of altitude in Psi.

ASHRAE Equation 3, page 6.1

$P (Psi) = 14.696 \times (1 - 6.8753 \times 10^{-6} \times Z)^{5.2559}$

Example: For 5,100 feet
P = 12.18 Psi

Step 2: Convert the indoor dry-bulb temperature (id DB) to degrees Rankine (id DBR) and calculate the natural log of id DBR

id DBR = id DB + 459.67
Natural log of id DBR = Ln (id DBR)

Example: For 75 dry-bulb
id DBR = 534.67 and Ln (id DBR) = 6.28165

Step 3: Calculate the natural log of the saturation pressure at the indoor dry-bulb temperature (iddb Pws)

ASHRAE Equation 6, page 6.2

Ln (iddb Pws) = - (1.0440397 $\times 10^4$ / DBR) - (1.129465 $\times 10^1$) - (DBR $\times$ 2.7022355 $\times 10^{-2}$) + (DBR^2 $\times$ 1.289036 $\times 10^{-5}$) - (DBR^3 $\times$ 2.4780681 $\times 10^{-9}$) + (6.5459673 $\times$ Ln (DBR))

Example: For 75 dry-bulb
Ln (iddb Pws) = -0.8438

Step 4: Calculate the inverse of the natural log of the dry-bulb saturation pressure to obtain the saturation pressure value (iddb Pws)

iddb Pws = Exp (Ln (indb Pws))

Example: For 75 dry-bulb
iddb Pws = 0.43007

Step 5: Calculate the humidity ratio of saturated air at the indoor dry-bulb temperature (iddb Ws) and the desired elevation (Lb water per Lb air).

ASHRAE Equation 23, 6.12

iddb Ws = 0.62198 $\times$ iddb Pws / (P - iddb Pws)

Example: For 75 dry-bulb
iddb Ws = 0.02276

Step 6: Calculate the degree of saturation at the indoor relative humidity (id u)

ASHRAE Equation 14, page 6.12

id u = RH / (1 + (1 - RH) $\times$ iddb Ws / 0.62198

Example: For 50% RH
id u = 0.491

Step 7: Calculate the absolute indoor humidity ratio (id W) for the desired indoor dry-bulb temperature and relative humidity at the desired elevation (Lb water per Lb air) .

ASHRAE Equation 12, page 6.12

id W = id u $\times$ iddb Ws

Example: For 75 dry-bulb and 50% RH
id W = 78.28

Step 8: Convert the humidity ratio value for the desired state-point to grains of water per pound or air

Indoor Grains = 7004 $\times$ id W

Example: For 5,100 feet, 75 dry-bulb and 50% RH
id Grains = 78.28

Appendix 4

Symbols and Terminology

ΔG	Grains difference or change in grains	IWC	Inches of water column (pressure unit)
A	Area (typically in square feet)	KW	Kilowatt
ACF	Altitude correction factor	KWH	Kilowatt hours
ACH	Air changes per hour	LEL	Latent evaporation load (Btuh)
AF	Activity factor (splashing and dripping adjustment)	Lb	Pound
ALF	Air loading factor (Cfm/SqFt)	LC	Latent capacity (Btuh)
ATR	Air turnover rate (supply air ACH for a space)	MA	Mixed air
Btu	British Thermal Unit	MAT	Mixed air temperature
Btuh	British Thermal Units per Hour	MWL	Make-up water load (Btuh)
CFH	Cold fill heat (Btuh)	OA	Outdoor air
CFL	Cold fill load (Btuh)	OAT	Outdoor air temperature
Cfm	Cubic feet per minute	PUL	Pool use load (Btuh)
DB or db	Dry-bulb temperature	R; R-value	Thermal Resistance (SqFt•F/Btuh)
DEF	Default evaporation flux (Lb/Hr•SqFT)	RA	Return air
DER	Default evaporation rate (Lb/Hr)	RH	Relative humidity
DOAS	Dedicated outdoor air system	RPM	Revolutions per minute
DP	Dew point temperature	SA	Supply air
EA	Exhaust air	SAG	Supply air grains
EAT	Entering air temperature	SAT	Supply Air Temperature
ER	Evaporation rate (Lb/Hr for the activity level)	SC	Sensible capacity (Btuh)
°F	Degrees Fahrenheit	SER	Sensible Effectiveness Rating (heat recovery device)
Fpm	Feet per minute	SHR	Sensible heat ratio
Ft	Feet	SqFt	Square Feet
Grain	1/7,000 of a Pound	TC	Total capacity (Btuh)
Gpm	Gallons per minute	TR	Temperature rise
Hg	Inches of mercury	TSP	Thermostat set point
Hr	Hour	U; U-value	Thermal Conductance (Btuh/SqFt•F)
IAG	Indoor air grains	WB or wb	Wet-bulb temperature
In	Inch	WUT	Warm up time (pool water)

A

Air Turnover Rate (ATR) The number of times per hour that the volume of space air is replaced by supply air.

Airway The cross sectional area of a duct.

B

Block Load The heating or cooling load for the entire space served by a heating equipment or cooling equipment.

C

Comfort Conditioning Equipment Manufactured equipment or equipment packages are optimized for the range of entering air conditions and sensible heat ratios that apply to comfort conditioning applications. The equipment may have components and materials that are not compatible with chemical laden air. The equipment cabinet and compartments may have leakage paths that will cause operational problems and materials problems. The warranty may be void if the equipment is used for pool-spa applications.

Contract Set Points Legally binding values for water temperature, space air temperature and space humidity (or dew point).

Chloramines Offensive chemical compounds produced by the water sanitation process. They are minimized by adequate water treatment.

Cooling Coil A refrigerant coil or chilled water coil that extracts heat from a flow of air. Key attributes are rows, fins per inch, face velocity, circuiting, and apparatus dew point.

D

Dehumidification Coil A cooling coil that is optimized for moisture removal. Construction is characterized by a low face velocity, six or eight rows, close fin spacing, and a relatively cold operating temperature. Dehumidifier manufacturers prefer to call this... *the evaporator.*

Dehumidifier An equipment package that has been optimized for moisture removal. The equipment may feature a dehumidification coil (evaporator) or a desiccant wheel. Equipment that has a dehumidification coil processes return air, with outdoor air inserted downstream from the coil; and the design may allow air to bypass the coil. Evaporator equipment also provides sensible cooling.

Dew Point Temperature The dry-bulb temperature and/or wet-bulb temperature of saturated air.

Drop Cold supply air that has noticeable velocity falls toward the floor after leaving a ceiling or high side wall outlet.

Dry-Bulb Temperature The temperature measured by an ordinary thermometer.

E

Engineered Ventilation Outdoor air that is purposely introduced to the conditioned space in a controlled manner.

Evaporator or Evaporator Coil The low pressure coil in a refrigeration circuit.

F

Fenestration or Fenestration Assembly A window, skylight or door.

G

Grains The moisture content of air in grains-water per pound of dry air units.

H

Humidity Ratio Moisture content of air in pounds-water per pound of dry air, or grains-water per pound of dry air.

Humid Zone The entire space that is subject to water vapor released from pool-spa evaporation.

HVAC A mechanical system that provides one or more of these functions: heat; humidification; sensible cooling; dehumidification; ventilation.

I

Indoor Air Condition The state point of indoor air (a specific set of values for dry-bulb temperature, humidity ratio, relative humidity, wet-bulb temperature, enthalpy and specific volume).

M

Mechanical Equipment An equipment package, or any component of an equipment package that processes air or pool-spa water.

N

Natatorium A space that houses a pool of any size. The space may or may not have spectator seating or a spa.

Noise Criteria (NC) A single value descriptor that quantifies the amount of noise a normal ear will hear. Typically found in performance data for supply air outlets, and other types of air distribution hardware.

O

Outdoor Air Condition The state point of outdoor air (a specific set of values for dry-bulb temperature, humidity ratio, relative humidity, wet-bulb temperature, enthalpy and specific volume).

Occupied Zone For air distribution, the portion of a room or space that is actually occupied by people (two feet inside of the walls and about 6.5 feet high).

R

Relative Humidity The degree of saturation. Air that is saturated has 100% relative humidity. Air that is partially saturated may has less than 100% relative humidly (determined by the psychrometric state point of the air).

S

Spa A pool or tub used for sitting and soaking.

Space Conditioning Equipment Equipment that controls the temperature; and/or moisture; and/or air movement; and/or amount of outdoor air Cfm in an occupied space.

Space Load The sensible heating load, winter humidification load, sensible cooling load or latent cooling load for a room, zone or the entire space served by the equipment (does not include system loads).

System Load Sensible heating, sensible cooling, humidification load or latent load produced by the HVAC system. (Typically duct loads, pipe loads, blower heat, engineered ventilation, reheat, etc. However, outdoor air introduced downstream from an evaporator coil is a space load because it is not conditioned before it enters the space.)

T

Throw Supply air leaves the face of the outlet at a relatively high velocity (say 700 Fpm) and slows as the momentum of the discharge air is transferred to room air. At some distance from the outlet, the velocity of the discharge air falls to a reference value specified by the outlet manufacturer (50 Fpm to 150 Fpm). This distance is the throw.

V

Vapor Barrier A membrane or surface that completely blocks moisture migration (permeance equals 0.00 Grains/Hr • SqFt per • InHg range). This would be an abnormal requirement for building construction. Codes and standards allow a small amount of moisture migration (see *vapor retarding membrane*).

Vapor Retarding Membrane or Vapor Membrane A vapor retarding material that has a low perm rating. For this manual, a material that has a permeance that does not exceed 0.10 Grains/Hr • SqFt per • InHg).

Ventilation Effectiveness ow well supply air is mixed or blended with space air.

Z

Zone Load he sensible heating load, winter humidification load, sensible cooling load or latent cooling load for one or more rooms and/or spaces that have the same point of control (a thermostat, for example).

Appendix 5

Summary of Tables and Equations

This appendix provides exhibits of the primary tables and equations used by *Manual SPS*. It does not provide guidance on each detail of a procedure, and it does not cover all options, alternatives or refinements.

A5-1 Tables

Table A5-1 provides water temperature values for various applications. Water temperature is selected first, then air temperature would be a few degrees warmer for less evaporation and lower operating cost.

Table A5-2 provides values for the condition of humid space air for various types of pool applications. Dry-bulb temperature is normally a few degrees warmer than water temperature. Space humidity may range from 50% RH to 60% RH.

Table A5-2 and Table A5-3 (next page) shows how indoor dew-point temperature varies for the range of dry-bulb and relative humidity values for each application. Table A5-3 also provides vapor membrane surface temperatures for minimum R-value calculations.

Table A5-4 (next page) provides evaporation values in Lb/Hr per SqFt of water surface area or wet deck area. These values are for a normal amount of water activity for a public natatorium.

Table A5-5 (page 147) provides activity factors for various applications. The evaporation rate for an application equals the product of the Table A5-4 value and the Table A5-5 value.

Table A5-6 (page 147) provides approximate altitude adjustment factors (ACF) for the psychrometric equations for a sensible heat process and a latent heat process. These factors are approximately correct for air that is 60°F dry-bulb to 80°F dry-bulb.

Table A5-7 (page 148) provides altitude adjustment factors (ACF) for the psychrometric equations for a sensible heat process and a latent heat process. These factors apply to air temperature that range from -20°F to 140°F.

Table A5-8 (page 148) provides altitude adjustment factors for common comfort cooling equipment that has an evaporator and an air cooled condenser. This table supplements Appendix 2 guidance.

Table A5-9 (page 148) provides altitude adjustment factors for an air cooled condenser. This table supplements Appendix 2 guidance.

Range of Water Temperature Values

Application	Temperature °F
Residential Pool	
Hotel or Motel Pool	76 to 86
Public, Institutional or Rec Pool	
Swimming Competition Pool	76 to 82
Diving Pool	80 to 90
Water Fitness Class	82 to 86
Elderly Swimmers	84 to 88
Therapeutic Pool	85 to 95
Spa or Whirlpool	97 to 104

Table A5-1

Indoor Air Conditions for Occupant Comfort

Application	Dry-Bulb Temp °F	Relative Humidity	Dew Point Temp °F
Residential Pool			
Hotel or Motel Pool			
Public, Institutional or Recreation Pool	78 to 86		57.8 to 70.5
Competition Swimming Pool		50% to 60%	
Diving Pool	82 to 86		61.5 to 70.5
Water Fitness Class	84 to 86		63.3 to 70.5
Elderly Swimmers			
Therapeutic Pool	86		61.2 to 70.5
Spa or Whirlpool			

1) Preferred air temperature 2 °F to 4 °F warmer than the design value for water temperature.
2) Maximum air temperature = 86° F
3) Maximum relative humidity = 60% (to prevent mold and mildew)
4) Relative humidity may drop below 50% RH when the negative moisture load produced by dry outdoor air Cfm exceeds the positive moisture load for the space.
5) Dew point temperature does not change with altitude.

Table A5-2

A5-2 Air Equations

This equation returns values for the sensible heat that isabsorbed or released by a flow of air during a heating or cooling process. The altitude correction factor is based on the condition of the entering air (see Table A5-6 and

Table A5-7). The change in air temperature (ΔT) is positive for heating and negative for cooling.

Sensible Btuh = 1.1 x ACF x Cfm x ΔT

This equation returns values for the latent heat that is absorbed or released by a flow of air during a humidification or dehumidification process. The altitude correction factor is based on the condition of the entering air (see Tables A5-6 and A5-7). The change in moisture (ΔGrains) is positive for humidification and negative for dehumidification.

Latent Btuh = 1.1 x ACF x Cfm x ΔGrains

A5-3 R-value Equation

An indoor surface temperature (T_s) depends on the overall R-value (R_t) of the structural panel (with the indoor and outdoor air film resistance), the indoor temperature (T_i) and the outdoor temperature (T_o).

$T_s = T_i - (T_i - T_o)$ x (K / R_t)

This version of the equation returns the minimum R-value (R_t) for a desired surface temperature (T_s).

$R_t = K$ x $(T_i - T_o) / (T_i - T_s)$

Minimum Vapor Membrane Temperature		
Application	**Indoor Dew Point Temperature °F**	**Membrane Surface Temperature °F**
Residential Pool	57.8 to 70.5	62.8 to 75.5
Hotel or Motel Pool		
Public, Institutional or Recreation Pool		
Competition Swimming Pool		
Diving Pool	61.5 to 70.5	66.5 to 75.5
Water Fitness Class	63.3 to 70.5	68.3 to 75.5
Elderly Swimmers	61.2 to 70.5	66.2 to 75.5
Therapeutic Pool		
Spa or Whirlpool		

1) Minimum dry-bulb temperature at the inside of the vapor membrane surface to prevent condensation.
2) Indoor dew point temperature depends on the indoor design condition, see Sections 2-2 and 2-3.
3) This surface temperature limitation applies to the coldest point on the vapor membrane surface, which is determined by the lowest conduction path R-value (from the outdoor air to the vapor membrane surface).

Table A5-3

Default Evaporation Flux (DEF)												
Water Temperature	**Space Air Temperature and Relative Humidity**											
↓	76 °F		78 °F		80 °F		82 °F		84 °F		86 °F	
°F	50%	60%	50%	60%	50%	60%	50%	60%	50%	60%	50%	60%
76	0.0456	0.0364	0.0424	0.0326	0.0392	0.0288	0.0356	0.0246	0.0320	0.0200	0.0280	0.0154
78	0.0482	0.0390	0.0450	0.0352	0.0418	0.0314	0.0382	0.0272	0.0346	0.0226	0.0306	0.0180
80	0.0584	0.0494	0.0554	0.0456	0.0520	0.0416	0.0486	0.0374	0.0448	0.0330	0.0410	0.0282
82	0.0656	0.0564	0.0624	0.0526	0.0592	0.0488	0.0556	0.0444	0.0520	0.0400	0.0480	0.0354
84	0.0730	0.0640	0.0700	0.0602	0.0666	0.0562	0.0630	0.0520	0.0594	0.0476	0.0554	0.0428
86	0.0810	0.0718	0.0778	0.0680	0.0746	0.0640	0.0710	0.0598	0.0674	0.0554	0.0634	0.0508
88	0.0894	0.0802	0.0862	0.0764	0.0830	0.0724	0.0794	0.0682	0.0756	0.0638	0.0718	0.0590
90	0.0984	0.0892	0.0952	0.0854	0.0918	0.0814	0.0884	0.0772	0.0846	0.0728	0.0806	0.0680
102	0.1634	0.1542	0.1604	0.1504	0.1570	0.1464	0.1534	0.1422	0.1496	0.1376	0.1456	0.1328
104	0.1764	0.1672	0.1734	0.1634	0.1700	0.1594	0.1664	0.1552	0.1626	0.1506	0.1586	0.1458

1) DEF = Pounds of water per hour per square foot of wet surface for a normal amount of Swimming, splashing and wet deck area.
2) Table values do not change with altitude.
3) Table values are for about 25 feet per minute air velocity over wet surface (the default for appropriate air distribution, see Section 12).

Air Velocity (Fpm)	5	10	15	20	25	30	40	50
Adjustment Factor	0.92	0.94	0.96	0.98	1.00	1.02	1.06	1.10

Table A5-4

Activity Factor (AF) for Water Churning	
Application	**AF**
Still water surface	0.50
Residential pool	0.50
Private multi-family, fitness club pool	0.80
Therapy, elderly swimmers pool	0.80
Hotel or motel swimming pool	0.65
Dive or swim competition in progress	0.65
Public swimming pool	1.00
Institutional swimming pool	1.00
Spa or whirl pool	1.00
Water slides Note 2	Speculative
Water fall and collection pool Note 2	No guidance
Fountains	No guidance
Wave pool, water cannon; etc.	No guidance

1) Multiply Table A5-4 values by the applicable adjustment factor.
2) See Sections 6-6 and 6-7.

Table A5-5

A5-4 Water Heating

The cold fill heat (CFH) is the amount of heat required to bring the temperature of cold fill water to design temperature (TR), as determined by this equation. See Section 4-6

CFH (Btu) = 8.345 x Fill Gallons x TR

Heat must be added to the water in a reasonable amount of time, which is the warm-up time (WUT) in hours. The warm-up time determines the cold fill load (CFL).

CFL (Btuh) = CFL / WUT

The pool water heater must compensate for the heat of evaporation to keep pool water at its design temperature. The evaporation rate (ER in Lb/Hr) is determined by Section 6 procedures. The latent evaporation load (LEL) is determined by this equation.

LEL (Btuh) = 1,050 x ER

The make-up water load (MWL) is the heat required to bring the temperature of cold make-up water to design temperature (TR), as determined by this equation.

MWL (Btuh) = 1.0 x ER x TR

When the pool is in use, the load on the water heating equipment equals the sum of the evaporation load and the make-up water load. This is the pool use load (PUL).

PUL (Btuh) = LEL+ MWL

Approximate Altitude Correction Factor [1,2]	
Feet	**ACF**
0	1.00
1,000	0.97
2,000	0.93
3,000	0.89
4,000	0.87
5,000	0.84
6,000	0.80
7,000	0.77
8,000	0.75
9,000	0.72
10,000	0.69
11,000	0.66
12,000	0.63

1) Approximate adjustment factors for entering air temperatures associated with comfort heating and cooling processes.
2) Calculations for air-to-air heat exchangers, desiccant wheels heat industrial process equipment, and special heating and cooling applications may require adjustment factors that include the effect of air temperature (see Table A5-7).

Table A5-6

A5-5 Space Air Turn Rate

The space air turn rate (ATR) depends on supply air Cfm and space volume (CuFt).

ATR = (Supply Cfm x 60) / Space Volume

A5-6 Evaporation

The evaporation rate (ER) depends on the default evaporation rate for one square foot of wet surface (DEF), an activity factor (AF), and the wet surface area (A). See Section 6-1.

ER (Lbs / Hr) = DEF (Lbs / Hr•SqFT) x AF x A (SqFt)

The latent load for evaporation (LEL) equals the product of the evaporation rate (ER) and the default value for the latent heat of evaporation.

LEL (Btuh) = 1,050 x ER

Altitude Correction Factor for Air Density Entering Air from - 20°F to 140°F										
Air DB (°F)	Altitude (Feet)									
	Sea Level	1,000	2,000	3,000	4,000	5,000	6,000	7,000	8,000	9,000
-20	1.20	1.16	1.12	1.08	1.04	1.00	0.97	0.97	0.93	0.89
0	1.15	1.10	1.06	1.02	0.99	0.95	0.92	0.92	0.88	0.85
20	1.11	1.06	1.02	0.98	0.95	0.92	0.88	0.88	0.85	0.82
40	1.06	1.02	0.98	0.94	0.91	0.88	0.81	0.81	0.79	0.76
60	1.02	0.98	0.94	0.91	0.88	0.85	0.81	0.81	0.79	0.76
70	1.00	0.96	0.93	0.89	0.86	0.83	0.80	0.80	0.77	0.74
80	0.98	0.94	0.91	0.88	0.85	0.81	0.78	0.78	0.75	0.72
100	0.94	0.91	0.88	0.84	0.81	0.78	0.75	0.75	0.72	0.70
120	0.92	0.88	0.85	0.81	0.78	0.76	0.72	0.72	0.70	0.67
140	0.89	0.85	0.82	0.79	0.76	0.73	0.70	0.70	0.68	0.65

Table A5-7

Altitude Adjustment Factors Cooling Evaporator with Air-Cooled Condenser				
Altitude (Feet)	Total Capacity		Sensible Capacity	
	Wet Coil	Dry Coil	Wet Coil	Dry Coil
Sea Level	1.00	1.00	1.00	1.00
1,000	0.99	0.98	0.97	0.98
2,000	0.98	0.97	0.94	0.97
3,000	0.98	0.95	0.91	0.95
4,000	0.97	0.94	0.88	0.94
5,000	0.96	0.92	0.85	0.92
6,000	0.95	0.90	0.82	0.90
7,000	0.94	0.89	0.80	0.89
8,000	0.94	0.87	0.77	0.87
10,000	0.92	0.84	0.71	0.84
12,000	0.90	0.81	0.65	0.81

1) Interpolation and extrapolation of values published by the
   Carrier Corp (*Engineering Guide for Altitude Effects*, 1967).
2) Use wet coil values for sensible heat ratios less than 0.95.

Table A5-8

Altitude Adjustment Factors Air-Cooled Condenser Capacity			
Altitude	Factor	Altitude	Factor
1,000	0.98	7,000	0.86
2,000	0.96	8,000	0.84
3,000	0.94	9,000	0.82
4,000	0.92	10,000	0.80
5,000	0.90	11,000	0.78
6,000	0.88	12,000	0.76

1) Sea level adjustment = 1.0
2) Interpolation and extrapolation of values published by the
   Carrier Corp (*Engineering Guide for Altitude Effects*, 1967).

Table A5-9

Part 4

Ancillary Guidance and Aids

Appendix 6

Summary of Dehumidification Methods

Space humidity can be controlled by refrigerant evaporating coils, dry outdoor air and desiccant wheels. These methods vary in concept, complexity, installed cost and operating cost.

- The mandatory concern is matching system capabilities with application needs.

- If two or more methods provide the required performance, installation cost and operating cost may determine the system of choice.

- The following summary covers basic concepts and configurations. For any given method, there are variations of the basic concept. See Section 8 for expanded discussions.

A6-1 Mechanical Dehumidifying Equipment

Mechanical dehumidifiers control space humidity and may control space temperature year-round (supplemental sensible cooling may be required, depending on the size of the moisture removal load and the size of the largest sensible load). The air by-pass feature allows 4-8 air turnovers an hour for the conditioned space. The latent heat of evaporation for pool water is recovered by an evaporator coil. Outdoor air is introduced downstream from the evaporator (equivalent to a space load). Since the evaporator coil processes 100% return air, the condition of the air entering the evaporator, and the coil sensible heat ratio are relatively constant year-round; and the latent heat of water evaporation is recovered year-round. Recovered latent heat can be used to heat pool water and/or supply air; excess heat is rejected to the outdoors. All capabilities are provided in one turn-key package. Supplemental supply air heat may be provided within the cabinet, or external to the cabinet. Reclaim heat shall not be the only source of water heat. Provide an independent, full capacity source of water heat.

A6-2 Outdoor Air Method

Outdoor air can control space humidity when the outdoor air is dry enough. This is a cold weather solution for a humid climate, and can be a multi-season solution for a dry climate.

- Outdoor air systems are once-through systems (introduce dry air, absorb moisture and exhaust moist air).

- A large amount of outdoor Cfm is not practical for technical, energy use and operating cost reasons.

- The outdoor air Cfm value for humidity control is a variable (automatic dampers and controls determine how much airflow is required for all possible combinations of latent space load and outdoor moisture, as the seasons change).

- During occupancy, the lower limit for outdoor air Cfm may be determined by the indoor air quality requirement (this is true for all types of systems).

- Outdoor air temperature is an energy use issue (cold outdoor air must be heated before it enters the conditioned space, warm outdoor air must be cooled before it enters the space)

- Condensation and freezing water is an issue when cold outdoor air is mixed with humid return air (preheat outdoor air).

- System efficiency is improved by an air-to-air heat recovery devices, which extract heat from exhaust air and use it to temper entering outdoor air.

- Condensation on heat recovery surfaces reclaims some of the latent heat in the exhaust air and has a dehumidification effect.

- Condensation on heat recovery surfaces may turn to ice during cold weather. Provide appropriate safeguards.

- The heat of evaporation contained in exhaust air is not fully recovered by air-to-air devices, and reclaimed heat is not available for pool water.

A6-3 Desiccant Dehumidifying Equipment

Desiccant dehumidifying equipment can control space humidity year-round. There is no bypass air feature, so supply air Cfm and space air turnover rate are determined when equipment is sized for the moisture removal load (if available space air turns are less than desired, use supplemental air circulation equipment). For dehumidification, an evaporator coil processes 100% return air, so the condition of the entering air and the coil sensible heat ratio are relatively constant year-round. The latent heat of evaporation in return air is recovered by the refrigerant coil. Then, recovered heat is used to regenerate the media in a desiccant wheel that is downstream from the evaporator (therefore, pool water is heated by other means). Then warm, dry air discharged from the desiccant wheel is mixed with outdoor air (in a downstream module or box), so the mixed air temperature determines supply air temperature at this point. This temperature is not compatible (except by coincidence) with the space heating load or sensible cooling load, so mixed air must be routed through a downstream device that increases supply air temperature (space heating load), or deceases supply air temperature (space cooling load). Supplemental heating and sensible cooling devices may be supplied with the desiccant package, or may be external to the package.

Desiccant dehumidifiers operate at a technical and economic disadvantage when processing return air (two dehumidifying devices in series, plus supplemental devices for sensible heating and sensible cooling; recovered heat consumed by the desiccant wheel not used for pool water). However, desiccant dehumidifiers can be competitive when processing 100% outdoor air (see the following commentary about DOAS equipment).

A6-4 Comfort Conditioning Equipment

HVAC equipment optimized for comfort conditioning applications is generally not suitable for institutional, commercial or residential applications that contain swimming pools and/or spas. The dehumidification capability of such space conditioning equipment may be inadequate for the large volume of moisture-laden air. Additionally, modified operating cycles, imposed duty-cycles and exposure to pool/spa-related chemicals may impact the reliability and longevity of typical space conditioning equipment.

There also are economic tradeoffs. Equipment selected for swimming pool and spa applications should balance first-cost with life-cycle cost. Life-cycle considerations include operating performance, energy recovery abilities, maintenance needs, and projected equipment/component replacements.

Under certain circumstances, it is possible for a knowledgeable practitioner, who has adequate experience with HVAC system design and indoor swimming pool requirements, to assemble a system from a combination of HVAC systems/components that meets all the psychrometric performance requirements, part-load requirements, materials requirements for chemical-laden air, and energy use requirements.

This manual does not provide adequate guidance for such efforts. (Some basic concepts are briefly discussed, with cautions and warnings, but this is not definitive guidance). Rather, this manual is specifically aimed at helping practitioners understand the unique design criteria for indoor swimming pools and spas, and the demanding performance requirements that are imposed on the dehumidification system and equipment.

A6-5 Dehumidification Methods for Outdoor Air

Outdoor air may be processed by the same equipment that dehumidifies space air, or by a dedicated outdoor air (DOAS) system that processes 100% outdoor air. The viability of DOAS equipment improves as the design value for spectator count goes up because it decouples an occasional load condition from the normal load condition. In any case, the system designer has the option to use some combination of space dehumidification equipment that has outdoor air capability, or a combination of DOAS equipment and space dehumidification equipment that has outdoor air capability.

A DOAS could feature a comfort cooling coil, a mechanical dehumidifying coil or a desiccant wheel. These considerations apply:

- Sensible heat ratio and capacity control are decisive issues because the sensible load can go from maximum to zero while the latent load remains significant or relatively large.

- For a viable solution, the coil sensible heat ratio must be compatible with the sensible heat ratio for the sensible and latent outdoor air loads for all relevant operating conditions.

- Outdoor air is required for normal operation because of the ventilation requirement for water surface area and wet deck area (i.e., a space air dehumidifier needs outdoor air capability if DOAS equipment only provides outdoor air for spectator events).

- Outdoor air requires heat during cold weather.

- For DOAS equipment, discharge air temperature is compatible with space air temperature year-round. For spectator comfort, discharge air temperature may be a few degrees cooler than space temperature.

- DOAS exhaust air Cfm must be compatible with DOAS supply air Cfm and the space pressure requirement. Heat can be reclaimed from exhaust air (condensation and freezing on reclaim surfaces is a cold weather issue).

- DOAS equipment has its own air distribution system.

Appendix 7

Codes, Standards and References

Guidance and information pertaining to natatoriums is provided by authored books, codes, manuals, standards, and good practice documents. Some sources are listed here. (References may go out of date and/or can be superceded. Some references are included in codes.)

A7-1 Authored Books and Papers

Humidity Control Design Guide for Commercial and Institutional Buildings: L. Harriman, G. Brundrett, R. Kittler

The book is generally applicable to the natatorium problem. Chapter 27 is devoted to Swimming Pools. Chapter 27 cites these references:

- "Thermal and moisture control in insulated assemblies." Chapter 23, ASHRAE Handbook of Fundamentals 2001. ASHRAE, Atlanta, GA.

- "Places of assembly." Chapter 4, ASHRAE Handbook of Applications 1999. Natatoriums, pp: 4.5–4.7.

- Design and dehumidification of swimming pools, 2001. Dectron Internationale, Atlanta, GA.

- Kittler, Reinhold 1983. "Indoor natatorium design and energy recycling."

- ASHRAE Transactions, vol 95, part 1, pp: 521-526.

- Künzel, Hartwig M. and Karagiozis, Achilles N. and Holm A., 2000. "WUFI ORNL/IBP; A Hygrothermal Design Tool for Architects and Engineers," ASTM Manual 40, Heinz Treschel, Editor. American Society for Testing And Materials, Philadelphia, PA. Note: The actual software is included on a CD-ROM supplied with ASTM manual 40. It was developed and published jointly by the Fraunhofer Institute of Building Science, Germany, Dr. Hartwig Künzel, 011-49-8024-64345 and by the US Department of Energy, Oak Ridge National Laboratory, Oak Ridge, TN, Dr. Achilles Karagiozis (865) 576-3924.

- Lotz, William A, 1990. "Considerations for swimming pool building design." Engineered Systems magazine. March/April, 1990. Business News Publishing Co. Troy, MI

- Lotz, William A, 1995. "Indoor pool design: avoid the potential for disaster." Heating, Piping and Air Conditioning magazine, November, 1995. pp: 47–63.

- Lotz, William A, 1996. "Are insulation specifications conjured up for magicians?" Insulation Outlook magazine, November, 1996. pp: 32–33.

- Lotz, William A, 1998. "Insulation failure and moisture problems resulting from inadequate installation of insulation and/or vapor retarders." ASHRAE Transactions, vol.104, pt.2. 1998

Moisture Control in Buildings: The Key Factor in Mold Prevention: 2nd Edition Heinz R. Trechsel, Mark Bomberg; ASTM International

Moisture Control For Buildings: Joseph Lstiburek, Ph.D., P.Eng., Member ASHRAE; ASHRAE Journal

Calculating Evaporation From Indoor Water Pools: M. Mohammad Shah, PHD, PE; HPAC Engineering, March 2004 (see also, ASHRAE Publications).

A7-2 ASHRAE Publications

The American Society of Heating, Refrigeration and Air-Conditioning Engineers (ASHRAE) publishes consensus standards and handbooks.

- ANSI/ASHRAE Standard 62.1-2007 *Ventilation for Acceptable Indoor Air Quality*

- ANSI/ASHRAE Standard 62.2-2007 *Ventilation and Acceptable Indoor Air Quality in Low-Rise Residential Buildings*

- ANSI/ASHRAE/IESNA Standard 90.1-2004 *Energy Standard for Buildings Except Low-Rise Residential Buildings*

- ANSI/ASHRAE Standard 90.2-2007 *Energy-Efficient Design of Low-Rise Residential Buildings*

- ANSI/ASHRAE Standard 129-1997 (RA 2003) Measuring Air-Change Effectiveness

- ANSI/ASHRAE Standard 139-2007 Method of Testing for Rating Desiccant Dehumidifiers Utilizing Heat for the Regeneration Process

- ANSI/ASHRAE Standard 146-2006 Method of Testing and Rating Pool Heaters

- ANSI/ASHRAE STANDARD 160-2009 Criteria for Moisture-Control Design Analysis in Buildings

- ANSI/ASHRAE Standard 169-2006 Weather Data for Building Design Standards

- ANSI/ASHRAE/ACCA Standard 183-2007 Peak Cooling and Heating Load Calculations in Buildings Except Low-Rise Residential Buildings
- 2009 ASHRAE Handbook of Fundamentals

  Chapter 1 Psychrometrics

  Chapter 9 Thermal Comfort

  Chapter 10 Indoor Environmental Health

  Chapter 11 Air Contaminants

  Chapter 12 Odors

  Chapter 13 Indoor Environmental Modeling

  Chapter 14 Climatic Design Information

  Chapter 16 Ventilation and Infiltration

  Chapter 18 Nonresidential Cooling and Heating Load Calculations

  Chapter 19 Energy Estimating and Modeling Methods

  Chapter 20 Space Air Diffusion

  Chapter 21 Duct Design

  Chapter 22 Pipe Sizing

  Chapter 23 Insulation for Mechanical Systems

  Chapter 25 Heat, Air, and Moisture Control in Building Assemblies—Fundamentals

  Chapter 26 Heat, Air, and Moisture Control in Building Assemblies—Material Properties

  Chapter 27 Heat, Air, and Moisture Control in Insulated Assemblies—Examples

  Chapter 32 Sorbents and Desiccants

  Chapter 38 Units and Conversions

  Chapter 39 Codes and Standards

- 2005 ASHRAE Handbook of Fundamentals

  Chapter 23 Thermal and moisture control in Insulated Assemblies—Fundamentals

  Chapter 24 Thermal and moisture control in Insulated Assemblies—Applications

  Chapter 25 Thermal and Water Vapor Transmission Data

  Chapter 26 Insulation for Mechanical Systems

  Chapter 28 Climatic Design Information

  Chapter 30 Nonresidential Load Calculations

  Chapter 33 Space Air Diffusion

  Chapter 40 Codes and Standards

- 2008 ASHRAE Systems and Equipment Handbook

  Chapter 1 HVAC System Analysis and Selection

  Chapter 22 Air-Cooling and Dehumidifying Coils

  Chapter 23 Desiccant Dehumification and Pressure Drying Equipment

  Chapter 24 Mechanical Dehumidifiers and Related Components

  Chapter 25 Air-to-Air Energy Recovery Equipment

  Chapter 26 Air Heating Coils

- 2007 ASHRAE Handbook of HVAC Applications

  Chapter 4 Places of Assembly

  Chapter 12 Industrial Air Conditioning

  Chapter 48 Water Treatment

  Chapter 56 Room Air Distribution

- Analytical Formulas for Calculating Water Evaporation From Pools; Mirza Mohammad Shah, PHD, PE; ASHRAE Transactions Volume 114, Part 2 (see also, Authored Books and Papers)

A7-3 AHRI Publications

The Air Conditioning Heating and Refrigeration Institute (AHRI) publishes consensus standards.

> *Standard 910 2006 Performance of Indoor Pool Dehumidifiers 2006*

A7-4 NSPF Publications

The National Swimming Pool Foundation (NSPF) provides consensus standards, guides and handbooks.

- NSPF® Pool & Spa Operator™ Handbook
- Certified Pool-Spa Inspector™Aquatic Play Feature™ Handbook
- Pool Math™ Workbook
- Aquatic Safety Compendium™S
- Hot Water & Healthy Living
- All-Weather Pool and Spa Log
- Health, Sanitation and Safety Facts Sheets
- Federal Pool and Spa Safety Act
- Pool and Spa Codes
- Material Safety Data Sheets
- Recommendations for Preventing Pool Chemical-Associated Injuries
- Vomit and Blood Contamination of Pool Water

A7-5 NSPI Publications

The National Spa and Pool Institute (NSPI) publishes Consensus Standards and Guides

- ANSI Z21.56-2001/CSA 4.7-2001, Gas Fired Pool Heaters
- ANSI Z21.56a (1996) Gas Fired Pool Heaters (supplement).

- ANSI Z124.7-97, Pre-fabricated Plastic Spa Shells
- ANSI Z535, Series of Standards for Safety Signs and Colors
- ANSI/NSPI-1, 2003 Standard for Public Swimming Pools
- ANSI/NSPI-2, 1999 Standard for Public Spas
- ANSI/NSPI-3, 1999 Standard for Permanently Installed Residential Spas
- ANSI/NSPI-4, 1999 Standard for Above-ground/Onground Residential Swimming Pools
- ANSI/NSPI-5, 2003 Standard for Residential Inground Swimming Pools
- ANSI/NSPI-6, 1999 Standard for Residential Portable Spas
- ANSI/IAF-8, 2005 Model Barrier Code for Residential Swimming Pools, Spas and Hot Tubs
- ANSI/IAF-9, 2005 Aquatic Recreation Facilities
- NSPI Workmanship Guidelines/ Practices for Residential Inground Swimming Pools and Spas 2004.

A7-6 ACCA Publications

The Air Conditioning Contractors of America (ACCA) publishes consensus standards and handbooks.

- ACCA *Manual N*, Fifth Edition Commercial Load Calculations for Small Commercial Buildings
- ACCA *Manual CS*, Commercial Applications, Systems and Equipment
- ACCA *Manual Q*, Commercial Low Pressure, Low Velocity Duct System Design
- ACCA *Manual D, Third Edition Residential Duct Systems*
- ACCA *Manual T, Air Distribution Basics for Residential and Small Commercial Buildings*

A7-7 ACI Publications

American Concrete Institute (ACI) related guidance

ACI 302.1R-96 (1996), Guide for Concrete Floor and Slab Construction

A7-8 ASTM Standards

ASTM International publishes standards pertaining to material used in natatorium construction and mechanical systems. See also; authored books and papers (A7-1).

A7-9 IAPMO Codes

The International Association of Plumbing and Mechanical Officials (IAPMO) published consensus codes and standards.

- IAPMO IS-2-90, Tile Lined Roman Bathtubs
- IAPMO IS 3-93, Installation Standard for Copper Plumbing Tube & Fittings
- IAPMO IS 21-89, Installation Standard for Copper and Copper Alloy Welded Water Tube Copper Tube Handbook, CDA
- IAPMO PS-33-93, Specification for Flexible Hose for Pools, Hot Tubs, Spas, and Jetted Bathtubs
- IAPMO SPS-4 2000, Special Use Suction Fittings for Swimming Pools, Spas and Hot Tubs (for Suction Side Automatic Swimming Pool Cleaners

A7-10 ICC Codes

The International Code Council (ICC) publishes consensus codes and standards.

- ANSI / ICC A117.1 (2003), Standard on Accessible and Useable Buildings and Facilities

A7-11 NFPA Standards

The National Fire Protection Association (NFPA) publishes safety Standards.

- ANSI/NFPA 54-2002, National Fuel Gas Code
- ANSI/NFPA 70-2002, National Electric Code

A7-12 NSF-ANSI Standards

NSF International publishes codes and Standards.

- NSF/ANSI 14 (2003), Plastics Piping System Components and Related Materials
- NSF/ANSI 50 (2004), Circulation System Components and Related Materials for Swimming Pools, Spas/Hot Tubs

A7-13 UL-ANSI Standards

Underwriters Laboratories (UL) publishes standards and codes.

- ANSI/UL 1081, Swimming Pool Pumps, Filters and Chlorinators
- ANSI/UL 1261 (2001), Electric Water Heaters for Pools and Tubs
- ANSI/UL 1563, Electric Hot Tubs, Spas, and Associated Equipment
- ANSI/UL 1995 (1999), Standard for heating and cooling equipment

A7-14 OEM Guidance

Dehumidifier manufacturers provide guidance for pool-spa applications. An incomplete list is provided below. Other sources may appear on an internet search.

- Desert Aire
- Pool-Pak International
- Dectron Internationale
- Seresco Technologies Inc.
- Nauatica Dehumidifiers
- Munters Corporation

Appendix 8

Comfort Conditioning Equipment

Under certain circumstances, it is possible for a knowledgeable practitioner, who has adequate experience with HVAC system design and indoor swimming pool requirements, to assemble a system from a combination of HVAC systems/components that meets all the psychrometric performance requirements, part-load requirements, materials requirements for chemical-laden air, and energy use requirements. The following guidance deals with issues that must be understood before proceeding with a design. This appendix does not provide guidance for producing designs that are suitable for a particular application in a particular climate.

- The building envelope for the humid space must comply with the requirements specified by this manual (see Section 1 and Appendix 1).

- Scenarios might range from a spa in a home to a small pool in a commercial building. (Difficulty and risk increase with the size of the project.)

- The attributes of the local climate are significantly different across the country.

- Mechanical system concepts depend on the application and the climate.

- The concept must be appropriate for the design conditions and load calculations for humid spaces (see Sections 2, 6 and 7 of this manual).

- The concept must be appropriate for all part-load conditions for every hour of the entire year (year-round system), or for every hour for part of the year (cold weather system).

A8-1 Comfort Equipment

Figure A8-1 shows a typical comfort system. Normally, the equipment provides space temperature control, and space humidity tends to drift. The challenge is to make space dew point temperature control the first priority.

A8-2 Comfort Equipment Issues

If the climate is humid or moist, outdoor air cannot be used to control space humidity when the outdoor temperature is moderate or warm (see Figure A8-2). A cooling coil (chilled water or refrigerant) may control space humidity, but it cannot simultaneously control space temperature.

- A swimming pool or spa space is not a normal application because cooling capacity is adjusted to control the space air moisture.

Comfort Cooling with Reheat

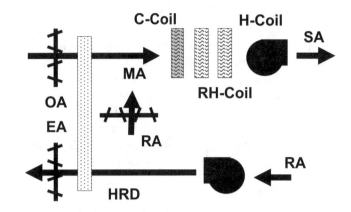

1) Outdoor Air (OA); Exhaust Air (EA); Return Air (RA); Mixed Air (MA); Supply Air (SA); Heating Coil (HC); Cooling Coil (C-Coil). Reheat Coil (RH-Coil); Heat Recovery Device (HRD); Pool Water Heater (PWH).

2) Operates in the outdoor air mode when the outdoor air is usefully dry (see Figure 8-12 for details). Compressor is off-line (no reheat).

3) The heating coil is an independent source of heat that may be in the air handler or external to the air handler.

4) Operates in the cooling coil mode when indoor humidity cannot be controlled with outdoor air. Activated by space humidistat. Outdoor air damper at minimum position for indoor air quality.

5) In the mechanical cooling mode, the reheat capacity is controlled by space thermostat.

6) The cooling coil could be a chilled water coil or a refrigerant coil.

7) Exhaust air heat recovery is optional.

Figure A8-1

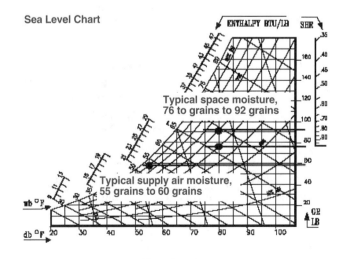

Figure A8-2

- For humidity control, a space dew point control and equipment controls try to match latent capacity with latent load as the latent load changes.

- Space temperature may drop below an acceptable level if the equipment operates after the sensible load has been satisfied (depending on the equipment manufacturer's control method).

Latent Capacity of Supply Air

For humidity control, the humidity ratio of the supply air must be usefully lower than the humidity ratio of the space air. Since the humidity ratio of the space air is relatively constant (about 80°F dry-bulb and 50% RH to 60% RH), the moisture differential depends on the dry-bulb and wet-bulb temperature (or relative humidity) of the supply air. Figure A8-2 shows that the moisture in comfort cooling supply air (dry-bulb about 55°F and 90% RH) is usefully lower than the moisture in space air.

Sensible Heat Ratio

For a cooling load calculation, there is a sensible load and a total load. In manufacturer's cooling performance data, there is sensible equipment capacity and a total equipment capacity. The sensible heat ratio equals the sensible fraction of total load, by this equation.

SHR = Sensible Btuh / (Sensible Btuh + Latent Btuh)

Sensible Heat Ratio Compatibility

Comfort cooling equipment packages (a roof top unit, for example) have relatively high sensible heat ratios when the condition of the entering air is roughly equal to the condition of the air in the space (80°F dry-bulb, 50% RH and 67°F wet-bulb, for example). This is demonstrated by Figure A8-3.

Figure A8-4 shows the cooling loads and SHR values for the Milwaukee, Wisconsin example (see Figure 8-8). Note that for 80°F dry-bulb and 67°F wet-bulb, the Figure A8-3 SHR value is not even close to being compatible with the SHR values for the example problem.

However, the entering air will be a little wetter and warmer than 80°F dry-bulb and 67°F wet-bulb because there is 1,296 Cfm of engineered ventilation. When the condition of the entering air is adjusted for mixing 1,296 Cfm of outdoor air (at the 1% DP condition) with 4,704 Cfm of return air (at the indoor design condition) we find that the Figure A8-3 unit has deficient performance (capacities for 85°F outdoor air are not exactly correct for 80°F outdoor air, but close enough).

- Occupied, with outdoor air at the 1% DP condition

- Mixed air db and wb = 81.6 °F and 69.5 °F

- Total Mbtuh capacity = 195,203 (interpolated)

Cooling Capacity (Mbtuh) for a 15 Ton Unit									
6,000 Cfm; 85 °F Outdoor Air									
Dry-Bulb °F	Wet-Bulb °F								
	61			67			73		
	Total	Sens	SHR	Total	Sens	SHR	Total	Sens	SHR
75	172.0	140.0	0.81	190.0	110.0	0.58	199.0	74.3	0.37
80	169.0	169.0	1.00	191.0	133.0	0.70	200.0	99.4	0.50
85	181.0	181.0	1.00	192.0	156.0	0.81	202.0	119.0	0.59

Figure A8-3

Abridged Version of Figure 8-8				
Loads	Cooling at 50% RH			
T - Total cool S- Sens cool L - Lat cool	1% DP		1% DB	
	Occ	Uocc	Occ	Uocc
T (Mbtuh)	166	82	160	84
S (Mbtuh)	56	35	69	43
L (Mbtuh)	110	47	91	41
SHR (S/T)	0.34	0.42	0.43	0.51

Location: Milwaukee, WI; 723 Feet
Indoor condition: 82.0 °F; 50% RH; 81.7 grains
Dew point condition: 71.4 °F; 80 °F db; 74 °F wb; 120.4 grains
Dry-bulb condition: 86.0 °F; 72 °F wb; 98.5 grains
Outdoor Cfm occupied: 1,296; Closed damper leakage: 432 Cfm

Figure A8-4

- Sensible Mbtuh capacity = 125,907 (interpolated)
- Latent Mbtuh capacity = 69,297 vs. 110,000 req'd
- Coil SHR = 0.65 vs. 0.34 required

But, 50% RH was used for space relative humidity when the outdoor air is at the 1% DP condition. Since the 1% DP condition is the worst case for humidity control, investigate what happens to the sensible heat ratios when 60% RH is used for space humidity. These results show that the equipment SHR is still too high.

- Occupied with outdoor air at the 1% DP condition
- Evaporation rate is reduced at 60% RH
- Latent outdoor air load is reduced at 60% RH
- Load SHR for 60% RH = 0.44
- Mixed air db and wb = 81.6 °F and 71.9 °F
- Total Mbtuh capacity = 198,931
- Sensible Mbtuh capacity = 112,031
- Latent Mbtuh capacity = 86,900
- Coil SHR = 0.56 vs. 0.44 for load SHR

Therefore, this particular roof top unit does not have enough latent capacity for this particular space in this particular city. So what happens if the same space is in Tucson, AZ where it is nice and dry?

It turns out that the SHR problem is not resolved because Tucson's 1% DP weather is 76°F dry-bulb, 70°F wet-bulb and 112 grains. This is not much dryer than the 120 grains for Milwaukee, so the wet weather SHR ratio for a Tucson space is still very low (about 0.40 when space humidity is 60% RH).

The Figure A8-3 unit might provide sufficient moisture removal if the application has a higher sensible heat ratio (for example, the 1% DP condition is much dryer at high altitude). Proceed as follows:

- Produce a set of the load calculations for the application (output similar to Figure A8-4).

- If the cooling load sensible heat ratios are 0.70 or higher, comfort cooling equipment might control humidity, if reheat is used at part load.

- Use the load calculations, related entering air conditions and manufacturer's performance data to investigate equipment performance (as demonstrated above).

- If there is any doubt about the equipment's ability to control humidity for any load condition, seek guidance from the equipment manufacturer.

- Note that a chilled water coil can be designed for a particular application. Give the design conditions and load information to the equipment manufacture and let them design the air handler.

Controlling Space Temperature at Part Load

The equipment will not maintain the space temperature set point unless the space SHR and the supply air SHR values happen to be equal. But, even if the SHR values are equal for a design condition, they will not be equal most of the time because the sensible load can substantially decrease while the latent load stays relatively constant.

For example, if the space SHR is 0.65 on a design day, there is 650 Btuh of sensible load and 350 Btuh of latent load for every 1,000 Btuh of total load. If it gets cool and cloudy (or at night), the sensible load could be 350 Btuh, while the latent load stays at 350 Btuh, so the SHR for part load drops to 0.50.

SHR for design day = 650 / (650 + 350) = 0.65
SHR for part load = 350 / (350 + 350) = 0.50

The simplest way to reconcile the part-load problem is to use reheat. This way the cooling coil "sees" the design value for sensible load, regardless of what happens outdoors or indoors.

For example, if the sensible load drops from 650 to 350 Btuh, 300 Btuh of reheat forces a 0.65 SHR, space humidity is maintained and space temperature is maintained.

SHR with reheat = (350 + 300 / ((350 + 300) + 350) = 0.65

Source of Reheat

A classical reheat system uses an electric coil or hot water heating coil to heat supply air. However, classical simplicity increases energy use and operating cost, fails to comply with ASHRAE Standard 90.1, and may violate local code.

To get past these problems, comfort cooling equipment could be modified to use hot compressor gas to reheat supply air, but now we are reinventing the dehumidifier. (Dehumidifier packages that reclaim the heat of compression are available in sizes that are as small as one ton.)

A8-3 Equipment Selection

Load calculation output and manufacturer's performance data is used to size cooling equipment (at design conditions); blower performance is evaluated; standard features, operating controls and safety controls are identified, evaluated and accepted; and/or optional features and controls are specified. ACCA *Manual CS* and manufacturer's engineering literature provides guidance.

Cooling Loads and Sensible Heat Ratios

Cooling equipment size is based on the grand total sensible load and the grand total latent load. Theses loads include space loads and system loads.

- A supply-side duct load is a system load that increases the dry-bulb temperature of the supply air. (When applicable, *Manual N* adds the supply duct load to the space loads).

- A return duct in an unconditioned space produces sensible and latent loads that affect the condition of the air that flows to the cooling coil. (When applicable, these system loads must be minimized by tight sealing and R-6 or R-8 insulation).

- For comfort cooling equipment, outdoor air is mixed with return air before it enters the cooling coil, so this produces sensible and latent system loads that affect the condition of entering air.

- Return-side system loads usually cause the space SHR to be different than the cooling coil SHR.

- The condition (dry-bulb and wet-bulb temperature) of the air leaving the cooling coil must be compatible with the coil SHR and the space SHR.

- Supply air dry-bulb and wet-bulb temperatures must be compatible with the space SHR.

- The practitioner uses expanded performance data to verify that there is adequate sensible and latent capacity for the summer design conditions.

- The cooling equipment shall have suitable components and adequate capacity control for part-load operation.

Design Loads

For warm weather, a pool-spa application has a sensible cooling load and a latent cooling load. However, there is a sensible and latent load for the 1% dew point condition, and a sensible and latent load for the 1% dry-bulb condition. And for cold weather, there is a sensible and latent load for the 99.6% dry-bulb condition. See Section 2 and Section 7 for guidance.

Entering Conditions

When outdoor air is mixed with return air upstream from the cooling coil, the condition of entering air depends on the condition of the outdoor air, and the outdoor air Cfm. This, in turn, produces large variations in the sensible and latent loads on the cooling coil, and the coil sensible heat ratio; and significant variations in cooling coil performance. Therefore, it is very difficult to match cooling coil performance to sensible and latent space loads as outdoor conditions change (i.e., remove a lot of moisture from return air when the outdoor temperature is below 70 °F, above 90 °F, or any where in between).

The dehumidifier arrangement avoids this problem by introducing outdoor air downstream from the evaporator coil. This way, the entering conditions are determined by the return air condition, which is relatively constant, year-round.

Performance Data for Comfort Equipment

Heating and cooling equipment manufacturers publish engineering guidance and performance data for their products. Related exhibits and commentary are provided by Appendix 9.

Excess Capacity

The capacity of the heating and cooling equipment shall be equal to or greater than the design load (which may be a sensible heating load, a sensible cooling load or a latent cooling load). Excess capacity should be minimized.

Other Issues

Comfort heating and cooling equipment may not be compatible with the 4 to 8 turnover requirement for space air. Comfort heating and cooling equipment does not reclaim the latent heat of evaporation for pool-spa water. Mixing cold outdoor air with warm humid return air can cause condensation in the mixing box. Comfort equipment may not be compatible with chemical laden air (there should be no leakage from the internal flow path to other compartments of the cabinet).

A8-4 Capacity Control

The ability of the HVAC equipment and its controls to track changes in heating and cooling loads affects indoor air quality, space air motion, space temperature and space humidity. This is critical for swimming pool and spa applications because there are serious health and moisture-damage consequences for not maintaining space conditions on a continuous basis.

- If the space is occupied, space air motion and an appropriate flow of outdoor air Cfm shall be continuous (this is a code requirement for commercial and institutional buildings).

- If outdoor air is used to control space humidity, outdoor air Cfm, return air Cfm and supply air Cfm must maintain the space humidity set point regardless of occupancy (to prevent condensation, space humidity must not exceed 60% RH; for occupant comfort, space humidity should not be less than 50% RH).

- Supply air can be relatively cold when a significant amount of cold outdoor air is mixed with return air. Bursts of cold supply air must not enter the conditioned space. Equipment that heats mixed air, or outdoor air, shall not have on-off control or inadequate capacity steps for staged control.

- The output capacity of the heating equipment must track the instantaneous heating load to maintain an appropriate supply air temperature on a continuous basis. Use proportional control (direct-fired furnace with modulating burner; hot water coil with an incremental valve, electric heating coil with electronic pulse control, hot gas coil with modulating control); or equipment that approximates proportional control (indirect-fired furnace with a 20:1 turn down ratio).

- Investigate all possible operating conditions, considering space use, hour of day and month of year, and determine the minimum loads (sensible and latent) on the cooling equipment.

- Note that if the system has an air-side economizer, the minimum load on the cooling equipment occurs when the system changes from mechanical cooling to outdoor air cooling.

- The output capacity of the cooling coil must track the instantaneous cooling loads (sensible and latent) to maintain space temperature and humidity on a continuous basis. Use modulating equipment (chilled water coil, for example) or use equipment that has adequate capacity reduction (multiple coils, row-split coils, face-split coils, for example).

■ The output capacity of a condensing unit or water chiller must track the instantaneous cooling load (use staging, unloaders, speed control, inlet vanes, hot gas by-pass, etc).

■ Conventional reheat, or hot gas reheat dramatically reduces the capacity control problem for cooling equipment. However, controlling a hot gas coil that heats air, a hot-gas heat exchanger that heats water, and a device that rejects excess heat to outdoor air or water equivalent creates a new set of design problems.

■ The practitioner, or the practitioner's proxy (i.e. guidance provided by an equipment manufacturer) shall identify all possible load condition scenarios and make sure that the HVAC system has the appropriate operating mode and capacity for any load condition.

A8-5 System Attributes

Mechanical cooling provides space humidity control when outdoor air is too humid to do the job. Since equipment operation is controlled for space air dew point, sensible capacity is excessive when the sensible load is less than the sensible load for a design condition. The excess sensible capacity problem is resolved by using supply air reheat (prohibited by ASHRAE Standard 90.1, and may be in violation of local code).

Common, packaged cooling equipment routes all the supply air though the cooling coil, so supply air Cfm depends on the design cooling loads and corresponding equipment size. Therefore, the space air turnover rate (see Section 5-9) is what it is. (Dehumidifiers have a bypass air feature that allows the supply air Cfm for the load to be compatible with the supply air Cfm for the air turnover rate).

When outdoor air conditions are suitable, the refrigeration equipment can be shut down, then outdoor air and some type of heating device are used to control space humidity and space temperature. Mixing cold outdoor air with warm, humid return air may cause condensation (preheat for outdoor air may be required).

Appendix 9

Equipment Performance Data

This appendix provides guidance that compliments Appendix 8. This information specifically applies to common comfort conditioning equipment. Related guidance is provided by ACCA *Manual CS* and *Manual Q*, industry handbooks and manuals, and engineering literature published by equipment manufacturers.

Some of this guidance applies to dehumidification equipment (blower, electric coil, water coil, for example). Parts of this guidance tangentially applies to dehumidification equipment (the concept may be relevant, but the details are different). See Section 8 and Section 9 for guidance that explicitly applies to dehumidification equipment.

A9-1 Performance at Altitude

Manufacturer's performance data documents sea level performance, but sea level data can be used for locations that are as high as 2,500 Feet. Appendix 2 provides equipment selection guidance for higher elevations.

A9-2 Blower Data

A blower could be in an equipment package that provides heating, or cooling, or heating and cooling, or desiccant dehumidification; or it could be part of a duct system, a duct-mounted return air fan, for example. In all cases - blower performance is summarized by a table graph, or computer program that correlates Cfm, external static pressure, wheel RPM and motor power (see Figure A9-1).

- Blower Cfm is determined from an equipment selection procedure that uses output from a load calculation and manufacturer's performance data, or blower Cfm may be equal to the design flow rate for a return duct system or exhaust system.

- External static pressure is determined by duct system pressure drop calculations (see Section 13-18).

- The blower table is published with the equipment manufacturer's performance data.

- The practitioner uses the blower table, a Cfm value and an external pressure value to determine wheel RPM and motor horsepower.

- The practitioner specifies wheel RPM (or a set of pulleys) and a suitable standard size motor when the equipment is ordered.

A9-3 Indirect-Fired Furnaces

Indirect-fired furnaces have an input capacity that depends on altitude, and an output capacity. The output

	Blower Performance — Standard Motor					
Cfm	External Pressure (IWC)					
	0.75		1.00		1.25	
	RPM	BHP	RPM	BHP	RPM	BHP
4,000	669	1.18	757	1.61	833	2.05
5,000	699	1.50	782	1.96	860	2.47
6,000	736	1.95	815	2.43	886	2.95
7,000	778	2.50	853	3.05	922	3.60
8,000	824	3.21	895	3.78	961	4.40

1) With a minor exception, blower motors for commercial duty are standard three phase or single phase motors, with pulleys for setting blower wheel speed. This exhibit shows the blower table format for this type of equipment (for a given RPM, Cfm depends on external pressure).

2) The exception is a small commercial equipment package (5-Tons or less) that uses a single phase, direct drive ECM motor (1 HP or less) to drive a blower wheel. The blower table for this type of blower shows that one Cfm value (selected by a speed tap or dip switch setting) is maintained over a range of external pressure values (typically 0.0 to 1.0 IWC, but could be as low as 0.0 to 0.5 IWC), as motor speed changes.

3) External pressure is the pressure drop for every air-path item that was not in place when the blower was tested. For example, if a furnace blower is tested with the heat exchanger and filter in place, these items do not add anything to external pressure. Blower table footnotes may list in-place items. If the blower table does not provide this guidance, question the equipment manufacturer about the issue.

Figure A9-1

capacity depends on the steady state efficiency of the furnace. The temperature rise across the heat exchanger is determined by the output capacity and the Cfm that flows through the furnace. Manufacturer's performance data provides capacity values, temperature rise limits, an efficiency rating and a blower table. Figure A9-2 (next page) provides an example of capacity data. Blower performance is summarized by a separate table. This equation determines temperature rise.

Output Btuh = Input Btuh x Steady State Efficiency
TR = Output Btuh / (1.1 x ACF x Cfm)

Where:
Adjust input Btuh for altitude, if applicable
TR = Temperature rise (°F)
ACF = Altitude correction factor
Cfm = Design Cfm for application (from blower table)

Furnace Model Size				
	150	**200**	**250**	**300**
Input Btuh	150,000	200,000	250,000	300,000
Output Btuh	112,500	150,000	187,500	225,000
Rise (°F)	25 - 60	25 - 60	35-60	40-60

Figure A9-2

A9-4 Direct-Fired Furnaces

The air that flows through a direct-fired furnace comes in contact with the burner flame. This will cause an air quality problem if the air contains chemicals that should not contact a flame. Therefore, direct-fired furnaces shall not be used to heat a blend of outdoor air and return air.

In regard to the combustion gases, a limited amount of return air may be safely mixed with outdoor air if permitted by local code (see ACCA Technical Bulletins 109 through 112 and engineering guidance provided by Rapid Engineering Inc., Comstock Park, MI).

For pool-spa applications, direct-fired equipment can be used to heat 100 percent outdoor air, but should conform to applicable codes, standards and manufacturer's installation instructions.

For a direct-fired furnace, input capacity equals output capacity, so steady state efficiency is 1.0. The temperature rise across the burner is determined by the input capacity and the Cfm that flows through the furnace. Manufacturer's performance data provides capacity values, temperature rise limits, and a blower table. This equation determines temperature rise:

TR = Input Btuh / (1.1 x ACF x Cfm)

Where:
Adjust input Btuh for altitude, if applicable
TR = Temperature rise (°F)
ACF = Altitude correction factor
Cfm = Design Cfm for application (from blower table)

A9-5 Electric Heating Coils

Manufacturer's performance data provides a kilowatt value, a minimum temperature rise and a maximum temperature rise. For furnaces, a separate table summarizes blower performance. Output heating capacity and the air temperature rise across the coil are determined by these equations:

Heating Btuh = 3.143 x KW
TR = Heating Btuh / (1.1 x ACF x Cfm)

Where:
KW = Heating capacity in kilowatts
TR = Temperature rise (°F)
ACF = Altitude correction factor
Cfm = Design Cfm for application (from blower table)

A9-6 Hot Water Coils

The parameters that affect hot water coil performance are listed below. Because there are many variables, many configurations can provide the required performance.

- Entering air temperature (EAT)
- Coil face velocity (Fpm)
- Entering water temperature (EWT)
- Water temperature drop (WTD)
- Water-side flow rate (Gpm)
- Velocity of the water in the tubes (Fps)
- Number of rows
- Number of fins per inch (Fpi)
- Circuiting
- Equipped or not equipped with turbulators

The easiest way to select a coil is to specify performance requirements and let the coil manufacturer choose the coil. At a minimum, the practitioner specifies:

- Heating Cfm
- Required heating capacity (MBtuh)
- Entering air temperature (°F)
- Discuss leaving air temperature or temperature rise (°F)
- If applicable, provide freeze protection

Other conditions that might be specified include:

- Entering water temperature (°F)
- Water temperature drop (°F)
- Water-side flow rate (Gpm)
- Maximum face velocity (Fpm)
- Maximum air-side pressure drop (IWC)
- Maximum water-side pressure drop (Feet or Psi)

After a heating coil design is selected by a computer program or manufacturer's representative, sea level performance is summarized by a few parameters:

- Output capacity (MBtuh)
- Airflow rate (Cfm)
- Water flow rate (Gpm)
- Entering air temperature (°F)

- Entering water temperature (°F)
- Air-side pressure drop (IWC)
- Water-side pressure drop (Feet or PSI)

The air-side and water-side performance of a hot water coil is summarized by these equations:

Air TR (°F) = Output Btuh / (1.1 x ACF x Cfm)
Water TD (°F) = Output Btuh / (500 x Gpm)

Where:
TR = Temperature rise (°F)
ACF = Altitude correction factor
Cfm = Design Cfm for application
TD = Temperature drop (°F)
Gpm = Gallons per minute

A9-7 Baseboard Heat and Cabinet Heaters

Space heat can be provided by baseboard radiation and cabinet heaters. These may be hot water equipment or electric fixtures. Manufacturer's performance data provides heating capacity per foot of length for baseboard elements, or total heating capacity for cabinet heaters.

- The performance of hot water equipment depends on the construction details of the fixture (rows, fins, etc.), entering air temperature and entering water temperature. There is a water-side temperature drop across the fixture and an air-side temperature rise through the fixture.

- The performance of electric equipment depends on the construction details of the fixture (rows, fins, etc.) and entering air temperature. There is an air temperature rise through the fixture.

- The water and air equations for hot water coils and electric coils (see above), apply to these devices.

A9-8 Hot Water Boilers

Hot water boilers are classified by pressure and temperature. Atmospheric boilers supply water at temperatures that range from 120°F to 212°F. Low pressure boilers operate at a pressure of 15 Psi or less and at temperatures that do not exceed 250°F. Medium and high pressure boilers (more than 15 Psi) operate at temperatures that slightly exceed or substantially exceed 250°F.

Atmospheric and low pressure boilers are preferred for small commercial applications. They have the right combination of operating temperatures and pressures and they do not require a licensed operator.

Hot water boilers may serve a space heating system or a heating and ventilating system. This depends on the type of terminal equipment. Space heating equipment could

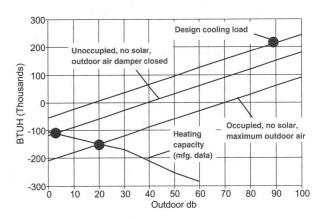

Air Source Heat Pump
Balance Point Diagram

Figure A9-3

be finned-tube radiation or some type of unit heater. Terminal equipment for space heating and ventilation could be an air handler equipped with a hot water coil and outdoor air damper, or a unit ventilator.

Hot water boilers also heat pool water (see Section 4-6). This could be a single purpose boiler, or the boiler can provide space heat and pool water heat.

Boiler input capacity depends on altitude, and output capacity depends on the steady state efficiency of the boiler. Manufacturer's performance data provides input and output capacity values (Btuh) for sea level, an efficiency rating and temperature rise limits. The temperature rise across the boiler is determined by the output capacity and the water flow rate (Gpm), per this equation:

Water TR (°F) = Output Btuh / (500 x Gpm)

Where:
TR = Temperature rise (°F)
Gpm = Gallons per minute

A9-9 Heat Pump Heating

In the heating mode, air source and water source heat pumps may or may not satisfy the total heating load (space load, outdoor air load and all other system loads). This depends on the balance point diagram for a particular set of operating conditions.

- The heat pump provides all the heat when the outdoor air temperature is above the thermal balance point.

- Supplemental heat is required when outdoor air temperature is below the thermal balance point.

An application will have multiple balance point diagrams because there are multiple operating scenarios, as demonstrated by Figure A9-3 (previous page). The practitioner shall identify the worst case scenario (warmest outdoor temperature, largest supplemental heat requirement).

- Since equipment heating capacity and building envelope load are fixed values at a given outdoor air temperature, the total heating load depends on ventilation rate, solar gain and internal gain.

- Outdoor air Cfm increases heating load, while solar gain and internal gain reduce heating load.

- If solar gain is zero (night time or heavy cloud cover), the heating load for a given outdoor air temperature depends on internal gain and ventilation rate.

- If space activity is at its maximum, internal gain is at its maximum and the ventilation rate is at its maximum. Investigate this scenario.

- If space activity is at its minimum (unoccupied), internal gain is at its minimum and the ventilation rate is at its minimum. Investigate this scenario.

- The ventilation rate for any scenario depends on whether outdoor air is controlling space humidity or maintaining indoor air quality.

- If operating controls close the outdoor air damper when the space is not occupied, the ventilation rate for this scenario depends on damper leakage.

The heating capacity line on the balance point diagram depends on the type of equipment (air source or water source), the temperature of the source fluid (air or water) and the size of the equipment, compared to the size of the maximum heating load.

- Heating capacity data for any type of heat pump equipment is provided by manufacturer's performance data.

- The heating capacity of air source equipment decreases linearly with decreasing outdoor temperature (with a jog for the defrost knee).

- The heating capacity of open-loop water source equipment (once through) is relatively constant for any outdoor temperature (depends on ground water temperature).

- The heating capacity of closed-loop water source equipment is at its maximum at the beginning of the heating season (water temperature above 90°F) and at its minimum at the end of the heating season (water temperature below 40°F, or below freezing). This is approximated by a capacity line that decreases linearly with outdoor temperature.

- If heat pump equipment is only used for heating, it can be sized for the design heating load. This will

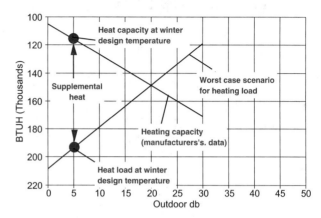

Figure A9-4

lower the thermal balance point and minimize the auxiliary heat requirement.

- For cooling, the sizing procedure for heat pumps is identical to the procedure used for cooling-only equipment.

- If air-source or water source equipment provides heating, sensible cooling and latent cooling, the excess cooling capacity shall not exceed the total cooling load by a factor of 1.15 (excess capacity degrades humidity control).

- If air-source or water source equipment provides heating and sensible cooling (no latent cooling), the excess cooling capacity shall not exceed the total cooling load by a factor of 1.25 (to limit capacity control problems at part load).

Output capacity for supplemental heating equipment is read from the balance point diagram (similar to Figure A9-4). At the winter design temperature used for the heating load calculation, subtract heat pump heating capacity from the total heating load.

- The amount of auxiliary heat that is actually installed may be greater than the amount of supplemental heat. This depends on the amount of back-up heat that must be available (by code or preference) if the heat pump heat fails.

- Supplemental heat is activated by the second stage of the thermostat. An emergency heat switch activates the total amount of auxiliary heat (Supplemental heat plus emergency heat).

- Incremental activation of supplemental heat is desirable when the design load for supplemental heat is relatively large.

Cfm	Ent Dry Bulb (°F)	Outdoor Temperature (°F)																
		85						95						105				
		Entering Wet-Bulb (°F)																
		61		67		73		61		67		73		61		67		73	
		Mbh	SHR	Mbh	SHR	Mbh	SHR	Mbh	SHR	Mbh	SHR	Mbh	SHR	Mbh	SHR	Mbh	SHR	Mbh	SHR
5,000	75	246	77	276	58	309	42	233	78	261	58	293	42	218	79	246	59	276	42
	80	246	87	276	67	309	50	233	88	262	68	293	47	218	88	246	69	276	52
	85	248	96	276	76	303	58	235	98	262	77	293	59	221	100	246	79	276	60
7,000	75	266	81	298	60	331	42	251	83	282	60	314	41	234	85	264	61	295	41
	80	267	93	298	67	331	51	253	95	281	72	314	52	237	98	263	73	295	52
	85	273	100	297	82	331	61	260	100	281	84	314	62	247	100	263	86	295	63
8,750	75	278	86	310	61	344	41	262	87	292	63	325	41	244	90	273	64	305	41
	80	280	100	309	74	344	53	266	100	292	78	325	53	250	100	273	78	305	54
	85	292	100	310	87	343	64	279	100	293	89	325	65	264	100	274	81	305	67

Cooling Performance for Air Cooled Equipment

1) Capacities not adjusted for indoor fan heat. To obtain effective cooling capacity, subtract indoor fan heat.
2) Mbh—Total cooling capacity (1,000 Btuh), SHR - Sensible heat ratio (percent of total capacity)
3) Sensible cooling capacity = MBh x SHR, Latent capacity = Total capacity - Sensible capacity

Figure A9-5

A9-10 Refrigerant Coil Cooling—Air Cooled

The total, sensible and latent capacities of an air cooled equipment package depend on the outdoor dry-bulb temperature at the condenser, the Cfm that flows through the indoor coil, the dry-bulb temperature of the air that approaches the indoor coil and the wet-bulb temperature of the air that approaches the indoor coil, as demonstrated by Figure A9-5. Equipment is selected so that total capacity is equal to, or slightly greater than the total load. Then, sensible capacity shall be equal to or slightly greater than the sensible load, and latent capacity shall be equal to or slightly greater than latent load.

- Outdoor dry-bulb and wet-bulb temperatures equal the temperatures used for the cooling load calculation.

- If there is no sensible and latent gain for a return duct, the dry-bulb and wet-bulb temperatures for return air are equal to the space temperatures used for the cooling load calculation.

- If there is a sensible gain for a return duct, the dry-bulb temperature for return air will be warmer than the space temperature used for the cooling load calculation.

- If there is a positive or negative latent gain for a return duct, the wet-bulb temperature for return air will be higher or lower the space temperature used for the cooling load calculation.

- Entering dry-bulb or wet-bulb temperature normally equals the temperature of a return-air, out-door air mixture, but could equal outdoor temperature (100% outdoor air) or return air temperature (100% return air).

- Blower Cfm is selected to provide the best match between cooling capacities and cooling loads.

- Cooling performance values shall be interpolated when one or more of the application temperatures does not equal the temperature value in the performance table.

- The total capacity values in the performance table are used without adjustment if an estimate for blower heat is added to the sensible cooling load calculation. If the load calculation ignores blower heat, subtract the estimated blower heat from the total capacity values in the performance table.

- If latent capacity exceeds latent load, add half of the excess latent capacity to the sensible capacity.

For example, the block load calculation for a sea level application says the sensible load is 151,250 Btuh (including blower heat), the latent load is 71,400 Btuh, so the total load is 222,650 Btuh. There are no return duct loads. The outdoor air condition is 95 °F dry-bulb and 74 °F wet-bulb, and 500 Cfm of outdoor air is used for indoor air quality. The space air condition is 80 °F dry-bulb and 50% RH. Looking at Figure A9-5, the total capacity of the 5,000 Cfm unit (at 95 °F), is the best match to total load. When equipment capacities are compared to equipment loads, the 5,000 Cfm unit satisfies the requirements of the equipment selection procedure, except it has a little more excess capacity then desired (1.18 vs. 1.15).

Blower Cfm = 5,000

Outdoor air fraction = 500 / 5,000 = 0.10

Elevation for psychrometric chart = Sea level

Outdoor air condition = 95 °F db and 74 °F wb

Space air condition = 80 °F db and 50% RH

Adjustments for return duct = None (no loads)

Mixed air condition = 81.5 °F db and 67.5 °F wb

Entering air look-up values = 80 °F db and 67 °F wb

Total capacity = 262,000 Btuh

Sensible heat ratio = 0.68

Sensible capacity = 0.68 x 262,000 = 178,160 Btuh

Adjustment for blower heat = None (in load calculation)

Latent capacity = 262,000 - 178,160 = 83,840 Btuh

Excess total capacity = 262,000 / 222,650 = 1.18 (+0.03)

Excess latent capacity = 83,840 - 71,400 = 12,440 Btuh

Sensible capacity conversion = 0.5 x 12,440 = 6,220 Btuh

Adjust sensible capacity = 178,160 + 6,220 =184,380 Btuh

Sensible load vs. sensible capacity = 151,250 < 184,380

Adjust latent capacity = 83,840 - 6,220 = 77,620 Btuh

Latent load vs. latent capacity = 71,400 < 77,620

Note: The excess latent capacity will cause the space humidity to be a little lower than 50% RH. This changes the load calculation, the condition of the air entering the equipment, and the equipment capacities. A new set of calculations could be based on 48% RH, or so, but this would only produce an incremental improvement in accuracy.

Note: If less excess capacity is desired (say 1.05 to 1.10 instead of 1.18), the blower Cfm could be marginally reduced (say 4,500 Cfm). However, the equipment manufacturer would have to provide capacity adjustment factors for the lower Cfm.

A9-11 Refrigerant Coil Cooling—Water Cooled

The procedure for selecting water cooled equipment is the same as the procedure for selecting air cooled equipment, except entering water temperature is substituted for outdoor air temperature. Figure A9-6 shows a performance table for water cooled equipment. Note that cooling capacity increases with an increasing water flow rate.

A9-12 Chilled Water Coil

The parameters that affect chilled water coil performance are listed below. Because there are so many variables, it is likely (but not certain) that some coil configuration will provide the required performance.

- Coil face velocity (Fpm)
- Entering dry-bulb and wet-bulb (EDB & EWB)
- Leaving dry-bulb and wet-bulb (LDB & LWB)
- Entering water temperature (EWT)
- Water temperature rise (WTR)
- Water-side flow rate (Gpm)

Cooling Capacity — Water Cooled Equipment 2,300 Cfm; Entering Dry-bulb 80°F							
EWB (°F)	EWT (°F)	Gpm 18.0			Gpm 14.0		
		TC	SC	KW	TC	SC	KW
71	55	78.0	41.3	4.65	76.3	40.7	4.81
	65	75.3	40.4	5.04	73.6	39.8	5.21
	75	72.6	39.5	5.43	71.0	38.9	5.61
	85	69.9	38.6	5.81	68.4	38.1	6.01
	95	63.0	36.3	6.20	61.6	35.9	6.41
67	55	73.3	50.8	4.53	71.7	50.2	4.68
	65	70.7	49.8	4.91	69.2	49.2	5.07
	75	68.2	48.9	5.29	66.7	48.3	5.46
	85	65.7	47.9	5.67	64.3	47.4	5.86
	95	59.2	45.4	6.04	57.9	44.9	6.25
63	55	68.6	60.2	4.42	67.1	59.5	4.56
	65	66.2	59.1	4.78	64.7	58.5	4.94
	75	63.9	58.1	5.15	62.4	57.5	5.32
	85	61.5	57.1	5.52	60.2	56.6	5.70
	95	55.4	54.4	5.89	54.2	53.8	6.08

1) Capacities (1,000 Btuh) not adjusted for indoor fan heat.
2) TC–Total cooling capacity; SC–Sensible Capacity (Btuh), KW–Kilowatt input
3) Latent capacity = Total capacity - Sensible capacity

Figure A9-6

- Velocity of the water in the tubes (Fps)
- Number of rows (Rows)
- Number of fins per inch (Fpi)
- Circuiting
- Equipped or not equipped with turbulators

The easiest way to select a chilled water coil is to specify performance requirements and let the equipment manufacturer choose the coil. At a minimum, the practitioner makes load calculations, then draws process lines for mixed air temperature, space sensible heat ratio and coil sensible heat ratio on a psychrometric chart to specify:

- Cooling Cfm
- Entering dry-bulb temperature (°F)
- Entering wet-bulb temperature (°F)
- Required sensible capacity (MBtuh)
- Required latent capacity (MBtuh)
- Leaving dry-bulb temperature (°F)
- Leaving wet-bulb temperature (°F)
- Entering water temperature (°F)

Other conditions that might be specified include:

- Water temperature rise (°F)
- Water-side flow rate (Gpm)
- Maximum face velocity (Fpm)
- Maximum number of rows.
- Minimum fin spacing.
- Maximum air-side pressure drop (IWC)
- Maximum water-side pressure drop (Feet or Psi)

After a chilled water coil design is selected by a computer program or manufacturer's representative, sea level performance is summarized by these parameters:

- Airflow rate (Cfm)
- Sensible cooling capacity (MBtuh)
- Latent cooling capacity (MBtuh)
- Entering dry-bulb and wet-bulb temperature (°F)
- Leaving dry-bulb and wet-bulb temperature (°F)
- Water flow rate (Gpm)
- Entering water temperature (°F)
- Water temperature rise (°F)
- Air-side pressure drop (IWC)
- Water-side pressure drop (Feet or PSI)

The air-side and water-side performance of a chilled water coil is summarized by these equations:

Sensible Btuh = 1.1 x ACF x Cfm x (EAT - LAT)
ΔGrains = Entering Grains - Leaving Grains
Latent Btuh = 0.68 x ACF x Cfm x ΔGrains
Water TR (°F) = Total cooling Btuh / (500 x Gpm)
Water TR = LWT - EWT

Where:
ACF = Altitude correction factor
Cfm = Design Cfm for application
EAT = Entering air temperature
LAT = leaving air temperature
TR = Temperature rise (°F)
Gpm = Gallons per minute
LWT = Leaving water temperature
EWT = Entering water temperature

A9-13 Water Chiller

Chiller packages are available with a water-cooled condenser or an air cooled condenser. Chiller size is defined by Tons of total cooling capacity. Manufacturer's performance data is used to select a chiller. Relevant equipment selection parameters are listed here:

- Temperature of fluid (air or water) entering condenser (°F).
- EWT - Entering water temperature (°F).
- WTD - Water temperature drop (°F).
- Chilled water flow rate (Gpm)
- Input power (KW)
- Water-side pressure drop (Psi)

Equations for chiller capacity and water flow rate (Gpm) are provided below. If the condenser is not part of a self-contained chiller package, manufacturer's performance data is used to select the condenser.

Minimum Tons = (Sensible load + Latent load) / 12,000
Chiller Gpm = (Tons x 12,000) / (500 x WTD)

Forms and Worksheets

On the following pages, Form DH and Form DC summarize the output of load calculations for selecting, sizing and controlling dehumidification equipment.

Heating Load Summary for Dehumidifier Equipment

City >			Water temperature (°F)			Pool Surface Area (SqFt)			Wet Deck Area (SqFt)		
Altitude	SqFt	CuFt	Pool 1	Pool 2	Spa	Pool 1	Pool 2	Spa	Pool 1	Pool 2	Spa

99.6% Dry-Bulb Loads for Maximum Water Activity and Full Occupancy

99.6% Dry-Bulb		Space		Latent Lb/Hr	Heating Load (Btuh)			62.1 Ventilation		Evaporation	
DB °F	RH	DB °F	RH		Space	OA Cfm	Net	Count	OA Cfm	Lb/Hr	Btuh

Include duct loads, use wet deck area, use maximum activity factors; you may deduct internal loads for lights, spectators and blower heat.

99.6% Dry-Bulb Loads for Maximum Water Activity and No Spectators

99.6% Dry-Bulb		Space		Latent Lb/Hr	Heating Load (Btuh)			62.1 Ventilation		Evaporation	
DB °F	RH	DB °F	RH		Space	OA Cfm	Net	Count	OA Cfm	Lb/Hr	Btuh

Include duct loads, use wet deck area, use maximum activity factors; you may deduct internal loads for lights and blower heat.

99.6% Dry-Bulb Loads for Vacant Facility

99.6% Dry-Bulb		Space		Latent Lb/Hr	Heating Load (Btuh)			62.1 Ventilation		Evaporation	
DB °F	RH	DB °F	RH		Space	OA Cfm	Net	Count	OA Cfm	Lb/Hr	Btuh

Include duct loads; outdoor air damper closed with default damper leakage rate; still water; no wet deck area; no deduction for internal loads.

Input for Evaporation Load Calculations

Space Air		Water Temp		DER (Lb/Hr)		Water			Wet Deck		
Dsn RH	DB (°F)	Item	°F	Dsn RH	50% RH	SqFt	Use AF	Still AF	SqFt	AF	Cfm/SqFt
		Pool 1									
		Pool 2									
		Spa									

1) Design value for space humidity when moisture load is positive = 50% to 60% RH = Dsn RH
2) Default value for space humidity when moisture load is negative = 50% RH
3) Default Evaporation Rate (DER) from Table A5-4; Activity Factor (AF) from Table A5-5

Issues that are Settled During Equipment Selection

1) The default value for outdoor air damper leakage (say, 5% of the maximum Cfm though the damper) is compared to the value for the actual damper, then the load calculations for a vacant space are adjusted if there is a significant difference.
2) The space air turn calculation requires a supply air Cfm value.
3) For dry outdoor air, space humidity may balance at some value that is less than 50% RH, calculate this value.
4) Preheat for outdoor air may be required. If required, determine the heat input value (this reduces the heating load on other equipment).
5) The design values for recovered heat is determined when equipment is selected. This heat may go to water and/or air, which reduces the operating load on other heating equipment, but does not reduce the installed capacity of other heating equipment.
6) If applicable, investigate purge cycle loads and effects, and provide the capability to control space conditions during the purge cycle.
7) Capacity control shall be appropriate for all load ranges (airflows, moisture load, heating load and sensible cooling load).

Form DH

Cooling Load Summary for Dehumidifier Equipment

City >			Water temperature (°F)			Pool Surface Area (SqFt)			Wet Deck Area (SqFt)		
Altitude	SqFt	CuFt	Pool 1	Pool 2	Spa	Pool 1	Pool 2	Spa	Pool 1	Pool 2	Spa

1% Dew Point Loads for Maximum Water Activity and Full Occupancy

1% Dew Point		Space		Latent Lb/Hr	Evaporator Loads (Btuh)			62.1 Ventilation		Evaporation	
DB °F	WB °F	DB °F	RH		Total	Sensible	SHR	Count	OA Cfm	Lb/Hr	Btuh

Include: Solar load, loads for lights, equipment and spectators; duct loads, blower heat, use wet deck area, use maximum activity factors.

1% Dew Point Loads for Maximum Water Activity and No Spectators

1% Dew Point		Space		Latent Lb/Hr	Cooling Loads (Btuh)			62.1 Ventilation		Evaporation	
DB °F	WB °F	DB °F	RH		Total	Sensible	SHR	Count	OA Cfm	Lb/Hr	Btuh

Include: Solar load, loads for lights and equipment; duct loads, blower heat, use wet deck area, use maximum activity factors.

1% Dry-Bulb Loads for Maximum Water Activity and Full Occupancy

1% Dry-Bulb		Space		Latent Lb/Hr	Cooling Loads (Btuh)			62.1 Ventilation		Evaporation	
DB °F	WB °F	DB °F	RH		Total	Sensible	SHR	Count	OA Cfm	Lb/Hr	Btuh

Include: Solar load, loads for lights, equipment and spectators; duct loads, blower heat, use wet deck area, use maximum activity factors.

1% Dry-Bulb Loads for Maximum Water Activity and No Spectators

1% Dry Bulb		Space		Latent Lb/Hr	Cooling Loads (Btuh)			62.1 Ventilation		Evaporation	
DB °F	WB °F	DB °F	RH		Total	Sensible	SHR	Count	OA Cfm	Lb/Hr	Btuh

Include: Solar load, loads for lights and equipment; duct loads, blower heat, use wet deck area, use maximum activity factors.

1% Dew Point Loads for Vacant Facility

1% Dew Point		Space		Latent Lb/Hr	Cooling Loads (Btuh)			62.1 Ventilation		Evaporation	
DB °F	WB °F	DB °F	RH		Total	Sensible	SHR	Count	OA Cfm	Lb/Hr	Btuh

Outdoor air damper closed, no internal loads, no wet deck area. Include solar load, duct loads, blower heat and default damper leakage load.

1% Dry-Bulb Loads for Vacant Facility

1% Dew Point		Space		Latent Lb/Hr	Cooling Loads (Btuh)			62.1 Ventilation		Evaporation	
DB °F	WB °F	DB °F	RH		Total	Sensible	SHR	Count	OA Cfm	Lb/Hr	Btuh

Outdoor air damper closed, no internal loads, no wet deck area. Include solar load, duct loads, blower heat and default damper leakage load.

Form DC

Index

D

E

F

G

H

T

U

V

W

X

Y

No Entries

Z

Zoning
For Space Pressure 23, 79–80
See also, Humid Zone

Notes

Notes

Notes

Notes

Notes

Notes